Dynamic Realism

Intersections in Continental and Analytic Philosophy

Series Editors
Jeffrey A. Bell, Paul Livingston and James Williams

Drawing on different traditions for new solutions to philosophical problems

Books in this series will bring together work in the analytic and continental traditions in philosophy. Although these traditions have until recently been thought of as separate, if not irreconcilable, these books will show how key philosophical problems can be addressed by drawing from work in both.

The intersections on display here will demonstrate the strength and vitality of a pluralist approach to philosophy, as well as its wide relevance to contemporary philosophical concerns.

Books available
Language and Process: Words, Whitehead and the World, Michael Halewood
Dynamic Realism: Uncovering the Reality of Becoming through Phenomenology and Process Philosophy, Tina Röck

Visit the Intersections website at edinburghuniversitypress.com/series-intersections-in-continental-and-analytic-philosophy

Dynamic Realism

Uncovering the Reality of
Becoming through Phenomenology
and Process Philosophy

Tina Röck

EDINBURGH
University Press

Edinburgh University Press is one of the leading university presses in the UK. We publish academic books and journals in our selected subject areas across the humanities and social sciences, combining cutting-edge scholarship with high editorial and production values to produce academic works of lasting importance. For more information visit our website: edinburghuniversitypress.com

© Tina Röck, 2022, 2023

Edinburgh University Press Ltd
The Tun – Holyrood Road, 12(2f) Jackson's Entry, Edinburgh EH8 8PJ

First published by Edinburgh University Press 2022

Typeset in Bembo
by R. J. Footring Ltd, Derby

A CIP record for this book is available from the British Library

ISBN 978 1 4744 8011 6 (hardback)
ISBN 978 1 4744 8012 3 (paperback)
ISBN 978 1 4744 8013 0 (webready PDF)
ISBN 978 1 4744 8014 7 (epub)

The right of Tina Röck to be identified as the author of this work has been asserted in accordance with the Copyright, Designs and Patents Act 1988, and the Copyright and Related Rights Regulations 2003 (SI No. 2498).

Contents

Acknowledgements   vii

Introduction   1

Part I Metaphysics as a Relation of Thinking and Being
1. Terminological and Methodological Clarifications   13
2. A New Metaphysics? Correlating Ontology with Epistemology   50

Part II Husserl's Phenomenology: Experience and Time
3. Phenomenological Experience: To the Things Themselves   69
4. Husserl's Philosophy as Correlated Transcendental Realism   92
5. Phenomenological Realism: The Argument from Temporality   119

Part III Process Thought
6. The Nature of Time: Time, Temporality and Being   141
7. Experience and Temporal Being   169

Part IV Dynamic Realism
8. What There Is: The Dynamic 'Object' of Experience   199
9. Being between Ontology and Epistemology   209
10. Uncovering the Real as Physical: Naturalism and Materialism   230

CONTENTS

11 Moving from the World of Science to the Life-World   253
12 From Phenomenology to Speculative Metaphysics   282

Bibliography   296
Index   304

Acknowledgements

As always, any work like this takes many people to believe in it and to support its growth. I received help from many people and institutions, and I will not be able to thank everyone, but I would like to mention a few.

My thanks go to the academic institutions that shaped my path and the taxpayers who support them; without you this type of work would be impossible. Here I want to thank especially the Royal Society of Edinburgh and the Czech Academy of the Sciences for granting me the space to focus on this book during some turbulent times.

Thanks to my philosophical colleagues past and present, for their challenges, suggestions and the shared laughter.

Thanks also to the series editors for their feedback, support and input, and to the lovely people from Edinburgh University Press, who helped birth this baby.

πεπαιδευμένου γάρ ἐστιν ἐπὶ τοσοῦτον
τἀκριβὲς ἐπιζητεῖν καθ' ἕκαστον γένος,
ἐφ'ὅσον ἡ τοῦ πράγματος φύσις ἐπιδέχεται.
It shows an educated mind to seek precision about anything
just to the extent that the nature of the subject permits.
Aristotle, Nicomachean Ethics 109b23–5

More than anything else the being of the world is
obvious. It is so very obvious that no one would
think of asserting it expressly in a proposition.
Edmund Husserl, Cartesian Meditations §7

Introduction

We live in interesting times. One aspect that renders current times interesting is a certain air of discovery, of change and revolution – the sense of a new beginning. However, the revolution shaping the contemporary world is one of conservation and return. In philosophy this takes the shape of a return of metaphysics and ontology, the return of the question of the real, of truth and knowledge. This return to (speculative) realism, materialism, to metaphysics and object(ive) ontologies is an attempt to come to terms with this, our, the modern world. Ours is a world that is shaped by two correlated insights. The insight of the twentieth century was the realisation of the weakness and fallibility of reason and a corresponding loss of certainty and (objective) truth. The second insight, which is shaping the twenty-first century, is the power of information to overtake physical reality if it is not limited in any way, the insight that the immense speed and complexity made real and accessible through modern information technology cannot be controlled by the tools of reason and logic. These insights have effects on all realms of thinking; in the academic, the scientific, the social, the everyday as well as the political realm, there is no escaping these developments. This leads to the present breaking point. Contemporary reality is so fundamentally connected and complex and is changing with such speed that traditional modes of thought, which anchor thought in the unchanging and the stable, are completely failing us.

What are the roots of these developments? During the twentieth century philosophers were split as to how best to approach these emerging issues of speed, change and connectivity, how to reground realism, truth, knowledge or objectivity (if that is even possible). Thinkers in the analytic tradition have been attempting to generate stability by focusing on knowledge, certainty and truth in science and by using mathematics and language (or logic) as objective tools for analysis. These attempts, however, were not able to address the human side of things, the need we have for a philosophy that can clarify and guide our attempts to live a good life in this complex, connected, changing environment. While the effectiveness of science, logic and mathematics as well as the fundamental role of language in 'embodying' our thoughts and intuitions is indubitable when they are employed to solve specific problems, their value is less certain when it comes to understanding the *conditio humana* – the nature and truth of the connected, temporal and complex reality we are living in. I argue throughout this book that conceptual-analytical approaches tend to abstract from the temporal, the complex, the experiential, the subjective, the human, the qualitative, the creative and the valuable in order to achieve clarity, simplicity, certainty.

Interestingly enough, these human issues are generally focused on in the continental tradition. While the analytic tradition is fairly united in its use of clear and exact reason, and argumentation, epistemology or scientific results as a basis to confront the problems of modern society, the continental tradition is much less unified in its approach. A variety of different paths are pursued in order to come to terms with the modern world. Some thinkers have even gone so far as to reject the possibility of regrounding reality or objectivity in light of the historicity, temporality, complexity and processuality of the world. These thinkers argue that reason, logic and language, if observed closely enough and over a long enough time, are just as mutable and thus ultimately untrustworthy as one's senses, experiences and feelings. What exists are changes, evolutions and differences, but no stable certainties. This position leaves nothing stable on which to ground objective or lasting truth or knowledge in any meaningful sense;

everything is possible. If anything goes, if there are no stable limits or grounds, then we deprive ourselves of precisely the choices that we thought we had gained through this apparent openness. This shift creates the loss of effective differences – of differences that actually make a difference – because we allow for the equality of all differences. If everything is different but equally valuable, different but equally meaningful, different but equally truthful, then nothing has real value, and nothing has a distinct meaning; no choice makes any difference – nothing is different if everything is different. Pure difference leads to absolute equality, and thus pure difference paradoxically erases all meaningful difference. Thus, this focus on the human, the changing and concrete in continental thought is often accompanied by a huge cost. Many thinkers in the continental tradition disregard questions regarding the logical, conceptual and law-governed aspects that the analytic tradition tends to investigate in detail. This leads to a philosophy that is just as one-sided in its focus on the concrete, the human and the lived. It is thus a tradition yielding answers and systems as unequilibrated as the linguistic or logical investigations and answers proposed by many analytic philosophers. A new balance is needed.

The substitution of realistic and pragmatic aims for big ideas and ideals that shaped both traditions further contributed in shifting society towards nihilism. We now live in a world that has lost faith in anything beyond immediate individual gratification, the immediate practical outcome. And thus, today, we are confronted with the realisation that pure creative openness, mere goal- and gratification-oriented pragmatism and absolute equality are also problematic, maybe even just as problematic as the blind and faithful adherence to traditional ideals and absolutes had been.

It is this situation of nihilistic, pluralistic and pragmatic groundlessness that the current revolution of return is replying to. It is an attempt to forge a new path that can cut across the extremes we are currently encountering. An attempt to mitigate between the sceptical uncertainty born of open creativity, difference, pragmatism and pluralism on the one hand, and abstract scientific-mathematical, logical or linguistic dogmatism on the other. How to mediate between creativity and reason, how to take productive genesis seriously without losing the moments of stability, certainty and objectivity? This search for a new path able to avoid the death of *reasonable open creativity* is the oldest, most traditional of philosophical paths. It mirrors Plato's attempt to avoid the *gigantomachia*, or Kant's attempt to forge a path between rationalism and empiricism.

The path that I propose in this book is a thoroughly Aristotelian one. It consists in combining a focus on direct experience (as *engaged experience*), in an attempt to avoid dogmatism, while also employing general, logically sound principles that are developed in correlation with engaged experience to avoid relativism and scepticism. What I have in mind here is the development of a middle way of thought, along the lines of Nagarjuna's path developed in the *Mulamadhyamakakarika*.

Due to its focus on direct experience, this investigation is anchored to a specific immanent issue. The issue that I will investigate using this Aristotelian approach is *the correlation between thinking and being*, that is, the correlation between a certain way of attaining knowledge (i.e. a certain epistemological stance) and a certain understanding of what there is (i.e. a specific ontology or metaphysical stance). This implies that any investigation into either epistemology or ontology/metaphysics needs to engage with both correlated elements in their correlation. And it is this correlation that, as I will argue, can ground truth, knowledge and certainty to an adequate degree and thus makes a genuine renewal of metaphysics as dynamic realism possible.

The intimate relation between thinking and being has shaped philosophy from the outset; epistemology and ontology are fundamentally intertwined. Nowhere is this close connection more obvious than in the question of realism. Before any investigation into realism can begin, however, a distinction has to be made. Are we looking at epistemic realism (how do we get to know what is real) or ontological realism (what is real)? If one approaches this conundrum by beginning with an ontological description of what there is, we encounter a distinct set of problems. First, we do not have a clear understanding of what the term 'is' should refer to, or what function it fulfils. Is it merely a copula, the element of language that connects subjects and predicates on a linguistic level and is thus of no logical importance? The sign of identity? Does it denote existence or being (and is there a difference between the two)? Is 'is' a predicate? And if it were a predicate what would the hallmark properties of 'existence' be? To be causally effective? To be material? To be substantial? Not only have these issues been debated since the beginning of Western philosophy, but there is still not even agreement on which method would allow us to answer these kinds of questions adequately.

Thus, it might be better to begin with an epistemic approach, by coming to an agreement as to which method we should employ to answer the question of what is real. However, this starting point immediately invites a different set of questions. How do we know that this approach actually uncovers what there is and not merely a mediated or (subjectively) constructed version of what there is? Can we discover what there is through our senses, or do only scientific results disclose reality? Is the true nature of what there is only accessible through speculation and reason? In order to answer these kinds of questions, we need to return to ontology, and depending on what we think reality is like, different epistemic approaches will reveal themselves as more or less adequate. If reality somehow shares the structures that shape thought, then speculation or conceptual analysis could prove to be adequate approaches; however, if what there is takes the form of mere chaotic matter, a speculative approach would be rather inadequate. So, which epistemic method is adequate to discover the nature of reality ultimately depends on what there actually is.

And thus we end where we started: in order to assess the adequacy of our epistemic stance we would need to know what reality is like, and in order to assess the adequacy of our ontological stance we need to provide a solid methodology, an epistemic approach that can disclose the nature of reality at least with a sufficient degree of intersubjective or objective certainty. Investigating these correlated aspects in separation has not led to convincing answers on either side. Instead of doing more of the same, it might be time to test a different approach, namely, to focus on the correlation between certain ontologies and certain epistemic approaches to generate a more resilient understanding of what there is. In a second step the adequacy of the resulting description can then be tested, using *all* of our investigative tools, including experience, scientific methodologies and discoveries as well as conceptual and logical analysis, to identify and hopefully balance any one-sidedness or bias.

In this book I will look at the correlation between thinking and being, but in order to further anchor this investigation I will focus on a specific form of this correlation. I will be looking at the correlation between a *phenomenological style of investigation of experience* and *dynamic (i.e. processual) realism*. To claim that such a correlation between phenomenological descriptions and a dynamic realism, as I propose it, is *adequate* (not true or certain, but adequate), is to claim that descriptions in the phenomenological style, if taken seriously, correspond to, imply, lead to or indicate[1] a dynamic nature of the world; in other words that any phenomenological description of experience suggests a dynamic *how of existence*. This approach presupposes the phenomenological claim that we can trust our senses to disclose something about the world, while requiring that we

---

1. Whether this relation between phenomenology and dynamic realism is most adequately spelled out as correspondence, implication, suggestion or indication depends on the precise perspective taken (for example, which precise phenomenological/dynamic stance is chosen) and the concrete aspect investigated using both the tools of phenomenology and dynamic realism (for example, the real, existence or identity). It is therefore context-dependent. But one of these characterisations will hold in any investigative context that is centred on unconcealing what there is from the correlation between phenomenological descriptions and dynamic ontologies.

remain sceptical about our interpretative judgements about these experiences. This approach also allows for the corresponding claim that a dynamic, creative and thus processual understanding of reality can only show itself from a certain epistemic stance, namely in beginning one's investigation with a clarified form of experience. This clarification of experience is to be understood as an attempt to exclude the distorting conceptual influences of our explanatory models, of our preconceptions regarding what is given in experiences, as much as possible. In sum, the claim I am defending throughout this book is that phenomenology can lead to a dynamic understanding of how reality exists, and that process metaphysics and process ontologies presuppose an active (quasi-phenomenological) dismantling of experiential preconceptions, in order to enable us to see what there is as it is actually experienced.

I first happened to encounter this correlation when re-reading Alfred North Whitehead's *Process and Reality*, while at the same time engaging with Edmund Husserl's phenomenology. And I could not help but wonder at the similarities, analogies and overlaps. In both traditions experience and temporality are foundational.[2] Furthermore, thinkers in both traditions emphasise the necessity of beginning one's investigation with a very specific epistemological attitude in order to be able to experience or disclose what there is (given) in the first place. Phenomenological descriptions and processual accounts of reality share one fundamental idea: *To experience the world without conceptual blinkers on is to see a temporal, relational and dynamic world.* And while a certain reading of Husserl's thought seems to preclude an ontological use of the phenomenological method, already Martin Heidegger prepared the path for a fruitful combination of ontological and phenomenological investigations in *Being and Time*. Thus, in this book I use phenomenology as an epistemological platform that

---

2. See, for example, the study on temporality and subjectivity in Whitehead and Merleau-Ponty by Luca Vanzago, which focuses on outlining these similarities (Vanzago, *Modi*).

allows me to disclose a dynamic reality, while process thought provides an ontological outline that grounds phenomenology as an epistemological approach able to uncover how what there is appears. The idea of such a correlation between epistemology and ontology allows me to fuse systematic and structural analogies between phenomenology and process thought and thus to fuse descriptions based in experience with speculative metaphysics, without remaining trapped within subjectivity on the one hand, and without losing experiential grounding for our metaphysical speculations on the other.

The fact that this book is published in a series that creates a space to combine continental and analytic modes of thought is hugely appropriate. The main thinkers shaping this account, namely Husserl, Whitehead and Bergson, are truly at home in both modes of thought; these thinkers combine the best traits of both traditions. Not only did Frege and Husserl work on similar questions around meaning and reference, but it is also well documented that it was Frege's critique of Husserl's *Philosophie der Arithmetik* that influenced the latter to attempt to clarify his stance on psychologism. This attempt affected the argumentation in Husserl's *Logical Investigations* and thus, in a sense, Frege's critique was a catalyst that contributed to the development of phenomenology. This is not to say that there are not numerous other influences that contributed to the development of Husserl's phenomenology, chief among them his teacher Franz Brentano's empirical psychology and the neo-Kantian lines of thought that shaped academic philosophy in Germany at the time. But it is questionable whether Husserl would have gone down this route without the initial spark provided by Frege's critique.

Alfred North Whitehead, on the other hand, was a trained mathematician who composed the *Principia Mathematica* in collaboration with Bertrand Russell. In his later career his focus shifted to the philosophy of science and then to metaphysics. These interests led him to develop process thought as an attempt to account for and unify mathematical, physical and experiential aspects. After moving to Harvard, he lectured on philosophy of nature and cosmology, influencing thinkers in the analytic tradition, most famously his doctoral student Willard Van Orman Quine.[3] Henri Bergson too was a precocious mathematician, and in quite an analytic fashion he developed (at least his early) philosophy in a close engagement with the physics, biology and mathematics of his time.

The main figures shaping this investigation thus in a way precede the continental–analytic distinction and were able to simply combine – as was always the case before the continental–analytic split in the twentieth century – logic with poetry, rigorous argument with sensory intuition and the vagueness of experience, the introduction of new terminology with an attempt to create precision and clarity. So, even if these thinkers are usually considered to belong to one or the other group, the main figures shaping this investigation are neither continental nor analytic thinkers. They are simply philosophers open to using any conceptual tool, any method, approach or language that seems helpful and adequate to tackle the philosophical problem at hand.

---

3. For a comparative account, see McHenry, 'Quine'. Quine himself replied to this account in the same issue, fundamentally agreeing with the claim that there is a large overlap between Whitehead and himself.

Part I Metaphysics as a Relation of Thinking and Being

> There remains the final reflection, how shallow, puny, and imperfect are efforts to sound the depths in the nature of things. In philosophical discussion, the merest hint of dogmatic certainty as to finality of statement is an exhibition of folly.
> Alfred North Whitehead, *Process and Reality* xiv

In this first part I introduce my terminology and methodology. I will defend the possibility of devising a new form of metaphysical realism that results from the intersection of ontology and epistemology. I introduce my precise understanding of realism and of experience in order to distinguish this investigation from other attempts to formulate a realistic position based on experience. In doing so I begin to spell out the correlation between phenomenology and process ontology as an adequate starting point to investigate the concrete, physical reality we are living in, and thus as an adequate method for developing a dynamic realism.

1

Terminological and Methodological Clarifications

In the second part of this chapter I introduce and justify the method(s) used in this investigation. There I will focus on characterising the method of speculation in order to distinguish it from a traditional understanding of speculation and from its use in the context of 'speculative realism'. I will also discuss and defend my use of phenomenology as a method that can help in developing a realist position. I will finally describe how I fuse speculation with phenomenology to achieve dynamic realism. Before I do so, in what follows I will introduce relevant terminology and clarify some central concepts and terms. This introduction of terminology is for the purpose of orientation only, and I agree with Santayana when he states that 'I do not ask anyone to think in my terms if he prefers others. Let him clean better, if he can, the windows of his soul, that the variety and beauty of the prospect may spread more brightly before him' (Santayana vi). However, argumentation is only possible when the meaning and the implications of basic terms is agreed; therefore I will quickly introduce my use of specific terminology at this point. Fuller definitions as well as more detailed arguments for the adequacy of these definitions will be provided throughout the book.

One presupposition that shapes my use of terminology should be addressed explicitly, namely the fact that I presuppose reality to be fundamentally temporal and thus changing or processual. While I will provide reasons for doing so throughout, many readers might wonder why they should go along with such an unusual presupposition and might demand to be convinced of this before they were willing to engage further. However, such arguments as to why a process ontology provides the most adequate description of what there is would result in a different book. A very thorough reader could, before proceeding, engage with texts already available that argue for a processual understanding of reality (for example Bergson, *Creative Mind*; Röck, *Physis*; Whitehead, *Process*). A more adventurous reader could simply go along and for the sake of the argument grant that the aspects of experience that show the world as changeable and evolving are at least as fundamental as those elements that show stability, which makes accounting for what there is as process at least as viable a strategy as any substantial account. If by the end of this book my arguments have failed to render the presupposition that reality is processual at least a viable strategy to account for what there is, then at least this idea will have been given a fair shot by the reader and can be safely ignored.

Terminology

Experience

I am interested in a specific understanding of experience that can disclose the objective, spatiotemporal world we live in as it is, while also accounting for the subjective elements involved in this disclosure. This form of experience is phenomenologically clarified and/or pragmatically/processually radicalised. This statement implies that 1) a phenomenological account of experience is comparable or largely analogous to a pragmatic/processual account of experience, and 2) that there are fundamental differences between such a clarified or radicalised understanding of (sense) experience and the way we commonly understand (sense) perception.

A first helpful approach to understand this difference between clarified or radicalised experience and our common-sense understanding is evident in the difference between the German terms

TERMINOLOGICAL AND METHODOLOGICAL CLARIFICATIONS

Erlebnis and *Erfahrung*.[1] While both are usually translated as 'experience' there is a distinct difference. *Erlebnis* refers to a direct lived experience that is not (or is only minimally) influenced by past experiences, education, socio-economic background; that is, it is not (or is only minimally) influenced by memories, background assumptions or concepts. It is not a pre-linguistic experience in the strict sense, but it is an attempt to grasp those experiences that are so intense that they shatter or at least crack the conceptual structures that shape most experiences. The birth of a child might be such an *Erlebnis*, or perhaps the experience of being shot. This form of experiencing can lead to an intimate familiarity with the content of experience that is not distorted by memories or ideas. It is a familiarity that is only truly available to someone who has actually had this experience. This is the level of concreteness and familiarity with what there is that phenomenologists are trying to achieve for every experience, to allow us to be moved by the experience itself and not our conceptual interpretations. Whether it is ultimately possible to liberate experiences from interpretations, and to what degree, remains a point of contentious debate. However, phenomenological descriptions have succeeded in disclosing aspects to experience that were usually overlooked or covered by preconceptions. So even if the promise of an experience that is fully freed from concepts can never be fulfilled, attempting to free experience from conceptual interpretations as much as possible has proven fruitful.

On the flip side, while this intimate, concrete familiarity can be very enlightening, it is not directly communicable and thus not easily shared with others who have not had this experience. The second term *Erfahrung* points towards experiences that include conceptual engagement (including memories, education and previous lived experiences) that supports, shapes and deepens the experience with a level of context and interpretation. This

---

1. I am not here following Heidegger's distinction between the two terms, but instead referring to general use.

corresponds to our everyday understanding of experience as perception, which involves a mixture of personal experience, interest, conceptual interpretation and theoretical, social and cultural background.[2] This means that 'perception is a process of interpretation; we get to the point of perceiving something as a result of the work of interpreting. The perceived object is therefore an interpretative construct, that is, a construction made by the subject through the act of interpretation' (Wiesing 23). The problem with perception is therefore, as Bergson argues, that while perceptions can be communicated more easily, they actually hide what there is and what would be available through direct experience behind a 'veil of prejudices', some of which are 'artificial, created by philosophical speculation, the others natural to common sense' (Bergson, *Creative Mind* 131).

This distinction between intimate lived experience and conceptually influenced perception has epistemological consequences with regard to how we can account for experience. It is connected to the distinction between subjective ways of experiencing (the actual experience of experience, for example either as *Erlebnis* or *Erfahrung*) and ways of thinking about experience (a conceptual account of what experience is). Possible ways of thinking about experience that have shaped philosophical thinking are, among many others, to consider experience an act that discloses primary and secondary properties, or an act that discloses phenomenal data. The way we conceptualise experience influences our ways of experiencing/perceiving as well as our interpretation of what is given in experience. The process of phenomenological clarification and/or pragmatic/processual radicalisation is a way to strip experience of such conceptual meta-interpretations and thus to focus the investigation on the actual subjective ways of experiencing.

While these definitions and distinctions are helpful to gain a better understanding of phenomenological clarification and/or pragmatic/processual radicalisation in the context of

---

2. For a different but correlated view on this distinction, see Levine 11.

experience, ultimately I am interested in an understanding of experience that goes beyond these distinctions, and especially the dichotomy between active and passive as well as subjective and objective. Such a complex interactive approach is necessary because of the complicated nature of actual experience. First, there is no position outside of experience from which we could investigate experience objectively; we are always already experiencing beings. Any investigation of experience is thus already fully immersed in and influenced by what it attempts to investigate. The being of humans is furthermore shaped by a most intimate connection between consciousness, its intentional nature, its directedness towards the world and our ontological, physical, biological existence. The way we are in the world is mediated by a human body – an extraordinarily complex and varied arrangement of physical, biological and experiential moments – a body that experiences and interacts with all the other beings-in-the-world. This is a basic fact of being that is actually given in experience. To make matters worse, insofar as we as experiencing subjects are part of this objective world, this radically subjective experience not only grants us a relation to this world, it is furthermore an ontological, an actual part of this reality. Experience, as it is performed by experiencing beings, is part of the world, and thus it is at the same time purely subjective givenness of the world as well as objectively present in the world. The fact that experience runs across the epistemic–ontological divide in these ways is the starting point of this investigation.

The aim is thus to understand experience as an encounter or a result of the coordinated interaction of world and mind, at once active and passive, subjective and objective. This is an encounter that is shaped by the givenness of what is experienced, ideally with as little conceptual distortion as possible. McDowell proposes such an understanding of experience as an in-between, in arguing that 'when we enjoy experience conceptual capacities are drawn on in receptivity, not exercised on some supposedly prior deliverances of receptivity' (McDowell 10). But these 'conceptual capacities that are passively drawn into play in experience' are not purely or simply passive, because they 'belong to a network of capacities for active thought, a network that rationally governs comprehension-seeking responses to the impacts of the world on sensibility'. Thus 'although experience itself is not a good fit for the idea of spontaneity, even the most immediately observational concepts are partly constituted by their role in something that is indeed appropriately conceived in terms of spontaneity' (McDowell 12). Beginning with experience as a coordinated interaction between mind and world, between passivity and spontaneity, allows us to push our investigation of experience towards uncovering how and to what extent our experience depends on subjective constitution, and by extension it allows us to push it in the other direction as well. It allows us to push towards the objective aspects of experience. The experience of things does not only depend on subjective constitution but is at the same time a self-giving (*Selbstgegebenheit*) of the object.

Thus, this turn towards what there is *as it is given in experience* does not imply a strict distinction between inner and outer, between subjective and objective. It describes an intimate unity of the given that is accessible to us in experience – be it a unity based on ontological processes or a unity based on intentionality. These conceptual shifts in the understanding of experience and the consequent focus on the actual act of experiencing make it possible to use subjective experience as the basis for dynamic realism, in a way that does not end in naïve realism, or in a position that negates the existence of or access to mind-independent reality. The proposed turn towards the real as that which is given in (clarified) experience is thus not a negation of consciousness and its active role, but is in fact the result of a reimagination of consciousness and at the same time a reimagination of what we mean by 'material', 'physical' or 'natural', as well as a reimagination of their respective active and passive contributions to any act of experience. It is furthermore not an attempt to naturalise phenomenology or process philosophy, as if natural were synonymous with material or law-governed. If nature can instead be thought as creative, spontaneous and open then this is indeed an attempt to naturalise these traditions.

Metaphysics, ontology and meta-ontology

Both *metaphysics* and *ontology* are ways to investigate and describe what there is; however, they have different focal points. Metaphysical systems are developed in order to grasp reality as a whole, to account for the ways we create hierarchies of value and the way we place ourselves against or with these values and what there is. Metaphysics, as I understand it, is concerned with how order, meaning and value are generated based on our sensual experience of what there is, and how they can be grounded, not in our concepts, but in what there is. In contrast to this outlook, ontology is the search for the basic qualities, fundamental entities or categories that capture and characterise what is, or what exists in *this* world. Ontology is the attempt to describe and situate these entities or categories (that stem from observance of what there is) within any given metaphysical system. While metaphysics is thus ultimately an attempt to structure and make sense of what there is as a whole, ontology is the study of the (structure of) elements or things that we are trying to make sense of within any given metaphysical framework.

This distinction can be spelled out in various ways. From a Quinean perspective and terminology, for example, ontology is the attempt to enumerate and list all that there is, and metaphysics becomes an investigation into the 'nature, structure and fundamental features of the kinds of things listed' (Berto and Plebani 4). If we take an Aristotelian perspective, metaphysics investigates the structures of *dynamis* (potential) and *energeia* (actuality) and how these relate to the unmoved mover, while ontology is concerned with the *ousiai* (forms/substances) and the other categories. From the perspective taken in this book, ontology is the attempt to describe and analyse the processes in their becoming, while metaphysics looks at their integration, the resulting creative potential and how this creative temporal integration forms, structures and orders reality as a whole. This, of course, implies that there is a certain interdependency and correlation between metaphysics and ontology, which makes a clear-cut or absolute distinction between these fields impossible.

We tend to distinguish two main methods of metaphysical inquiry, namely descriptive metaphysics or revisionary metaphysics. And while I do focus on (phenomenological) descriptions in this book, it is not an exercise in this traditional kind of descriptive metaphysics. While descriptive metaphysics 'is content to describe the actual structure of *our thought* about the world' (Strawson 9), the kind of metaphysics I am interested in attempts to describe the actual structure of the world. It attempts to go beyond conceptual and theoretical structures in order to uncover the actual structure of the world that is given in radicalised sense experience. So, with Husserl, Bergson and Whitehead, I am developing a descriptive metaphysics that does not describe our (pre)conceptions of what we think we experience, that is not guided by the semantic and syntactic structures of our propositions and judgements about the contents of our experience, but that orients itself on what we are actually given in experience.

As stated above, it is not the aim of this book to develop a processual ontology or metaphysics; I simply presuppose a generalised form of process thought.[3] The main thrust of this investigation is the development and grounding of a meta-ontology. A meta-ontology is an investigation that attempts to determine which questions or methods should guide ontological (and in consequence influence metaphysical) investigations. As I laid out in the introduction, not every epistemic position is able to come to terms with any metaphysical stance. Some epistemic positions exclude certain metaphysical/ontological accounts of what there is and vice versa. Taking the epistemic position, for example, that only reason can adequately uncover and represent what there is correlates with an understanding of *true* reality as

---

3. For an outline of this form of process ontology, see Röck, *Physis*.

TERMINOLOGICAL AND METHODOLOGICAL CLARIFICATIONS

fundamentally rational, ideal and conceptual. However, if one takes what there is to be fundamentally singular, material and concrete – as that with which we practically engage – it seems intuitively plausible that a close phenomenological description would provide a much more adequate point of departure. I am thus following a dual approach to learn the nature of what there is. I am not only investigating what we mean when we ask what there is, but at the same time I am looking for the most adequate methodology to access this knowledge and thus generate a realist ontology/metaphysics.

To engage in meta-ontology also means to investigate what we actually mean when we ask what there is and how what there is exists. I take these questions that probe the structure and nature of being as attempting to pick out those elements of reality which make an actual difference in our lives, in our reality. It means to ask about that which has the ability to affect and the ability to have an effect on itself or other beings over time. From the outset, this way of conceptualising the question of what there is and how what there is exists presupposes a quite relational and temporal understanding of what there is. This is where many more traditional meta-ontological approaches fall short in their attempt to describe actual reality. For example, compiling an exhaustive list of everything that exists is not an adequate approach if reality turns out to be fundamentally dynamic and relational. Not only does this enumerative approach sever all relations, but it also abstracts from the fact that things do change – they become and perish. Such an enumerative framework cannot account for the interconnected (relational) and temporal aspects of the world that we live in, because it breaks what there is into distinct, unchanging identities and thus turns creative, correlated becoming into enumerable entities.

Nor does an analytic/reductive approach that moves towards discovering the fundamental constituents of reality and cataloguing the basic types of ontological existents seem a fruitful meta-ontological approach for present purposes. Why should it necessarily be the case that the atoms that make up the chair provide a better or more informative basis for the characterisation of what makes an actual difference than the chair I bang my shin against? To me, the one seems to be as relevant as the other. And since I cannot bang my shin on an atom, but merely what is composed of atoms, i.e. the chair, the chair might even be the more relevant level of detail or resolution to provide a basis for an investigation of what caused the pain in my shin. What level of detail is adequate of course depends on the precise aspect investigated, the context and the aim of the investigation. In determining the impact of chemical compounds docking on to certain receptors, for example, a different level of resolution will be adequate than macroscopic objects. My argument is simply that the level of resolution should be adequate to the situation investigated as well as the investigative aim, and that it is a mistake to default to the lowest or lower levels alone, without also addressing intermediary as well as higher levels. Applying this strategy to the case of biochemistry, I would argue that merely investigating the chemical compounds and their effect on the organism is insufficient. Depending on the compound, in the case of humans, for example, convictions or beliefs can have as much of an impact as the chemical itself (if not more so), as studies into placebo and nocebo effects have shown, and will impact the measurable results. Ultimately it might be that different descriptions or models[4] of the same phenomenon will always be needed to account for different investigative aims:

> The multiplicity of models is imposed by the contradictory demands of a complex, heterogeneous nature and a mind that can only cope with a few variables at a time; by the contradictory desiderata of generality, realism and precision, by the need to understand and also to control; even by the aesthetic standards which emphasize the stark simplicity and power of a

---

[4]. Both a 'concept' and a 'model' provide a generalised or idealised account of some state of affairs, a set of ideas or processes. While concepts are purely linguistic in their account, a model can be a mathematical, physical or conceptual representation of an event, a process or a system of ideas.

general theorem against the richness and the diversity of living nature. These conflicts are irreconcilable. (Levins 431)

This, however, does not lead to relativism or scepticism, but simply accounts for the fact that the complexities of living nature cannot be captured in a single, unified conceptual system. It simply means that some models map general features and are thus less adequate to capture a specific concrete system, while other models map more specific features and are thus less insightful when it comes to discovering general structures.

While analytic and reductive approaches can generate valuable insights, they are not adequate methods for the issues this book is concerned with. So, instead of compiling lists of what there is or trying to find the most basic elements of what there is, the present meta-ontological approach consists in investigating the qualitative differences in the ways in which being can be thought and experienced. What there is can be thought as existing in an abstract or ideal manner, in a material or physical manner, in a potential manner, or – and this is the position I will take – as enduring, dynamic and relational. This last *how of existence* (manner of being) as enduring, dynamic and relational is also the most compatible with the way we actually experience what there is, and thus the most adequate basis for the construction of a dynamic ontology and a realist metaphysics.

Change

The problem of change shaped Western philosophy from the outset. Plato's Socrates presents this problem in the most concise way I have encountered so far:

> SOCRATES: Can we, then, if it is always passing away, correctly say that it is this, then that it is that, or must it inevitably, in the very instant while we are speaking, become something else and pass away and no longer be what it is?
> CRATYLUS: That is inevitable.

> SOCRATES: Then if it never stays the same, how can it be something? [...]
> CRATYLUS: There's no way.
> SOCRATES: Then again it can't even be known by anyone. For at the very instant the knower-to-be approaches, what he is approaching is becoming a different thing, of a different character, so that he can't yet come to know either what sort of thing it is or what it is like — surely, no kind of knowledge is knowledge of what isn't in any way. (Plato, *Cratylus* 439d–e)

While our lives and our senses are inundated with changes, philosophers have denied the reality of change (and in some cases also of time), because the reality of change leads to conceptual contradictions in describing or accounting for reality. But this doubt, this denial of change, involves 'an assumption much grosser than that which they discard' (Santayana 27). To deny the existence of change on conceptual grounds alone presupposes that conceptual contradictions are a clearer guide to truth or falsehood than our experience or our senses. This means assuming that 'if a thing is dialectically unintelligible, as change is, or inexpressible in terms other than its own, it cannot be true' (Santayana 27). This is a presupposition that, to my knowledge, has often been held, but never proven or even clearly and concisely argued on an ontological level.

One way to account for change while avoiding the conceptual problems mentioned is to engage the problem on the level of language. Taking this route, Bertrand Russell, for example, defined change as

> the difference, in respect of truth or falsehood, between a proposition concerning an entity and a time T and a proposition concerning the same entity and another time T', provided that the two propositions differ only by the fact that T occurs in the one where T' occurs in the other. (Russell, *Principles* §442)

This definition of change as a difference in the truth-value of two propositions about the same entity, at different points in time, is known as Cambridge change. While Cambridge change is a way to express a change in properties (intrinsic as well as extrinsic) without contradiction, it does not grasp the ontological phenomenon of change itself and thus cannot provide a workable solution for us.

Ontological changes have, however, also often been investigated in a similar way: something is changing if at t it has property x, which at t' has been replaced by property y. Change is what happens between t and t'. This interval account of change does not deal with or account for any actual movement, nothing is actually undergoing changes. One (static) state at t is contrasted with another (static) state at t', therefore effectively circumventing the phenomenon in question, namely the process of change. This procedure limits our ability to investigate change. It can only be investigated as a fait accompli, diagnosed in retrospect, but we cannot catch in its processual actuality. This focus on the effect of a process of change enables us to disregard the actual goings-on between the limit points. In any such *interval description of change*, change becomes a mysterious thing that happens between two points in time. In conceptually transforming change into something unknown happening between two points, we transform an immediate and obvious experience into a conceptual problem.

This understanding of change thinks movement and change through immobility, distils from movement and change all that is dynamic, and reduces it to intelligible and enduring static elements. Therefore, this account of change is not a viable route for the present project, rooted in the attempt to do justice to the phenomenon of change as an ongoing process. Actual change can only be properly understood if the flow and dynamicity of change is considered in its actuality, as given in experience. Thus, we do not understand actual change by comparing an entity at one point in time with the same entity at another point or by considering linguistic accounts of change. We understand change by looking at what actually happens between these points, when we look at the actual growth, flow and passage, since, as Whitehead put it, 'we live in durations, and not in points' (Whitehead, *Aims* 159).

When I use the term 'change' I do not distinguish between 1) accidental change or the change of properties of an unchanging underlying entity and 2) substantial change as the non-identity of things over time or the change involved in becoming or perishing. The main implication of this is that the term 'change' does not necessarily imply an unchanging entity undergoing change. Therefore, I use change as a general term (much like the ancient Greek term *kinesis*) to refer to all sorts of processes, including becoming, movement, qualitative changes, quantitative changes and perishing, and also the processes referred to in expressions such as 'the times are changing' or 'it's changeable' (referring to the weather). The term thus does not merely describe accidental changes, which do in fact presuppose something that undergoes these changes, but instead refers to all possible forms of change. The reason why I can dispense with the distinction between accidental and substantial change is that from the perspective of dynamic ontologies, there are no substances that any change could stand in an accidental relation to.

However, change as it is understood here is not a form of hyper-chaos, where anything can transform into anything else in an instant. Changes remain law-governed, at least to a certain extent. Thinkers who presuppose genuine change do not claim that changes are chaotic or are transformations that are completely lawless or arbitrary. There is continuity in most changes. The world we experience is mostly one of continuous process. Wooden tables do not simply turn into swimming pools. There is a certain style to actual change, a certain calm continuity. If change were completely ungoverned chaos, the experience of absolute change, without any connection to the past, would simply create the impression of changelessness. 'A certain actual persistence is requisite to perceive a flux, and an absolute flux, in which nothing was carried over from moment to moment, would yield, in each of these moments, nothing but an intuition of permanence' (Santayana 31). The claim that everything flows or that all is process merely amounts to the claim that there is not one single spatiotemporal element or thing that, given a suitably thorough investigation, remains unchanged over long periods of time. The claim is that, if we observed our environment over a sufficiently long period, let's say thousands of years, and if we investigated it at all possible scales from the atom to the galaxy, then we would not discover one single element, aspect or entity that had remained completely unchanged. One might now interject that this position is self-refuting, as it tacitly presupposes an eternal unchanging observer, but descriptions as well as knowledge can be the result of collaboration and accumulation. Different observers can describe different events at different times, and these descriptions can then be compared to detect continuities as well as changes. This collective and collaborative engagement is in fact how science progresses and how knowledge expands.

Being

Consequently, I do not consider the term 'being' to denote an atemporal entity underlying changes, nor do I consider the term to imply an atemporal form of existing. On a purely grammatical level, the term 'being', much like the German *Seiendes*, is a gerund. As a grammatical structure this suggests a temporal process, a going on, and not an atemporal entity. Taking this linguistic form of 'being' seriously, I take it to denote a continuously ongoing existence. This definition of being as an ongoing existence renders the expression 'being is temporal', which I also use, a tautology. However, since we are generally not accustomed to think of being in its temporal extension, the use of this tautology provides a handy reminder of the temporal and processual nature of being. In contrast, the term 'existence' does not have a temporal connotation and can thus be used to refer to potentially ideal or possibly unchanging (non-temporal) entities. In its use as a gerund (i.e. existing) the term becomes synonymous with being.

However, even if change and temporality are as fundamental as I claim, is it adequate to identify this processual nature with 'being' as I did in the last paragraph? In his article 'Meta-ontology', Peter van Inwagen addresses this issue. He argues that '"lasting" or "enduring" or "getting older"' is 'a most general activity' and that this 'most general activity [is shared] with everything – or at least with every concrete inhabitant of the natural world'. However, he also claims that it is 'just wrong to call this activity "existing" or "being"' (van Inwagen 234). This amounts to the claim that 'being' cannot be thought as process, and that the 'most general activity' that 'is shared with everything' should not provide a characterisation of what there is. If correct, this line of argument would make the present project unviable. However, at this point van Inwagen's line of thought is rather confusing. Instead of defending this claim, he merely states that enduring is not more intimately connected to being than 'colour or shape or intelligence', 'for the plain reason [. . .] that one idea is not another idea' (van Inwagen 234). That one idea is not another is a tautology that, I have to admit, at this point simply makes no sense, as it does not seem to explain or justify his stance in any way. Granted, it is true that 'blue' is not the same as 'shape', since one idea is not the other. But 'blue' refers to a concrete, qualitatively determined colour and not a shape, just as becoming is a concrete, qualitatively determined (temporally extended) form of existence that characterises at least spatiotemporal entities (though it might not apply to ideal entities, possible entities, abstract entities and so on), and not some other form of existence. Therefore, I will argue that the process of enduring (going on) is not only most intimately connected to what there is in the spatiotemporal realm, it is one of its hallmark characteristics.

Van Inwagen goes on to argue that there is no informative difference between ascribing being and existence to something, that 'being' or 'existence' are univocal, and that this single sense of being or existence is adequately captured by the existential quantifier in formal logic. This is a position that simply presupposes that being or existence can be adequately understood in purely functional terms. This, according to van Inwagen, is the case because, following Kant, being or existence taken as 'mere existence' should not be understood as a property or a first-order predicate. Being or existence are purely quantitative or functional terms and cannot confer any qualitative content on what is considered to exist (Tegtmeier 34). If 'mere existence' were not understood in purely functional terms, so the argument goes, we would end up with the contradictory qualitative description of existence as having the quality of *having no qualities*. Therefore, the claim '*x* is or exists' does not add any informative content to the statement '*x*' – functionally these statements are identical. This of course is not compatible with my above distinction between existence and being. If 'being' is understood to further qualify 'mere existence', to indicate a specific how of being, namely as being temporal, as existing in a processual fashion, then being does confer a qualification that differs from existence. At the same time it is not a predicate in the traditional sense, since it does not add further information about *what something is*; instead it adds information about *how something is*. Thus adding 'is a being' adds a qualification about how something exists and it certainly does make a difference whether something is ascribed temporal being or mere existence.

Time and temporality

My focus on the phenomenon of time implies that I am not concerned with the more abstract or theoretical, reflective aspects of time such as eternity, infinity, the beginning of time and so on. Instead, I am interested in 'actual time', i.e. time that can be experienced. There can be no doubt that in our experience, temporality proves fundamental to the world. There is no such thing in inner or outer experience as timelessness. The fact that there is no practical escaping from temporality led me to posit the thesis that reality is fundamentally temporal and fundamentally changing, thus dynamic. Ideal or eternal entities are not focal objects of this investigation because, first and foremost, we cannot experience them as spatiotemporal objects; that is simply not how ideal objects are present to us. Ideal, eternal objects are qualitatively distinct from the spatiotemporal, phenomenal entities that we can actually experience, and these entities are the object of investigation in this book.

There is a difference between a logically sound conceptual account of *time* and a description of *temporality* that is grounded in experience. Bergson's distinction between clock time and duration is a helpful example to clarify this difference. According to Bergson, there is a 'cardinal difference between concrete time, along which a real system develops, and that abstract time which enters into our speculations on artificial systems' (Bergson, *Creative Evolution* 25). He argues that, in the case of *linear, abstract* or *measurable understanding of time as clock time* (or physical time as expressed through variables such as t_1, t_2 or Δt), time is thought as a linear extension between the past and the future. On this timeline any point in time can be situated. The selection of any point in time (on the timeline) creates a relative past and relative future (or a relative before and a relative after) with regard to the chosen point. This metaphor renders time linear and progressively ordered; consequently changes are usually conceptualised as moving from the future along the timeline towards the present and then into the past. Bergson now argues that this view does not reflect the way we actually experience time; it is highly abstract and conceptual account. As I will argue in Part III, we experience time as a duration, as a temporal going on, not as a line that is extended between the past and the future.

As a little aside, since time and its measurement through clocks as well as measuring in general is a prominent issue throughout this book, it seems apt to take a closer look at its role in modern physics: 'A term like "clock" [. . .] cannot appear in the statement of any fundamental physical law. Einstein was aware of this, and acknowledged that any discussion of physics couched in terms of "clocks" or "measuring rods" could be only a temporary expedient' (Maudlin 106). Why is the mention of a measuring tool so problematic for physics? Because measuring tools are relatively arbitrary ways to translate prima facie unmeasurable, qualitative, perceptible phenomena into standardised units, rendering them measurable. This procedure is problematic, as it introduces subjective elements, and a lot of care has to be taken to minimise, standardise and idealise these aspects (Maudlin 106–25). Developing standardised measurements to grasp actual reality and generate adequate definitions is a complex procedure and often involves choices between non-trivial alternatives. This even applies to the definition of what a measurement is. Some current theories consider measurements (or quantity terms) either to be conventional or realistic (i.e. the best empirical account of a specific quality or relation), as a unit of information (van Fraassen 141–85); or else measurements can be taken to be operationally defined through the steps necessary to yield such measurements. The potential problem that all of these theories of measurement imply is the need for (non-ideal, physical) measuring tools as well as (potentially non-conscious AI) subjects using these tools to perform the measurements, thus potentially introducing non-ideal aspects, subjectivity and action into the heart of physics.

While it seems indubitable that change involves time, it is now time to argue the inverse, namely that time involves change. The claim is that there is no *experiential* awareness of time, no experience of endurance or temporality, that is not connected to or even coextensive with an experience of some form of change, be it an experience of the flow of consciousness, of movement or of property-alteration. The claim that there is no experiential awareness of time without change does not imply that we cannot abstractly conceive of time without change; we clearly can, as Sidney Shoemaker's thought experiment proves.

Shoemaker argues that we can conceive of a scenario where time passes without any changes taking place. He invites us to think of a world that is comprised of three regions A, B and C. Each of these is undergoing a 'local freeze' of a year. During this freeze nothing changes from the perspective of the region undergoing the freeze, while observers from one of the other regions would still perceive changes and could communicate as much to the inhabitants of the frozen region, after the end of the freeze. This is a regular occurrence in Shoemaker's thought experiment and each region freezes at different intervals (three, four and five years); thus the inhabitants can predict a simultaneous freeze every sixty years and know when this event occurs. During the period where all three regions freeze at once, there is no experience of change, since there is no subject who could experience any changes or who could report on such changes. However, there is a passage of time and general knowledge of it. While Shoemaker might thus succeed in proving the logical possibility of time without change, to the best of my knowledge there is in fact no such world existing, nor are there such regions that freeze regularly. Should such regions and worlds be discovered one day, this argument would gain relevance for our purposes; as it stands, it merely describes a logical possibility, but not a possible experience. My claim is that we cannot actually perceive and bring to mind as present the experience of time without change. It simply is not a possible phenomenon that our senses could ever grasp. Time without change is thinkable but it cannot be experienced.

If we fail to acknowledge this difference, if in our explanations we eliminate the relevance of our experience in favour of a conceptual description, we commit what Whitehead called the *fallacy of misplaced concreteness*. This consists in mistaking an intellectual abstraction for a concrete reality and thus in treating such an abstraction not as a heuristic tool, but as a concrete, existing entity. It is a specific form of reification. Committing this fallacy means, for example, holding that the conceptual descriptions of what there is grasp a more fundamental reality than the reality that we can access in experience, and that thus it is sufficient to engage with laws, data graphs representing particles, mathematical formulae representing movements or other conceptual constructs in our attempt to understand the world. While concepts, mathematics and mathematical physics are powerful tools in helping us to understand aspects of what there is, there are moments of reality that have to be excluded in any conceptual or mathematical approach. Nowhere is this more evident than in accounts of temporal reality that are based on mathematical approaches, because '[m]athematics [. . .] represents a world eviscerated of time and phenomenal particularity. It is a visionary exploration of a simulacrum of the world, from which both time and phenomenal distinction have been sucked out' (Unger and Smolin 15).

This fallacy of misplaced concreteness is also at work in our tendency to reify abstractions. As soon as conceptual abstractions or models are taken as fundamental entities or as an accurate description of the situation, instead of tools that aid in thinking, problems rooted in concepts and abstractions take precedence over actual reality. Again, this is not to say that such abstractions are irrelevant; on the contrary, abstract ideas such as place, value, justice and so on are extremely relevant to our lives, just as models can have an immense power to generate deeper insights. However, it is not productive to put all the explanatory weight on the abstract concept or the simplified model alone.

On a side note, these thoughts also imply that there is a correlation between being in time and being changeable. Material beings are in time and are thus fundamentally changing, temporal, i.e. dynamic, processes. There is not one physical being that did not become at one point, just as there is (most likely) no physical being that will not perish. Between becoming and perishing there is a phase of relative stability – continuity – and this is the phase we refer to when we talk about being. Nonetheless, becoming and perishing are just as much part of being as the phase of continuity and relative stability.

While spatiotemporal or physical objects are in time and thus have the ability to change, ideal objects such as numbers, a priori laws, concepts and the like are not capable of change in the same way, if they are conceived in an abstract, Platonic or ideal fashion. A law, for example, describes how things have to be and is 'a true generalisation that is *spatiotemporally unrestricted*; it applies to all of space and time' (Godfrey-Smith 11). This means that a law, thus understood, is not subject to temporality, to change or to spatial location. When I talk about objects in time, I always refer to material or spatiotemporal objects, and not to objects that are outside of time, or entities or laws that are unrestricted by time.

How about cases where the spatiotemporally located and the ideal are connected? For example, the act of thinking an ideal object? In this case all depends on the exact aspect investigated and the investigative aim. While there might be ideal, not spatio-temporal objects that are eternal or unchanging, these kinds of entities fall outside of the scope of this investigation. The act of thinking such ideal entities, of gaining insight or understanding of such abstract objects, however, is temporal and thus implies the flow of time as part of the actual experience of consciously engaging with such an entity. Therefore, there is no experience of thinking such entities that does not involve change. This reflects the traditional Platonic distinction between διάνοια (*dianoia*, thinking, intellect) and νόησις (*noesis*, understanding or insight). The nous can access the ideas and is beyond time, but the act of our dianoetic thinking it is of a different quality and connected to temporality.

To sum up, I would just like to flag the two fundamental shifts in thinking that this understanding of a temporal reality implies. The first is concerned with the nature of time and implies the introduction of a concrete, ontological temporality. The second concerns the status of 'being'. Concrete beings are to be understood as fundamentally processual, dynamic and temporal, which means there is no static 'to be' (i.e. static object, substance, essence or substrate) at the heart of changing beings. These two shifts are interrelated: if being is fundamentally temporal, then temporality is just as real and ontological as concrete beings.

Adequacy

This meta-ontological project that investigates the methods capable of discovering reality as truly dynamic necessitates engagement with the problem of propositional knowledge in a world of genuine change. Thus, if we wish to come to terms with *dynamic being* on *a conceptual level*, a shift in our understanding of knowledge and truth is necessary. I use the term 'adequate' to express this shift from the traditional definition of knowledge and truth (which implies that all items of knowledge or truth have to clear the exact same standard of certainty) to a well-defined and limited plurality of standards of acceptable certainty.

The idea of various standards of truth as adequate for certain types of objects or judgements has its roots in the history of philosophy. Aristotle, for example, argues that judgements about *asyntheta* (i.e. simple or non-composed entities) cannot be true or false – in contrast to judgements about composed entities – but can only provide access (i.e. allow us to know) or fail to provide access (i.e. not lead to knowledge) (*Metaphysics* IX, 1052a). This implies that there is a different standard of truth and knowledge adequate for *asyntheta* than for composed entities. Similarly, Husserl's claim that positing sentences cannot be true or false, but merely fulfilled or unfulfilled, as he argues in his 6th logical investigation, provides an adequacy standard for positing sentences only. Heidegger's understanding of truth as *aletheia* provides an adequacy standard for phenomenological unconcealment, i.e. insights created through a description that focuses on unfamiliar aspects of familiar phenomena. Along similar lines, Wilfrid Sellars describes *picturing* as an adequacy relation that is 'a mode of "correspondence" *other than truth* that accompanies truth in the case of [basic] empirical statements' (Sellars, 'Truth' 54).

So how do we determine the standards of acceptable certainty when it comes to the concrete, creative, dynamic reality that we are living in? The concept of truth proposed in the pragmatic tradition provides a first stepping stone: 'What was originally a correspondence is transformed into an analogy between two movements: *the movement of things in the process of becoming* and *the movement of ideas as they are constructed*' (Debaise, *Speculative Empiricism* 10). I take this to mean that the closer the movement of ideas resembles the process of becoming, the stronger the analogy, the more adequate the resulting judgements are. Departing from this thought, I take the term '*ad-aequatio*' to point towards a process of making similar or aligning, thus towards the process of creating a correspondence between matters of fact and our propositions or judgements about them. Knowledge and truth, in this reading of *adaequatio*, does not simply exist, it is created in a process of alignment.

However, the term 'adequate', at least in its modern English use, has also taken on an additional meaning. We generally use adequate to refer to a set of qualities, namely the acceptability, appropriateness or suitability of something. I am using the term adequate in both of its meanings. This approach thus combines the idea of adequacy as the quality of *being appropriate* with *adaequatio* as a *process of making or creating similarity or alignment*, in such a way that the quality of adequacy (of being suitable) characterises both the result of the process but also the process itself.

The concept of adequacy thus replaces the role that certainty, evidence or *adaequatio rei et intellectus* have traditionally played, and allows for degrees of adequacy concerning knowledge and truth. It furthermore allows for truth and knowledge to be understood as processes, making it possible to generate truths about continuously changing objects or matters of fact. So, judgements or propositions that refer to dynamic events or entities cannot be simply considered to be either true or false (or certain, evident, or a straightforward correspondence/*adaequatio*) in the traditional sense; however, there is a standard of adequacy that they can either pass or fail. Thus, judgements or propositions can be more or less *effective* in grasping or expressing the processes in questions, they can be more or less adequate or faithful. This shift acknowledges that there is no ideal language that fully grasps its object; every system of symbolisation is only faithful to a degree:

> Logic, like language, is partly a free construction and partly a means of symbolising and harnessing in expression the existing diversities of things; and whilst some language, given a man's constitution and habits, may seem more beautiful and convenient

to him than others, it is a foolish heat in a patriot to insist that only his native language is intelligible or right. No language or logic is right in the sense of being identical with the facts it is used to express, but each may be right by being faithful to these facts, as a translation may be faithful. (Santayana vi)

To this I would just add that some languages, some logical systems and systems of symbolisation have the ability to be more faithful to the factual dynamic processes than others.

It is, however, also important to emphasise that the concept of adequate truth does not necessarily lead to scepticism or relativism. While there is generally a range of possible interpretations that suitably (i.e. adequately) fit, symbolise, encode or present the (constantly changing) phenomena, there are also interpretations that simply do not fit them. These are inadequate interpretations, judgements or propositions. Furthermore, any categorisation as (more or less) adequate or inadequate can and should always be reassessed in light of further changes and further discoveries. And, just to be clear, this shift towards truth as adequacy is not advisable for all contexts, especially not in those cases where precision and clarity are desirable and actually achievable.[5]

What there is – reality – world

Philosophers have proposed a wide range of ways to order and account for what there is: sense data, phenomena, material objects, the physically given, propositions, universals, relations, first principles and so on. For now, I will leave the meaning of 'what there is' undetermined, since it is the main aim of this book to come to terms with this question and how to pose it. However, the thrust of my arguments will be to claim that 'what there is'

---

5. More argumentative work needs to be done in order to make this use of 'adequate' a truly viable position, which I will do in my next book, *An Adequate Truth*.

should first and foremost be understood as the spatiotemporal and everyday world. The expression 'everyday world' should not be taken to imply that this world is everyday in the sense of being average, typical or standard. On the contrary, the everyday world that we encounter in living our lives is extraordinarily varied, complex, *dynamic* and *temporal*. The term 'everyday' merely refers to the fact that this world is inescapable, it is always present, it is every day. Furthermore, I use the expressions 'what there is' and 'what is real' or 'reality' synonymously and vary between them for stylistic reasons only.

One final clarification in this context. I use the expression 'the world' as a general term denoting the kinds of things and environments we engage with on a daily basis with a maximum of inclusivity. This, however, does not imply, as Markus Gabriel suggests in his book *Fields of Sense*, that there is 'a world', i.e. one unified region that could be understood as the sum total of all its elements (plus itself). I take the expression 'the world' to express the maximum extension currently present without implying any form of totality, since what is currently present is continuously evolving. This maximum extension does not imply an ultimate totality, since the world is truly temporal, constantly changing. Even if the world could be conceptualised as a totality, this could only be done if its potential future is disregarded. This totality could only capture the world in its current form, up to an artificially fixed moment of now, and thus by ignoring and artificially cutting off the ongoing developments now taking place. If, however, the temporal dimension is taken into consideration, it becomes clear that what there is, or the world, does constantly change in not fully predictable ways, and thus it could never be grasped fully as a final totality or understood absolutely. This dynamic and ever-changing world is thus much closer to Lacan's Real, which can never be fully grasped or expressed through symbols, than the traditional philosophical understanding of reality.

Due to the evolving creative openness of the world, which goes on even while we attempt to account for this maximal extension at one point in time, the problem is moot. While we attempt to formulate the maximal extension, this maximal extension keeps expanding. Thus, Gabriel's argument that the world (as an absolute or sum total of everything) does not exist in a full, final, eternal or atemporal manner turns out to be trivial.

Methodology

After having clarified some central concepts, I will now address the issue of methodology. I am aligned with Peirce when he argues that:

> Philosophy ought to imitate the successful sciences in its methods, so far as to proceed only from tangible premises which can be subjected to careful scrutiny, and to trust rather to the multitude and variety of its arguments than to the conclusiveness of any one. Its reasoning should not form a chain which is no stronger than its weakest link, but a cable whose fibres may be ever so slender, provided they are sufficiently numerous and intimately connected. (Peirce, *Chance* 3)

Consequently, I am not presenting a single line or chain of arguments that can act as proof for a specific metaphysical system. I am not devising a final system stabilised by a tight sequence of arguments, with one argument implying or leading to the other, thus creating one clear line of evidence. Instead I am connecting and interweaving various strands of reasoning from different traditions, in order to create a flexible metaphysical growth that remains able to change and adapt in light of new problems, challenges or arguments. I am combining a variety of arguments and points, however minor, that align and move thought in a similar direction. While I will focus on process thought and phenomenology, I also use strands of reasoning rooted in the analytic and the pragmatic tradition as well as the history of philosophy. I will also use insights gained by the natural sciences where appropriate.

Where to begin?

As Hegel already argued, beginnings are always problematic. This is the case because every beginning has a history, a process leading up to it, a certain way it came into being. It is therefore impossible to truly begin at the beginning. On the other hand, a beginning is not a mere continuation of what has come before; something new emerges. A beginning is the space between continuation and revolution, between sameness and difference. This is the space from which my investigation departs. The aspect of continuity is addressed by integrating lines of thought from the history of philosophy as well as traditional concepts into my argumentative network. The aspect of revolution is woven into this tapestry in the form of a revolutionary shift in the focus of investigation and a corresponding shift in the use of traditional concepts and ideas, as my redefinition of traditional concepts above indicates. Simply put, this shift consists in moving away from the methodological ideals of *clarity* and *simplicity* and the resulting ontological ideals of *oneness* and *substantiality*, while moving towards the ideal of *adequate clarity, actual temporality* and *related complexity*. This preserving and at the same time revolutionary approach is inspired by and mirrors the nature of processes: a process is a going on that preserves and transmutes at the same time.

This type of processual mediation between conservation and revolution is often connected to Hegelian thought in the form of a negation of negation. There are, however, two main differences between the movement of the concept in Hegelian philosophy and thinking of reality as a process. First, mediation in the case of process thought does not imply a linear progression towards higher or more inclusive levels, towards some form of higher fulfilment. Processes are neither rational nor structured or guided by reason. There are processes of dissolution and disintegration, which are just as real and fundamental as the processes of creation and growth. Thus, later stages in the process are not necessarily more evolved, more elaborate or in any other way preferable to earlier stages of the process.

The second difference between a Hegelian movement of the concept and the understanding of reality as process is that in the latter case, the resulting dynamic realism is a fundamentally realist position applying to what there is, including nature and the mind-independent material world, and not an account of the evolution of subjectivity, reason, consciousness or concepts. I am aware that this last claim is controversial and that any true Hegelian would simply argue that the Hegelian system is not a system of concepts only, that it is a fully fledged ontology. However, it is an ontology only in a post-Kantian sense, whereas process thought implies an ontology in the pre-Kantian sense.

Understanding the world as process implies that there are non-rational processes that make up, that *are* the physical world. Thinking the world as process in this way does not apply the laws of (dialectical) thought to nature, but claims that nature as process creates and brings forth its own structures that we need to learn to see, that we need to attune to, that we need to learn how to experience, describe and account for. Thus, my project has much in common with Maurizio Ferraris's vision of realism:

> My starting point, in a nutshell, is a thought experiment. Let's adopt Husserl's *epochē* and suspend for a moment Kant's Copernican revolution, to follow – as far as possible – a hypothesis: the coexistence and interaction of different beings in the world depend primarily on the properties of the latter, and not on the conceptual schemes of the 'I think' [. . .] In short, if we want a Copernican revolution, let's do it for real. So, instead of placing Man at the centre of the universe like Kant did, let's turn him/her into a secondary spectator of a world that is much greater and older than s/he is. (Ferraris, *Positive Realism* vii)

While I agree with Ferraris's move towards a pre-Kantian approach to ontology and metaphysics, my starting point remains phenomenologically grounded. This seems a contradiction only as long as one considers phenomenology as a form of idealism or as a correlationism with no access to the 'great outdoors'. I will argue that phenomenology can be read in a more realistic fashion, and that I can thus avoid this apparent contradiction. But there is an additional reason why beginning with phenomenology is advantageous in this case. Departing from phenomenological descriptions (and a continuous return to them) provides an essential limiting function on conceptual investigations and speculations.

In order to make this point I will use a reinterpretation of Nicolai Hartmann's distinction between *Realmöglichkeiten* (real possibilities) and *Denkmöglichkeiten* (possibilities of thought): While real possibilities are limited by what is actually possible in this world that we live in,[6] possibilities of thought are only limited by the syntax of thought. Quantum physics, for example, like any science, aims at disclosing real possibilities. However, the scientists involved seem to describe aspects of nature that run counter to our logical and semantic intuitions; they describe a world that seems to go beyond what we would generally think possible. The claims, for example, that there is instantaneous communication, or that there is some form of dual existence as particle and wave, are examples of apparently real possibilities that seem to go beyond what we would generally consider intuitively likely, thinkable or logically consistent. Thought experiments and arguments based on intuitions, on the other hand, both describe possibilities of thought. Such conceptual scenarios are conceivable, they follow the syntax of thought, but they do not describe the reality we live in, nor is it clear that they have any bearing on this reality. An excellent case in point is Shoemaker's thought experiment probing our intuitions with regard to time and change. While his thought experiment might tease out our deep intuitions around the possibility of *thinking* time without change, it does not have any bearing on the question

---

6. While what we consider to be really possible might change over time, with new discoveries and new developments, possibilities of thought – given a certain logical structure – should remain constant. What is logically thinkable (coherent, consistent and non-contradictory) within any given logical system cannot change.

whether time without change actually exists, nor does it pretend to be able to provide such clarity.

And while the investigation of possibilities of thought has its advantages, for the purposes of this book I am more interested in investigating real possibilities than possibilities of thought, and thus I try to tie my generalisations and speculations continuously back to what can be phenomenologically described, i.e. actually experienced, and, if appropriate, to what can be disclosed by science. Philosophy should not be limited to 'the analysis and definition of our fundamental concepts, and the clear statement and resolute criticism of our fundamental beliefs' (Broad 18); it needs to include, especially in the form of a speculative ontology and realist metaphysics, a move towards what there is, what there is beyond our concepts and beyond our fundamental beliefs: in short a pre-Kantian account of what there is.

Thinking as the flight of an aeroplane and the role of speculation

Basing metaphysical speculation on real possibilities grounded in and guaranteed by (phenomenological) descriptions of the spatiotemporal world as given in experience thus allows for a form of speculation that does not immediately fall prey to the lure of intellectualism or rationalism, since it is not bound by the possibilities of thought alone. Whitehead's understanding of philosophical progress as the flight of an aeroplane illustrates this approach well: 'The true method of discovery is like the flight of an aeroplane. It starts from the ground of particular observation; it makes a flight in the thin air of imaginative generalization; and it again lands for renewed observation rendered acute by rational interpretation' (Whitehead, *Process* 5). For Whitehead, discovery begins with the particular, an actual experience, a concrete experience of surprise or of disappointment, an experience of obsession, of puzzlement or of wonder; this is the ground from which the aeroplane of thought takes flight. In taking flight this concrete actual experience is then intellectually manipulated, generalised, abstracted or imaginatively altered (as in eidetic variation), in order to derive knowledge that is not only relevant for the individual case, but that can ground general insights. When this metaphorical aeroplane lands, the results of its flight, the results of intellectual manipulation, can be compared with and tested against what we began with, the original experience as well as further concrete experiences.

In our case it becomes necessary to leave the phenomenological ground to soar into generalisation, abstraction and speculation, because of the singular nature of our object of investigation – reality. The more all-encompassing and/or singular the object of investigation is, the less we can learn through the traditional method of comparing and contrasting or through repeatable experiments. We simply cannot learn about the nature of reality by contrasting it with 'non-reality', just as we cannot learn about the beginning of the universe through repetitive varied experiments – the Big Bang cannot be re-run. For the investigation of singularities imaginative generalisation is indispensable. However, as the history of metaphysics and ontology shows, speculation as well as imaginative generalisation can be dangerously seductive and misleading, since it is often skewed by the interests and conceptual preferences of the thinker, the current intellectual climate, the sociopolitical environment and so on.

The free flow of speculation should thus be tamed and restricted by phenomenologically clarified experiential as well as scientific data in order to avoid the untethering of philosophical imagination from the concrete reality it seeks to understand. In order to allow for such an influence of what there is over how we think, without renouncing logical or conceptual structures, I am following Whitehead's understanding of 'speculation', which is defined as 'the endeavour to frame a coherent, logical, necessary system of general ideas in terms of which every element of our experience can be interpreted' (Whitehead, *Process* 3).

This understanding of speculation as the development of a rational understanding in terms of which *every experience*, including emotions and dreams, religious experiences, scientific experiences (i.e. scientific discoveries) and so on, can be interpreted strikes a delicate balance between rationalism, empirical description and experiences. The radical concrete, processual and creative situatedness of experience (i.e. not perception) ties speculation to what there is and balances the rationalistic framing. What is given in experience (i.e. phenomenological data) has precedence over logical structures and concepts. It is experience that guides and limits speculation. However well developed the rational side of the system, if there are experiences that cannot be 'adequately' accounted for, or if there are aspects of the system that are not 'applicable' to any experience, then the entire system has to be adapted (Whitehead, *Process* 3). This means that 'every experience has to be interpretable as an "illustration" of a scheme of ideas' and that 'experience must be conceptually thinkable' (Debaise, *Speculative Empiricism* 13).

Whitehead's equally strong emphasis on coherence, logical structures and necessity, on the other hand, forces us to transcend the concrete singular, the given and lived experience, precisely because this experience must be rendered conceptually thinkable in order to be communicable. The rational side of the system constrains the creative openness disclosed in experience and thus enables us to theoretically and systematically engage with what is given in experience, but in such a way as to continue to be able to account for and interpret *any* experience (Debaise, *Speculative Empiricism* 11–12) adequately. This is the method of speculation as I understand and use it.

(Ab)using phenomenology as a method to develop dynamic realism

In this book I am using phenomenology as a tool. However, phenomenology as a method is rooted in a certain tradition, and while I will attempt to respect its historical and traditional dimensions, I am not concerned with preserving its historical form nor with discovering the true essence of the phenomenological method. In using phenomenology to answer the present call to realism and metaphysics, I attempt to meet and encounter realist forms of criticism of the phenomenological method, and in learning from them, to grow and expand it, instead of simply attempting to disprove these challenges. In doing so I follow Marie-Eve Morin when she states that 'I want to look at how phenomenology can take up the realist challenge [. . .] Whether or not what we will be left with still deserves the name "phenomenology"' (Morin 138) is not my concern.

What is my concern, however, is the puzzle of phenomenology: 'The puzzle of phenomenology is how spatiotemporally individuated (factual) acts of consciousness can give rise to Objectivity, that is, to something that is true, and is experienced as being so independently from consciousness' (Morin 140). In order to unravel the puzzle as to how subjective experience can lead to objective knowledge, I depart from Husserl's claim that every experience discloses a realm of *immanent transcendence*: we do experience spatiotemporal things as transcendent, but this transcendence is given immanently. It is this understanding of experience as an encounter of immanence and transcendence that enables me to use phenomenology as a path towards realism. The realm of 'immanent transcendence' thus discloses intentional givenness as a continuum bridging the space between what is given, the subjective or the immanent, and the objective, the transcendent. A thorough investigation of givenness shows that these elements are so intimately correlated and connected that a clean distinction, a clean-cut separation of the for-me from the in-itself of spatiotemporal phenomena, is impossible. Phenomenological investigation of *actual experience* of the spatiotemporal, i.e. the physical world, thus *discloses experience as a unified relational structure encompassing the subject, the object and their mode of relation.* The precise nature of this experiential integration can be spelled out in different ways. It can, for example, be rooted in intentionality (Husserl) or it can be rooted in our ontic-ontological being-in (Heidegger), or our relational being-with (Heidegger and process thinkers).

TERMINOLOGICAL AND METHODOLOGICAL CLARIFICATIONS

If we follow Husserl's path for now and root this integration in intentionality, then phenomenology is a way to research the 'enigma of enigmas', which is 'the essential correlation between reason and what is in general' from within intentional consciousness (Husserl, *Crisis* §5).

> The knowledge of the essential two-sidedness of intentionality [. . .] brings this consequence with it, that a systematic phenomenology should not direct its effort one-sidedly [. . .] On both sides in truth there open up vast domains of eidetic inquiry, and these are constantly related to each other, yet as it turns out keep separate for a long stretch. (Husserl, *Ideas I* §128)

This leads to a systematic openness and enables us to use phenomenology as a tool to investigate either the subject or the object, which turn out to be two sides of a unified correlated structure.

Since the intentional relation is fundamentally integrated with no clear cut-off points, there is no clear point on this intentional correlated continuum between the subjective and the objective where the influence of the subject ends. Its influence slowly fades towards being negligible, the more the investigation is focused on the objective aspects. Similarly, the influence of the object on this correlated structure does not stop at a specific point either. It too simply fades in importance and influence, the more the investigation focuses on the role of the subject in this structure. The subject and the object are thus simply the extreme ends of the intentional correlation, between which actual experience happens.[7]

Take the example of me loving you. This intentional relation can be investigated with a focus on me (but has still to include the relation of loving as well as 'you', otherwise the investigation could not be about the act of me loving you). It could, however,

---

7. This insight of gradation can be applied to any internal relation, but I will focus these arguments on the phenomenon of experience and on intentional relations.

also be investigated with a focus on the intentional act of loving (while still including 'me' and 'you'). Finally, it could be investigated with a focus on 'you' (an investigation in which the act of loving and I still play a role). All three investigations will yield somewhat different results, will disclose different aspects of the whole structure. But none of these investigations will disclose the pure I independent from the intentional relation, in complete independence from you or the intentional act of loving. Nor will any of these investigations disclose the object of the loving, you, in complete independence from me loving you.

It is this integrated relatedness of intentionality that explains the multiple forms of phenomenology that we can engage with today. The phenomenological method can be understood and practised with a focus on consciousness or the cogito, rendering it a form of transcendental idealism. It can also be practised more materialistically or realistically, namely as an investigation into the role that the embodied, embedded and incarnated flesh plays in this correlation, or as an investigation of how the phenomenological object-matter structures and shapes forms of givenness in passive synthesis. These different readings of phenomenology need not be mutually exclusive, and they might be equally appropriate for different questions and different investigative aims.

So far, I have argued that any attempt to understand actual experience adequately leads one to conceive of a holistic integrated and continuous structure encompassing the subject, the object and their intentional correlation. From this it followed that phenomenology is neither *a form of naïve realism,* nor does it necessarily presuppose *a pure subject.*[8] Ultimately, there is no pure ego-subject without a body or its world, nor is there a pure, completely unrelated world of objects.[9] These pure and

---

8. I will address the issues around Husserl's world-destruction argument and the consequent reading of phenomenology as a traditional form of idealism in Part II.
9. As I will argue in Part II, relatedness is not limited to being related to human consciousness, and thus does not imply a traditional form of idealism. From the perspective of process ontology, every being can be considered to be

extreme limit cases are regulative ideals limiting and thus binding the space opened up through investigations of intentionality (or *being-in* in the case of Heidegger and *being experientially related* in the case of process thought). The prevalent Western mode of thinking, however, in its struggle for absolute (and ideally pure) knowledge, has a tendency to overemphasise and (over)analyse these extremes. We tend to focus on either the in-itself as the other-of-thought, as that which is mind-independent and causes experiences, or we focus on the experiencing subject in as pure a form as possible. I take the great insight of process philosophy and phenomenology to be that the pure subject and the pure object are both empty, barren possibilities of thought. These are purely conceptual options that force us to choose between extremes that do not actually exist. A pure subject without a body, without a world, does not exist, and the pure object is of no concern until it is discovered and thus related.

---

both the subject of its relations as well as (and at the same time as) the object of some (other) relation(s), and is thus both a subject and an object.

2

A New Metaphysics?
Correlating Ontology with Epistemology

Over the last twenty years many forms of realism have emerged, in both analytic as well as, more recently, continental philosophy. This resurgence of metaphysics in both traditions is somewhat surprising. In the case of analytic philosophy, it is surprising because analytic philosophers have, at least in part (especially between 1930 and 1950), rejected metaphysical speculations as nonsense or meaningless. Today, however, analytic metaphysics is a well-established field within the analytic tradition. Its resurgence began in the 1950s with the work of Quine and Strawson, among others, whose focus on 'logical and linguistic semantics afforded a ready avenue for the re-establishment of metaphysics as the ontic counterpart to language' (Simons, 'Metaphysics' 710). It is this focus on semantics that contributed to the return of ontological questions. In particular, Quine's introduction of the concept of 'ontological commitment' as a tool to reflect on the kinds of ontological commitments that are implied by one's philosophical stance moved thinkers in the analytic tradition towards hypothetical ontological considerations. However, these reflections remained quite subtle. Full-fledged metaphysics only re-emerged as a consequence of the difficulties concerning the semantics of truth and the idea of 'possible worlds' as a solution to these difficulties. In *Naming and Necessity* (1972), Saul Kripke argued that a proper name refers to the same individual in every possible world.[1] These reflections influenced David Lewis's

---

1. For a more detailed account of these developments, see Simons, 'Metaphysics'.

defence of modal realism in *On the Plurality of Worlds* (1986). This was not a direct influence since, strictly speaking, Kripke is not a modal realist in Lewis's sense, and Lewis's framework is not rooted in issues around rigid designation. Nonetheless, it is the idea of (re-)identification across possible worlds that formed the bedrock of Lewis's modal realism, which paved the way for the return of ontological and metaphysical issues in analytic philosophy, since it 'had philosophers "doing" metaphysics with little thought for the linguistics' (Simons, 'Metaphysics' 723).

As this quick outline shows, the return of metaphysical reflection in the analytic tradition is rooted in the possibilities of thought (mainly in semantics and modal logic), and thus cannot guide the present investigation. However, since then, and especially since the turn of the century, many forms of analytic metaphysics and especially of metaphysical realism have been developed that seem at least to be partially grounded in real possibilities, including scientific and structural realism. I will be engaging with some of these developments in the last part of this book.

In the continental tradition, the current return of realism is characterised by a rejection of positions that are rooted in the possibilities of thought, a rejection of linguistic and conceptual approaches. It often takes the form of a denial of two central tenets of postmodernism, namely 1) that reality is a construct (thus denying constructivism) and 2) that concepts such as 'truth', 'reality' or 'objectivity' merely refer to socially enforced standards and norms and are in no way mind-independent, intersubjective or objective (thus denying relativism). Both aspects are interconnected. Rejecting the claim that reality is the result of social (conceptual, conscious) constructions means rejecting the idea that reality is infinitely malleable, simply because facts cannot be reduced to interpretations (Ferraris, *Manifesto* xi) However, just to be clear, I do not consider this an adequate understanding of postmodern thought. Many postmodern thinkers, such as Derrida and more recently Bruno Latour, have accepted the claim that facts cannot be reduced to interpretations.

Still, realists and metaphysicians in both traditions agree that such a return cannot be a return to the naïve search for the given that shaped pre-Kantian metaphysics, and have devised various ways to avoid this. The way proposed in this book is rooted in the acknowledgement of the fact that there is a fundamental interdependence or correlation between the epistemological stance describing whether (and how) we can get access to the real and the ontological (or metaphysical) description of what there is. Ultimately I argue that what there is can only be known adequately through an investigation that departs from the correlation of epistemology and ontology. This leads to my strategy of rooting the present account of what there is in the correlation between process ontology and phenomenology. But before I can move on to discuss this specific correlation in more detail, I first need to introduce the concept of 'correlation' and defend my application of it to the issue of realism.

What are Correlations?

My use of the term 'correlation' is best introduced in reference to Husserl's idea of the correlational a priori, and then contrasted with Meillassoux's use of the term. According to Husserl the insight into the a priori correlation between phenomenological objects and their intentional givenness was the cornerstone on which he built phenomenology. In *The Crisis of European Sciences*, Husserl explains that:

> [t]he first breakthrough of this universal a priori of correlation between experienced object and manners of givenness (which occurred during my work on the *Logical Investigations* around 1898) affected me so deeply that my whole subsequent life-work has been dominated by the task of systematically elaborating on this a priori of correlation. (Husserl, *Crisis* §48)

For Husserl the term 'correlation' describes a specific intentional relation that holds between certain types of objects or phenomena (i.e. imaginary, spatiotemporal, ideal) and the way these phenomena are given in experience (as imaginary, as spatiotemporal, as ideal). This relation is in no way arbitrary; on the contrary, according to Husserl, it is an a priori as well as necessary relation. So spatiotemporal objects, for example, can only be given in the manner of spatiotemporal objects, namely as having different sides (i.e. sides distributed in three dimensions, including a front and a back) and resistant materiality. Logical or ideal objects, on the other hand, can only be given as ideal (i.e. as not having a front or back) as well as being completely penetrable by consciousness.

To clarify this difference, it is helpful to compare the experience of a seen phenomenon, let's say a wheel (i.e. a spatiotemporal round object), with the experience of visualising an ideal phenomenon, such as a perfect (ideal) circle. While I cannot change the shape of the wheel I see with my physical eyes, in my mind's eye I can fully manipulate the shape I imagine. I have full control over it. If I bend and stretch the imagined circle long enough it will stop being a perfect circle and turn into an ellipse, but this doesn't change the fact that I can manipulate it as imagined, while I cannot manipulate the wheel as seen in the same way. This a priori correlation between the type of given object (whether spatiotemporal or ideal) and the type of intentionality (seeing or imagining), as well as the possibilities that these various types of intentionality allow for, holds necessarily.

Speculative realists criticise this position as a form of 'correlationism',[2] a philosophical stance that considers access to the *great outdoors* as in some sense impossible:

> By 'correlation' we mean the idea according to which we only ever have access to the correlation between thinking and being, and never to either term considered apart from the other. We will henceforth call correlationism any current of thought which maintains the unsurpassable character of the correlation so defined. (Meillassoux, *After Finitude* 5)

---

2. I will discuss the critique of correlationism in more detail in Part II.

The problem with Meillassoux's interpretation and presentation of correlations in *After Finitude* can be traced back to the fact that he seems to understand 'correlation' as synonymous with relation in general, instead of taking into consideration the *differentia specifica* separating correlations from other relations. He does acknowledge that the 'co' in 'correlation' is relevant, but he simply states that the '"co–" (of co-givenness, of co-relation, of the co-originary, of co-presence, etc.)' is 'the grammatical particle that dominates modern philosophy' (Meillassoux, *After Finitude* 5), without further discussion. It is this 'co-' that renders phenomenological investigations a potential bridge towards realism.

In order to argue this point, in what follows I will first take a closer look at the metaphysics of relations, arguing that relations do in fact exist and that they are not fully reducible to intrinsic qualities or properties of the relata. I will then investigate the distinction between internal and external relations, and finally introduce the specific nature of correlations.

The metaphysics of internal and external relations

I will begin this discussion of the nature of relations with Aristotle, whose discussion of the category of *pros ti* (literally 'toward something') has fundamentally shaped the way relations were and are still conceptualised in Western philosophy. This discussion in the *Categories* not only sums up many of the conceptual issues involved in thinking relations, but it also highlights the fundamental correlation between our understanding of relations and the ontological structure of the relata. First, it is unclear whether the *Categories* should be read as an ontological or a logical discussion; both readings have a long tradition. Secondly, the discussion in the *Categories* lets one trace the influence of the ontological conception of the relata on the way we conceive of relations very easily.[3] Due to the Aristotelian

---

3. See, for example, the connection between the ontological nature of relata and the nature of relations traced in Marmodoro and Yates 4 or in Brower.

conception of the nature of substances, nothing can be both a substance and relational at the same time. A substance is that which is self-contained, that which does not rely on anything else to be what it is.[4] So the question is, how can substances and relations be thought together? The answer is to introduce the following distinction: 'being relative' can mean two things – either a being *related to something* or a *relational being*:

> On the one hand, we can say that a is a relative because a is related to something. In this sense Aldous being taller than someone, can be called a relative. On the other hand, 'relative' could be taken to mean 'relational' and from this point of view, Aldous is not a relative, since 'Aldous' by itself does not express any reference to something else. (Mignucci 102)

So, if being relational means being an entity, for which being is the same as being somehow relative to something (Aristotle, *Categories* 8a31), substances, qua substances, cannot be relational. Aristotle argues that only secondary substances (i.e. species and genera of primary substances), as well as properties or accidents, could be relational in this sense. These reflections are often taken to imply that relations cannot be integral to the relata, if these relata are the basic constituents of reality (i.e. primary substances). Thus, in most traditional ontologies based on a substantial paradigm, relations do not fundamentally characterise what something is; they are not connected to a substance's identity or essence, and thus relations are not internal to the substance, but merely external to it.

At this point I need to clarify the term 'internal relation'. For present purposes I will only discuss two ways of defining internal relations. $Internal_1$ relations can be read as relations that are grounded in intrinsic (but accidental) properties of the relata (i.e. the substances). $Internal_2$ relations, on the other hand, can be read as integral to the identity of one or all of the relata. To hold that relations are internal in the first sense is to hold that

---

4. For a detailed discussion, see Duncombe 121.

they are in a sense external to the relata in their essence, which means that the relata maintain their self-identity, with or without the relations they stand in. A good example is spatiotemporal location. What something is does not change if its spatiotemporal location is altered. This does not mean that the substance does not have a spatiotemporal location and various relations to other spatiotemporal locations; it simply means that the location is not integral to what the substance is. This example is taken to be illustrative of many relations and is used to conclude that many (or even all) relations are not fundamental to what there is, that they can be either eliminated or reduced to intrinsic monadic properties of the relata.[5] Predicates such as 'smaller than' or 'larger than', to use a different example, in this view do not indicate some mysterious additional relational property, but are instead considered to be fully explainable through the intrinsic but accidental properties of the relata. This view of relations can be characterised as internal$_1$, because relations are taken to be nothing above and beyond the fixed intrinsic (i.e. internal) but accidental properties of the relata.

However, this cannot be the whole story, since an intrinsic property cannot simply constitute a relation by itself or by simply being brought into the vicinity of another sized entity. These entities or their properties also need to become related somehow, in order to actually relate to each other. Secondly, properties (as well as concepts/terms) do not exist in isolation, they cannot be fully intrinsic or detached from other properties. In the words of Leibniz: 'There is no term which is so absolute or so detached that it does not involve relations and is not such that a complete analysis of it would lead to other things and indeed to all other things' (Leibniz 228). Furthermore, not all relations fit this picture neatly. Consider relations such as *being a slave to* or *being a master of*, a further traditional Aristotelian example. I do not

---

5. This assessment of the relevance of spatiotemporal location for the identity of something changes somewhat in different contexts, for example when it comes to Max Black's arguments around the identity of indiscernibles.

think that any reference to intrinsic properties is or ever could be adequate to account for such relations. This to me seems a fairly obvious stance, if relations are not merely considered theoretically, as possibilities of thought, but also considered in their ontic-ontological reality.

Let me now move on to clarify my understanding of internal$_2$ relations. This is an understanding of relations generally ascribed to the British Idealist Francis Herbert Bradley.[6] His definition of internal$_2$ relations is as follows: 'every relation [. . .] essentially penetrates the being of its terms and is, in this sense, intrinsic; or, in other words, every relation must be a relation of content' (Bradley, *Appearance* 347). This means that relata exist only as thus-and-so related and would cease to be these precise relata (they would cease to be self-identical) if any single relation was changed. Or, in the words of Blanshard: 'A relation is internal[$_2$] to a term when in its absence the term would be different [. . .]' (Blanshard 451). In understanding relations as internal$_2$, relata and relations form a complex but fundamentally integrated structure that can be investigated by focusing on one or more of the relations, or on the seemingly substantial intersections of relations (i.e. what is usually referred to as the relata). Internal$_2$ relations are constitutive of the relatum they generate and the relata do not exist in independence from these relations.

We are as precise as Bradley in thus acknowledging that the simple opposition of internal and external relations is ultimately an abstraction. Bradley argues that '[e]very relation [. . .] has a connexion with its terms which, not simply internal or external, must in principle be both at once' (Bradley, 'Relations' 641), because 'every relation does and again does not qualify its terms, and is and is not qualified by them' (Bradley, 'Relations' 638). This is because at the same time relations perform contradictory functions: they distinguish what they relate and they connect

---

6. To be clear, Bradley actually denied the reality of all relations in favour of a non-relational monism, but his arguments are often taken as a simple attack against the reality of external relations and as a defence of internal$_2$ relations.

what they relate. This contradiction is only a fundamental conceptual problem from within the perspective of possibilities of thought in the Western tradition; from within the logical system established by the *catuskoti*, this is much less problematic. However, this is not to say that thinkers such as Nagarjuna would consider relations any less empty than Bradley does. To be clear, Bradley argues for the dual nature of relations in order to expose their inexistence, while I am arguing for the dual nature of relations because of the processual nature of reality. For me, most relations can be regarded as internal and/or external to any given set of processes, depending on how the limits of the processes in question are defined. While Bradley concluded from his investigations that no relations can exist as part of ultimate reality, which to him is consistent, harmonious, ordered, perfect and timeless, I am taking a different stance. Reality, ultimate reality, is open, creative and as harmonious as Heraclitus' various accounts of the unity of opposites imply; what there is is a harmony that is full of strife and movement.[7]

The present view of internal$_2$ relations is thus the result of not grounding relations in pre-existing substances or monadic entities or properties, but considering relations and the resulting relata to be processes, actions or other forms of ongoing dynamic engagement. Let me give you an example in Aristotelian terms:

> the masterhood of Themistocles is ontologically dependent on the slavery of Sicinnus, on account of the fact that certain types of actions of Themistocles constitute, together with certain types of actions of Sicinnus, a single unified activity or subject. It is the oneness of this activity (and not any polyadic property) that grounds the ontological dependence between master and slave. (Marmodoro and Yates 6)

This is to say that the master–slave relation is rooted in the fact that Sicinnus acts (or better, is forced to act) like a slave to the master, while Themistocles chooses to act out the role

---

7. Compare Röck, *Physis* 93–143.

of the master. In this account relations can be read as unified complexes, involving relata[8] as well as their interaction over time, that together constitute some form of ontological whole or unity, in this case generating a specific master–slave activity structure.

If reality as a whole is considered to be processual or fundamentally dynamic, if *being* is a process, then this activity-structure reading can be applied to what there is in general, which means that every relation is internal$_2$ and only all of the actual relations together constitute the full identity of a relatum. Relations thus not only distinguish and connect, they also constitute both individuality as well as difference. There is no difference and no individuality until there is relation. It is relations that 'make individuals distinct' (Ramey 39). Obviously the term 'individual' has to be taken with a grain of salt: in this case, it does not refer to an indivisible, unchanging entity (i.e. a traditional substance), but instead is used to refer to continuous and fairly stable processes. Let me give a concrete example. The ongoing process that I am, the individual that I am, is the result of all the evolving relations that I have stood in, which led to all the relations that I am standing in right now. Every single relation past and present – physical, conceptual, biological and so forth – contributes to my current identity. Some of these relations have a large impact, some an almost imperceptible one, but all of them together constitute my present existence and all of them together will *contribute* towards co-forming my future. Missing just one of these relations, or entering into it later or leaving it earlier, would render me a (even only slightly) different individual in the present. One could argue that some relations' influences are so imperceptibly small that their effect, depending on the investigative aim, can be disregarded – and I would claim that it is this strategy that led to substance ontologies. The trouble with the

---

8. The relata too are ultimately effects of processes and relations, in this case Sicinnus and Themistocles themselves constituted by interrelated physical, biological, cultural and social processes.

real world, however, is that it is never quite clear which relations will turn out to have lasting impacts and which will not.

Correlations

While understanding relations as internal$_2$ already suggests a unity of relations and relata, correlation describes an integration that goes even further, because it also includes a temporal dimension. The term 'correlation' stems from the Latin *correlatio* which means 'mutual reaction', 'interdependency' or 'reciprocal action'. It does not describe a static (internal) relation, but a relational interaction between the correlated moments over time. Correlation thus describes an internal relation that has a temporal dimension, i.e. the relata can and do change, and these changes are not localised. They affect the whole correlated system. A correlational system should not be thought along the lines of a stable construction made out of (somehow) connected (substantial) blocks; it is best visualised by bringing to mind a child's mobile. Like a mobile, with all its connectors and hangers responding to the slightest influence on any aspect of the network, the whole correlational system is affected by any internal and/or external influence. Any shift in any aspect of the mobile influences the whole structure and not just some aspects. Correlations constitute a mobile (i.e. mutable) integrated system, where everything has its place in the network, but its sphere of influence is not simply located; the potential for influencing or being influenced is distributed (with varying degrees of freedom) over the whole system.

The Correlation between Thinking (Knowing) and Concepts of Being

Having established the difference between correlations and other relations, I will now provide a first general introduction to the (co-)relation between epistemic approaches and the resulting descriptions of reality. As should be clear from my account of correlations, any investigation into correlations implies a very delicate study that pays attention to every detail and tracks these and their influences over time. And while I will attempt to provide this level of delicate attention to detail in my investigation of the correlation between phenomenology and process ontology, for now, in what follows, I will simply argue that there is in fact an internal relation between epistemological approaches and ontological entities. It is this internal relatedness that makes it impossible to begin either investigation without addressing preconceptions rooted in the other.

I will illustrate the relations between epistemology and ontology, between thinking and being, by beginning with a naïve question: *If this everyday world that we live in is to be taken to be what is real (as our actual, direct experience would suggest), what would be the hallmark properties that characterise all of what there is? In other words, given these premises, how should we characterise what there is?* The ancient Greeks provided us with a simple and straightforward answer to this question. They considered this world to be fundamentally temporal, instable, chaotic or surprising, changing, material and concrete. And to my knowledge, there is not one philosopher who has disputed this claim. What has been argued by many philosophers, however, is that this apparent reality is not 'really real', that it is a mere appearance or phenomenon, and that the concrete, chaotic instability of the empirical world given to our senses has to be disregarded in order to gain access to 'true reality'.

The reason for this devaluation of the everyday and its concrete temporality is generally an epistemic one. The hallmarks of the concrete – being temporal, changeable, creative, surprising or chaotic and concrete – are problematic with regard to knowledge, certainty and planning. How can we understand, grasp and hold fixed in our minds what is constantly changing? How could one gain general (i.e. conceptual) insight into that which is singular and concrete? And consequently, how could one master or prepare for that which cannot be held fixed in our minds, that which cannot be known through general or conceptual insight? The simple answer to the problem that the everyday world is at best somewhat intelligible was to conclude that it could therefore only be somewhat real. There had to be something genuinely real below, behind or above this chaos disclosed by the senses. Only an effort of the intellect, be it rational or empirical, so the argument went, could disclose the actually real and thus guarantee certainty. This short (and rather oversimplified) account shows the correlation between thinking and being that shaped the beginnings of Western philosophy. These interlocking convictions, namely that knowledge has certain characteristics, that what is knowable has to share these characteristics and that knowability is a characteristic of the real, provide an example for the correlation between a way of understanding knowledge and a corresponding understanding of how being or existence has to be thought.

A critic could now object that this result might simply be an effect of my ontological starting point. So, let me leave the original question and thus the attempt to uncover the hallmark properties that characterise all of what there is, and instead try my hand at beginning the investigation with an epistemological stance. There are many traditional epistemic stances to choose from. There are many methods available to account for the generation of knowledge, for example empiricism, constructivism or pragmatism. However, each of these presupposes a view of reality. Empirical investigations presuppose that reality is in some relevant way independent of our knowing it. Constructivism necessitates an interpretative stance, holding that reality depends on our interpretation of it. Pragmatism requires a pragmatic stance, holding that reality depends on our engagement with it. But the choice between these stances and methodologies is not arbitrary; it is immediately obvious that any of these positions pre-selects and limits the possible nature of what there is, depending on what the respective method can come to terms with or disclose.

Any choice imposes limits on the possible ontological structures that can be captured and described through my chosen stance and method. If one considers the real to be what can be known through intellect and reason, this leads to an emphasis on a relatively stable, lawfully ordered reality. If, on the other hand, one considers the real to be what there is irrespective of consciousness, and/or reduces 'being' to material existence, then the objective methods of the natural sciences provide an adequate method to uncover the nature of reality. If we consider reality to be the result of natural forces, then looking at the structure of judgements or logical thought seems a ridiculous epistemic approach. This is not to say that for every epistemological position there is one and only one metaphysical and/or ontological correlate (or vice versa). It is to say, however, that every epistemological position creates a framework for which some ontological systems are more adequate than others.

The fundamental difficulty in coming to terms with the 'real' is the fact that any engagement with this issue needs to address epistemological, metaphysical as well as ontological issues – at the same time and in correlation. We can now either conclude that our search for knowledge and the real as an unmediated in-itself is futile and that we can never truly know the world around us; or, and this is the answer I would prefer, we could conclude that knowledge and reality are too complex, too inter-related, too temporal and dynamic to be fully grasped once and for all by one single method or to be ultimately described within one single metaphysical framework. This standpoint is mirrored in Husserl's explanation of the lack of absolute understanding when it comes to spatiotemporal objects. Husserl argues that the things of this world are not mysterious. The fact that objects are only partially knowable *correlates* with the kind of being physical objects (i.e. things) have.[9] Things are, they exist in a way that cannot grant the kind of clear and absolute insight that we can

---

9. Compare, for example, Husserl's arguments in *Analyses* §55.

achieve in investigations of logical structures or mathematical relations. To demand the same quality of clarity and certainty from spatiotemporal things that we can achieve in investigations of mathematical and logical structures is to misunderstand what spatiotemporal things are. Similarly, to expect one epistemological approach, one ontological description to grasp reality in its totality, once and for all, is simply to misunderstand the nature of reality. This view is the result of disregarding the extreme complexity, relatedness and creative temporality of what there is.

If neither epistemology nor ontology can provide certainty or at least a stable basis able to ground the investigation, what should guide our search instead? The answer seems quite straightforward at this point, namely that it should be grounded in the correlation between epistemology and ontology. The path I will follow to do this is to ground the investigation in the precise question to be investigated, in order to grasp the precise correlation this question asks for. As my example of the intentional structure of 'me loving you' showed, there are always various perspectives and aspects that can be investigated regarding any one correlation. Depending on the exact question asked, depending on what precisely is questioned and in what way, different epistemological and ontological choices immediately appear as more fruitful options. So, ultimately, I argue that the ontological and epistemological choices that frame any investigation into what is real should be determined by the precise question that is asked and by the specific correlation that is investigated.

The question shaping this investigation is the one mentioned above: If this everyday world that we live in is to be taken to be what is real, as our actual, direct experience would suggest, what would its hallmark properties be? How would we characterise what there is as we encounter it in our everyday lives? Beginning with this question establishes my framework in the following way: my investigation is shaped and limited by the correlation between a descriptive-phenomenological approach to direct experience and a general, i.e. conceptual, understanding of what there is that is able to account for every experience.

In what follows, I will introduce the relata of this correlation, namely phenomenology and process ontology, to then apply the results of this investigation in the fourth part to ground dynamic realism in this correlation.

Part II Husserl's Phenomenology: Experience and Time

> No ordinary 'realist' has ever been so realistic and so
> concrete as I, the phenomenological 'idealist'.
> Edmund Husserl, *Briefwechsel* 16

3

Phenomenological Experience: To the Things Themselves

Phenomenology is an empirically oriented philosophical method that focuses not on the objects of experience, but on describing and studying the various *qualitative differences* of *how we experience* in every act and every kind of experience, which is why the term

> [p]henomenology neither designates the object of its researches nor is it a title that describes their content. The word only tells us something about the *how* of the demonstration and treatment of *what* this discipline considers. Science 'of' the phenomena means that it grasps its objects in such a way that everything about them to be discussed must be directly indicated and directly demonstrated. (Heidegger, *Being* §7, c)

It is precisely this return to what there is, as directly indicated by experience and directly demonstrable in experience, that attracted many thinkers to the method of phenomenology. In the words of Heidegger:

> The term 'phenomenology' expresses a maxim that can be formulated: 'To the things themselves!' It is opposed to all free-floating constructions and accidental findings; it is also opposed to taking over concepts only seemingly demonstrated; and likewise to pseudo-questions which often are spread abroad as 'problems' for generations. (Heidegger, *Being* 26, §7)

It is this focus on what there is as given in everyday direct experience that renders this method so useful for the present question, namely *how are we to characterise what there is as we encounter it in our everyday lives?* This is Husserl's principle of all principles, which he introduces in *Ideas I*: 'every originary presentive intuition is a legitimizing source of cognition, that everything originally (so to speak, in its "personal" actuality) offered to us in "intuition" is to be accepted simply as what it is presented as being, but also only within the limits in which it is presented there' (Husserl, *Ideas I* §24). For Husserl, this aim should provide the ultimate basis of any investigation, be it scientific or philosophical: 'the most universal principle of all methods, [is] the principle of the original right of all data' (Husserl, *Ideas I* §26). In coming to terms with any given phenomenon, data, i.e. what is given, comes first. We cannot simply disregard aspects or interpret before we have described the data: what is given needs to be fully explored before conceptual ordering or interpretation is adequate, which means to 'take our start from what lies prior to all standpoints: from the total realm of whatever is itself given intuitionally and prior to all theorizing, from everything that one can immediately see and seize upon' (Husserl, *Ideas I* §24).

However, phenomenologists are not merely interested in our experience of the world that we encounter in our everyday lives, but in every aspect of experience. This includes experiences of thinking, understanding, dreaming, imagining, hallucinating and so on. Thus, for this second part of the investigation, it is necessary to mention the distinction between experience (*Erfahrung*) and perception (*Wahrnehmung*). Whereas 'experience' refers to the sheer givenness of something (including hallucinating, remembering, fantasising or imagining), 'perception' describes a specific mode in which experience shows up for us through a sense act – such as seeing, touching or hearing. According to Husserl it is perception that gives the spatiotemporal world. Direct and immediate sense perception is furthermore the most basic form of givenness or experience. This is the case because other modes of givenness such as remembering or imagining are at least partially dependent on (or more precisely, founded on) this kind of basic perception or sense experience.[1] Thus direct, immediate sense perception is ground-giving, i.e. foundational (Husserl, *Einleitung* §3) and cannot be grounded by something else. I will, however, use 'experience' and 'perception' largely synonymously, and will only distinguish them explicitly if it is relevant for the argument. This imprecision should not be problematic, since in my discussion of experience I focus on the sense perception of spatiotemporal objects and disregard many of the problems and issues involved in investigating the experience more generally.

What is Phenomenological Experience?

In the phenomenological tradition experience in general is understood as an intentional act that allows the inner as well as the outer world to be there for us. Fundamentally, to experience is to be given something, to have something showing up in consciousness, in such a way that it can be qualitatively described. In this sense *to experience* an object is *to be conscious of* that object.

Husserl distinguishes a phenomenological understanding of experience from the phenomenalist, sensualist and causal accounts of experience prevalent at his time. In engaging with phenomenalism Husserl argues that it is simply not the case that we perceive a series of distinct phenomena or appearances when we perceive an object. We do not perceive 'a collection of [sense] data floating in an insubstantial void' (Husserl, *Formal* §100) that are then combined in a second step to form the objects of perception. For this same reason, it is also not appropriate to identify the experience of 'a material thing with an array of sensory appearances' (Smith 306) as sensualist accounts do. Finally, it is also the case that we do not actually perceive a causal connection between perceived objects and our perception:

---

1. While it is quite obvious that remembering something is founded on a prior experience of what is remembered, this is not quite as clear in other cases. For a discussion of this primacy of sense experience in relation to imagination, see Drost.

> Husserl is clear that perceiving an object does not involve an awareness of a causal connection between the thing and us, rather there is just the conscious sense of the unmediated presence of the object. To hear the doorbell ringing is not to hear the button being pressed even given that the button's being pressed initiates the causal chain that results in hearing the doorbell. For Husserl, we don't hear the button at all; we only know that the button is being pressed because we assume a certain scientific and causal view already. We read causation into the perceptual scene rather than finding it there. (Moran 239)

All these ways of understanding and explaining perception, either as a collection of phenomena, of sense data, or as a perceptible effect of an external cause, are actually themselves not phenomena given in perception. These are speculative, conceptual constructions meant to explain what perception is; they do not describe the actual process of experiencing. These traditional ways of accounting for experience were developed in order to discover what it is that gives rise to perception, or what the fundamental elements of perception are. Phenomenology, on the other hand, is not an attempt to understand what experience is or what causes it; instead it is an attempt to describe *how we experience* and *how the objects of experience are given*. It is an attempt to focus on actual experience and what is given in experience, and nothing more. On the basis of these descriptions we can then formulate a tentative answer as to what experience is, but such a definition of experience can only be the result of phenomenological investigations, not their starting point. Husserl's phenomenological descriptions, for example, show perception to be an intentional act that *gives* its object in a certain correlated and law-governed manner.

Husserl furthermore clarifies that a phenomenological understanding of perception should also not be confused with representationalist accounts, as proposed by Berkeley, Hume or Mill. Husserl acknowledges that we tend to think of experience as a means to 'get at' the objects of perception out there. We thus tend to understand perception as a relation between consciousness and the objective world. This preconception implies a split, a doubling of objects as part of every experience. There is the object of sense experience 'out there' as well as a second object, a copy of the first one, that is experienced 'in here'. Perception thus understood gives only a representation or copy instead of providing access to the original 'out there'. However, this account does not adequately describe how we experience. We tend to be able to competently distinguish between perceiving an image, a copy or a picture and perceiving something directly. When we experience something as a picture, given within this experience there is both the picture itself (as a picture) as well as whatever is pictured in it. In order to be able to perceive something as a picture we need to be aware that it is just a picture, otherwise we would simply perceive it as the real thing and not as a picture. The picture thus acts as a sort of mediator through which we become conscious of what is pictured. But this structure does not describe sense perception. We do not perceive the world as a picture directly indicating or depicting some deeper reality somewhere else. We furthermore do not live as if our senses merely provided images of something that is beyond our reach (Heidegger, *History* 42). On the contrary, we perceive the world and its things as directly there for us: the table, the cup, the keyboard are given in experience, not as an image, but as themselves.

We are given the phenomena directly, phenomenologists argue, because experience by its very nature is intentional, i.e. directed towards and thus disclosing that which is experienced. The intentional structure of experience means that there is no need to connect the inner life of the mind to an independent outer reality, since experience is both intrinsic to consciousness and at the same time essentially open to and always already with-the-world. We are not worldless minds locked into a cage of flesh with no access to the outside world besides our rational faculties. We are always already in-the-world. There is no cage, no boundary separating us from the world we live in, except the conceptual boundaries of our own making, rooted in conceiving ourselves as worldless minds detached or detachable from our bodies and the world we live in.

The intentional nature of perception bridges the distance between the perceiving consciousness and the thing perceived and thus implies a certain form of phenomenologically mediated direct realism. What do I mean by this? Two things. First, that these investigations into the intentional correlations between the 'objective' and the 'subjective' aspects of givenness, between what has traditionally been called 'immanent' and 'transcendent', led phenomenologists to suggest that one actually cannot clearly distinguish between the transcendent and the immanent. 'Phenomenology solves (or dissolves) the "riddle" of knowledge by redefining the relation between "inner" or "immanent" subjectivity and "outer" or "transcendent" objectivity, such that one attends only to what is transcendent-within-immanence' (Moran 49). Thus, the object of any sense perception is immanently transcendent – it is given, immanently, but as being transcendent (Husserl, *The Idea* 2nd Lecture).[2]

Secondly, phenomenologists claim that things that are given in perception are given as a 'bodily presence', as 'itself there' (*selbst da*). To engage in a perceptual act thus means to experience the self-appearance of the object (Husserl, *Logical Investigations II* VI, §14). But this directness and this emphasis on the self-givenness of the perceived object as itself is not to be conflated with a naïve realism. This intentional openness to the world and

---

2. This claim, that objects of sense perception are given as immanent-transcendent, does not, however, violate Husserl's agnosticism with regard to the actual existence of the object, since the 'intended object as such can be grasped in its sense of transcending the act, without reference to its actual worldly existence or non-existence' (Moran 53). Thus, spelling out the concept of 'intentionality' in terms of 'immanent-transcendence', phenomenological research can be used to walk the fine line between the kind of objectivism present in naïve realism and the subjectivism prevalent in many transcendental approaches. Put simply, in intentionality we can discern a correlation between the *object that is intended*, the *object as it is intended* and the intentional act.

connectedness does not mean that we always come to correct judgements about the things we experience:

> It is not the case that a perception first becomes intentional by having something physical enter into relation with the psychic, and that it would no longer be intentional if this reality did not exist. It is rather the case that perception, correct or deceptive, is in itself intentional. Intentionality is not a property which would accrue to perception and belong to it in certain instances. As perception, it is *intrinsically intentional*, regardless of whether the perceived is in reality on hand or not. (Heidegger, *History* 31)

While phenomenological accounts of perception and naïve realism concur in their assessment of perception as directly giving, they differ in the kinds of conclusions that we can draw from this givenness. While the naïve realist would deduce the possibility of knowing what the object of perception is from direct experience, the phenomenologist chooses to suspend judgement about what something is and limits herself to a description of how this object is given. The aim of phenomenology is thus to focus on a description of the phenomena as they are given in sense experience, without making judgements about their existence, or drawing conclusions about what they are in themselves. It is the equation of direct access (or naïve realism) with epistemic transparency and certainty in knowledge that led to many forms of epistemic confusion, including the idea of a clear and clean distinction between the inner and the outer in the first place. If our investigation, however, remains tied to the descriptions, instead of leading to judgements and speculations, we cannot be mistaken. It is our tendency to over-interpret of what is given that fails us, not our senses.

The famous broken straw illusion illustrates this point well. If a straw is inserted into a container of water without being fully submerged, the straw will appear to be bent, due to the different refractive qualities of air and water. So, if one were to conclude something about what the straw is (bent or not) based on this givenness, misinterpretations and mistakes would arise. But if one merely describes the process of creating the appearance of the straw as bent and how the phenomenon of the bent straw appears, mistakes can be avoided. This description of the bent straw is furthermore relevant, because there is no obvious reason why we should consider the 'actually' unbent straw to be more real or more fundamental than the appearance of a bent straw. On the contrary, it is the phenomenon of the bent straw that discloses something about the light-refracting properties of water that the 'real' unbent straw cannot teach us. So why should one account be allocated more reality or more truth than the other?

Ultimately which aspect is more revealing and thus more relevant for any given investigation simply depends on the investigative focus, the aim with which the experience is examined. And while it is true that we cannot perceive objects with senses other than the ones we actually have, and thus that our perceptions are filtered, this does not mean that what we perceive is somehow not real or not actual. The fact that further information is available does not imply that the given information is necessarily flawed, or that we have no adequate information at all. Nor does the possibility of further knowledge mean that the partial information we do have now is somehow necessarily less relevant or less objective that the potential further insight that might be gained one day.

What is the Actual Object of Phenomenological Experience? The Object as Intended

Before I discuss what the object of phenomenological experience actually is, I need to acknowledge that asking this is actually quite un-phenomenological. From the perspective of phenomenology, the question of what the phenomenon is – whether it exists objectively, i.e. as a transcendent object, or whether it exists as a subjective construction, i.e. as an immanent object – is a misleading way of putting things. The only appropriate phenomenological answer to this question would be that the object exists both as an immanent and a transcendent object at the same time, and that this does not constitute a contradiction, since it describes precisely the way phenomena are given. The phenomenon is neither simply a mind-independent object nor is it merely formed through our faculties – it is both. In the *how* of givenness both the structure of the object and the structure of the subject come together, and thus the *how* of givenness can be a point of departure to investigate both the life of the mind and the life of the world. However, the question whether something that is phenomenologically given actually exists is crucial when it comes to the question of realism, and simply stating that this question is not phenomenological is inadequate. Thus, let me look at what Husserl has to say about the matter.

The difficulty that we have to confront in determining the object of phenomenologically clarified sense experience is the fact that Husserl uses various different concepts when talking about the spatiotemporal object as it appears. Sometimes he refers to it as the intentional object, sometimes as noema or as cogitatum. There are, furthermore, instances where he identifies the noema with the object, while at other times he distinguishes the two.

Husserl's idiom 'the object as intended' has encouraged several different models of the noema and its role in intentionality. This idiom echoes Kant's 'phenomena' or 'things-as-they-appear', where natural objects are 'phenomenal'. Alternatively, Husserl sometimes speaks of the 'intentional object' rather than the 'intentional content' of an act. In the *Cartesian Meditations* (§§15–18) he speaks interchangeably of the 'objective sense', the 'intentional object' and the 'cogitatum qua cogitatum' of an experience. These idioms echo traditional medieval ontologies where objects exist *in intentio*, suggesting that the noema be assimilated to the object itself (Smith 270).

All of this renders rather complicated the issue of understanding precisely what Husserl thought that the *object as intended* was. His student Martin Heidegger provides a good first step to help us to address the issue. The objects of experience, he argues, are simply the phenomena. But what are phenomena? In *Being and Time* Heidegger provides a very clear and exhaustive definition of the various possible meanings of 'phenomenon'. In §7 he introduces the concept by first explaining the etymological roots. Phenomenon comes from the Greek verb *phainesthai*, which means 'to show itself' and is often interpreted as 'appearance' or 'mere appearance'. But it is precisely this reading of phenomenon as mere appearance that is problematic. Heidegger explains that mere appearance is often understood as indicating something that in fact does *not actually* show itself. This understanding of appearance as mere appearance characterises a symptom of an illness, for example. The appearance of a fever or a cough is a form of mere appearance, namely the appearance as a symptom, that in turn indicates something more fundamental (i.e. more real), namely the underlying illness, which does not appear itself. In this case something precisely does not show itself; it is precisely not the illness itself that appears or gives itself directly. This case is an example of (mediated) appearance: the underlying illness does not show itself; instead it makes itself known through something that does show itself (the cough or the fever).

Even though this type of appearing is not a self-showing, the *mediated appearance* of the illness is only possible on the basis that something is showing itself (in this case the symptoms). Without the symptoms we would never know that there was an illness in the first place. Such mediated appearance presupposes the self-showing of phenomena, in this case the phenomenon 'fever' as a symptom. So whether we are talking about direct appearance or mediated appearance, '[a]ppearing is a making itself known through something that shows itself' (Heidegger, *Being* §7, a). Whatever we can experience, learn, grasp, think of this world and of ourselves needs to be given, it needs to appear. So, appearance is never mere appearance. At the very least it is appearing as a symptom or a sign, and as such disclosing the fact that something is not directly given or absent (mediated appearance), which does not render this kind of appearance somehow deficient or less real or less relevant. In the case of direct appearance, what is given in experience is the appearing object itself. We are never deceived by the phenomenon, it is the self-giving of what is. What can deceive us is our interpretation of its meaning or our judgement about its relevance.

Husserl provides more precision in his account of what phenomena are and how they are given than Heidegger did in this passage. In the *Logical Investigations* Husserl distinguishes three moments of phenomenological experience: 1) the conscious intentional act (the seeing, imagining or hearing of something), as well as two objects of the act, namely 2) the object intended (the vase, the dream or the song) and 3) the intentional matter (how I am actually experiencing these objects, how they are given to me). What I have actually given in experience, Husserl claims, is the intentional matter, and this intentional matter is both shaped by the kind of intentional act that is disclosing the object and the kind of object the intended object is. I can feel the vase, see the vase or remember the vase. All these intentional acts have the same object, in the sense of the object intended, but the object will be disclosed a little differently in each and every one of these acts, thus leading to variations in the intentional matter. One way to read phenomenology as a realist enterprise is to take these early distinctions and simply claim that the object intended and the intentional matter jointly constitute the phenomenon, rendering the phenomenon something that is neither reducible to the mind-independent object (the object intended) nor merely that which is formed through our intentional structure (the intentional matter) – *it is both*. In the intentional act, the *how* of givenness is shaped by both the structure of the object and the structure of the subject. In any intentional act both aspects come together, and thus the *how* of givenness can be a point of departure to investigate both the life of the mind or the life of the world, rendering phenomenology a potentially realist enterprise.

Phenomenology as Idealism:
Moving towards Transcendental Philosophy

While there is certainly some tension between a transcendental-idealist and a transcendental-realist reading of Husserl's philosophy, there is more than enough material in his writings to support both. While the transcendental-idealist reading might be more familiar, there are passages throughout his work that suggest a direct givenness of the object itself in perception. For example: 'External perception too (though not apodictic) is an experiencing of something itself, the physical thing itself: "it itself is there"' (Husserl, *Cartesian Meditations* §9). Or: 'Perception in itself is perception of a perceived; its essence is to bring some object to appearance and to posit what appears as something believed: as an existing actuality' (Husserl, *Thing* §40). Claims such as these led some interpreters to believe that, in its basic form, perception is the 'perceiving of material, spatial objects, their properties and relations to other objects' (Moran 237). If this is the case, why is it that phenomenology is often read as a straightforward form of idealism, effectively ignoring the many references Husserl makes to the realist nature of his own philosophy?

One reason for this overemphasis on the idealistic interpretation is surely rooted in Husserl's move towards transcendental phenomenology through the introduction of the 'noema', the 'reductions' and the '*epochē*'. Together these concepts create a quite idealistic impression of the intentional object. One of the most famous instances of this confluence is the passage in *Ideas I* (§§87–96) where Husserl explores the correlation between *noesis* and *noema*.[3] Since a lot of work in the context of the phenomenological realism–idealism debate focuses on the nature of

---

3. In the 1908 Lectures on the *Theory of Meaning* Husserl proposed a quite realistic, if not much investigated, way to flesh out this relationship between intentional givenness and what is given. Here Husserl distinguishes between the 'ontic' object as such and the 'phansic' or 'phansological' object as it is intended (Husserl, *Vorlesungen* §8).

noesis and noema (even though Husserl did not use this distinction much in his later work),[4] I too will focus on this distinction in my discussion of Husserl's 'idealism'. This way of proceeding seems appropriate since this distinction between noesis and noema creates and addresses problems which, *mutatis mutandis*, apply to many of Husserl's ways of expressing the distinction 'between the radically opposed and yet essentially interrelated regions of Being' (Husserl, *Ideas I* §128) – i.e. consciousness and ontological reality.

However, a clear view of the noema can only be had from within the phenomenological attitude. To truly understand the object of phenomenological investigation as noema, we first need to discuss the move from the natural to the phenomenological attitude through the methodological steps of *epochē* and the reduction(s).

From the natural attitude to the phenomenological attitude

We behave in conceptually informed ways; we hold a specific attitude towards what there is and how best to engage with it. Every attitude is conceptually informed, because it is characterised by a certain presupposed understanding of truth, of reality and of objectivity, and therefore allows for certain assumptions, beliefs and behaviours, while excluding others. From a religious attitude, for example, a prayer is truly sustaining. From a scientific one, it is nonsensical. Any attitude towards the world is more than a theoretical understanding of the world or a perspectival view on it, it is a way of being in the world. It is a stance or orientation towards the world that involves and correlates both who is taking the stance and that towards which this stance is taken; it is an internal relation, correlating the acting, being thinker and his or her world. This also implies that the world we live in shows itself as a correlate of a specific attitude.

---

4. For further details, see Moran 133.

The natural attitude is the primordial ground from which all other attitudes grow. Every attitude, every engagement with the world, be it a religious, scientific or any other attitude towards what there is, is rooted in the natural attitude. Husserl characterises this attitude as 'natural', but also as 'straightforward' and somewhat 'naïve' (Husserl, *Crisis* §38). In it 'attention is turned towards things given in whatever manner they are given, in a mode of acceptance' (Moran 217). From within the natural attitude the world appears as already given, as out there, simply and fully present, as an independent (set of) object(s) that we can engage with theoretically and practically. This attitude is shaped by this *Generalthesis*, i.e. the *universal thesis* or *general positing*, that the world and the entities within it exist in independence from consciousness and experience (Husserl, *Ideas I* §§30/31). This conviction shapes all of our everyday interactions, since the *Generalthesis* 'is after all, something that lasts continuously throughout the whole duration of the attitude, i.e. throughout natural waking life' (Husserl, *Ideas I* §31). But while this attitude is foundational, it is not a good basis for phenomenological descriptions. In the natural attitude we are caught up in the phenomena, the practical aims and tasks. In order to get clear phenomenological descriptions, we need to take up a different attitude, a phenomenological one.

Due to the entangled nature of these attitudes, they cannot simply be shaken off or taken up; some attitudes might be impossible to take up for a specific subject. It is fundamentally difficult to shift one's stance in relation to the world. An exception is the phenomenological attitude, which, according to Husserl, can be taken up by anyone. However, this is still not a simple process. To reach the phenomenological attitude, an attitude that allows for a genuine, critical reflection on the implicit biases and presuppositions inherent in the natural attitude, some effort is needed. We need to learn this new attitude, we need to train to see from this new vantage point, and even after much training, in our everyday lives we will continue to take up the natural attitude instinctively (which is a very good thing – we would not want to be stuck in the phenomenological attitude while cooking eggs!)

In order to create this reflective distance to the natural attitude a rigorous approach is needed (Husserl, *Ideas I* §51). For Husserl these are the methodological steps of the reduction(s) and *epochē*,[5] which are intended to help the existing, embodied thinker to move from the *natural attitude*, i.e. the way that we engage with and experience the world and its objects in everyday life, to a *philosophical* or *transcendental attitude* (Husserl, *The Idea* 15).

The first step, the *epochē*, is simply the suspension of the *Generalthesis*, i.e. the claim that there is an objective world 'out there'. This is a step back from our natural attitude in order to enter into the 'transcendental' or 'phenomenological attitude', which renders any 'intellectual experience [. . .] into an object of pure seeing and apprehension while it is occurring. And in this act of seeing it is an absolute givenness' (Husserl, *The Idea* Lecture II, 24). In ancient Greek the term *epochē* expressed 'a way of refraining from making epistemic commitments based on inadequate evidence' and a way of 'withholding assent' (Moran 106). Thus *epochē* simply indicates a bracketing, a suspension of judgement, in this case about the *Generalthesis*, i.e. whether something 'really exists'. In *Ideas I* Husserl takes great pains to argue that this disregard for the existence of a corresponding world, this exclusion or parenthesising (*Ausklammerung*) through the *epochē*, is not a loss: 'Strictly speaking, we have not lost anything but rather gained the whole of absolute being which, rightly understood, contains within itself, "constitutes" within itself, all worldly transcendencies' (Husserl, *Ideas I* §50). Therefore the *epochē* is not a sceptical step implying the denial of the representative truth of experiences (Husserl, *Ideas I* §31). Nor does the methodological suspension of the *Generalthesis* imply a judgement about the adequacy or relevance of the

---

5. The relation between the *epochē* and the reduction is not very clear. For reasons of simplicity I consider the *epochē* as the first step of the various reductions. For a thorough discussion, see Moran 273.

natural attitude. The natural attitude is not wrong or defective in any way. In most cases we actually do want to know what something is in the mode of the natural attitude. The phenomenological attitude simply allows for a different, additional approach to understanding. Fundamentally the methodological step of *epoché* implies suspending judgements about *what the experienced objects 'really' are*. This suspension in no way amounts to a denial or negation of the independent reality of any object. It merely facilitates a sustained focus on how it is given without the distraction of questions concerning its reality. The *epoché* is thus nothing but the injunction not to investigate whether there is something 'out there' corresponding to whatever is given in experience, but to remain with the phenomenon when engaging in phenomenological investigations.

After the *epoché* the reduction(s) can be applied. The *epoché* is the condition of possibility of the reduction (Husserl, *Crisis* §43), as it allows for the a priori correlation between subjectivity and the world to become an explicit object for investigation. The term 'reduction' is rooted in the Latin verb *reducere* and refers to a 'return' or a 'leading back', which indicates that the reduction is designed to neutralise various prejudices and to lead back to the phenomenon itself, the experience of originary givenness. Its aim is to reduce the additional information, the conceptual noise, that distracts from the experience as it is given.[6] There are various types of reduction and various ways into the reduction, from 'philosophical' to 'eidetic' and from the 'Cartesian way' to the 'way through the critique of the natural sciences' (Moran 274).

The great advantage of introducing these transcendental methods is that a phenomenologist does not have to immediately engage with questions around whether something is real

---

6. The idea that the reductions could lead to a virtually presuppositionless starting point for philosophical investigation was not shared by many later phenomenologists. Heidegger, for example, denied this possibility and developed his 'hermeneutic phenomenology' to come to terms with the fact that we always necessarily start somewhere, with some presuppositions.

or constituted, or how it is treated in the other sciences. This allows one to begin one's investigation of a specific phenomenon afresh, so that the phenomenologist can establish an experiential baseline that can act as a guideline for our judgements, scientific accounts or other conceptual interpretations of the phenomenon. The transcendental methods of reduction and *epochē* are thus helpful in disclosing the realm of pure phenomena, by eliminating or minimising distractions. But they are also helpful in moving from psychological analyses of singular experiences to knowledge, because to 'every psychological experience there corresponds, by way of the phenomenological reduction, a pure phenomenon that exhibits its immanent essence as an absolute givenness' (Husserl, *The Idea* 34).

This, however, also means that these methodological steps do not resolve the issue of realism either way. The *epochē* and the reductions merely open up a path towards a field of research that would be easily overlooked had we not taken these methodological steps. They do not imply or point towards a specific ontological commitment. While Husserl was very explicit about using these tools to develop a 'transcendental idealism' based on a 'pure cogito' in this manner, thus devising what he called an 'eo ipso transcendental idealism', he was also very vocal in his insistence that his project was not a straightforward form of idealism. Husserl himself situated his philosophy in a letter to Émile Baudin in the following way: 'No ordinary "realist" has ever been so realistic and so concrete as I, the phenomenological "idealist"' (Husserl, *Briefwechsel* 16).

Thus, with regard to its phenomenological dimension, this book can be taken as an attempt to develop a realist position from the application of the reductions. It does so by focusing the investigation on the intentional object as disclosed, and thus the passive constitution as much as possible, while not engaging with the side of the cogito shaping the correlation. However, it is impossible to clearly distinguish between the ideal and the real, the pure cogito and the cogitatum. In order to render phenomenology a realist enterprise, a further reduction needs to be introduced. This is the preconception that there is any correlation between simplicity and truth. It is the tendency of Western thought to strive for the clear and simple, its tendency to want to deal in absolutes and ideals, that renders the complex, messy, interrelated nature of what there is almost invisible. To truly develop a dynamic realism and thus a realist phenomenology, a different mode of thought is needed, one that does not engage in a form of purification or reification – of the subject or the cogito, as well as the object or the existing processes.

The intentional object after the epochē: the noema

Having introduced the transcendental methods of *epochē* and reduction, I can now move on to discuss the nature of the intentional object as it is given after the application of these methodological steps, namely the noema. It is precisely this process of bracketing that allows the phenomenon to appear as phenomenon, as noema, instead of being given in the natural attitude as the familiar empirical-psychological object. Husserl also refers to the noema (Greek: what is thought) as *Sinn* (sense); to him it is 'sense giving'. The intentional act is directed towards the noema, it is the 'direction of regard of the pure ego' (Husserl, *Ideas I* §88). The noema is thus the intentional object as appearing meaning, freed from questions concerning psychology, science and ontology.[7] The relevant question for us is now how this noematic sense (or the noema) relates to the 'real' object of experience. How this question is answered will make a substantial difference as to whether Husserl's phenomenology can be read in a realist fashion or not.

Determining the exact nature of the noema is one of the most controversial issues in Husserl scholarship. The noema can,

---

7. The noema is the appearing sense, but that is not all that the 'full noema' is: it is composed of this remaining, self-same nucleus of appearing noematic sense and the further predicate-noemata, i.e. the further properties characterising the noema (Husserl, *Ideas I* §131).

for example, be interpreted along the lines of a Fregean sense (*Sinn*) (Føllesdal, 'Husserl's Notion'). The noema is then taken to be the aspect of the intentional act that mediates between the I-pole and the object-pole, and cannot be identified with the object. In this case the noema is what gives the intentional act its sense, which means that the noema is not actually an object, but the sense-giving component of intentional acts. A different way of understanding the noema has been proposed by Aron Gurwitsch, who emphasises not only the sense-giving moment, but also the perspectival and abstract aspect of the noema. From this perspective the noema is an ideal entity (i.e. an abstract, ideal sense) through which any intentional act is able to refer to its intentional object. The intentional object itself is *constituted* in experience through the unfolding network of noemata that disclose the intentional object from various perspectives and within different contexts. It is this network or system of noemata that every object is 'reduced' to in the phenomenological reduction. Both John Drummond and Robert Sokolowski, on the other hand, argue that the noema is nothing but the actual object of experience itself, considered from a phenomenological perspective – they argue that the noema is simply the intentional object as intended (Sokolowski, *Introduction*). Finally, the noema can also be read as some form of combination of these positions. For example: 'With the noema, Husserl is positing a single complex entity that will take combinations of what Frege includes under the term "sense" (*Sinn*), mode of presentation, and the referential function of the act, i.e. the intentional object of the act' (Moran 223).

Husserl does not provide a clear answer as to which of these (or any further possible) interpretations is ultimately correct. In fact, Husserl explicitly denies the identification between noemata and physical objects on the one hand, while also denying the possibility of distinguishing them. In *Ideas I*, for example, he argues that there is a substantial difference between objects and noemata. They cannot be identified, since any natural object, such as a tree for example, can burn or be destroyed, but the noematic sense in its purely immanent form that is correlated with the tree cannot burn; it cannot be physically destroyed in any way:

> Whatever in purely immanent and reduced form is peculiar to the experience, and cannot be thought away from it, as it is in itself, and in its eidetic setting passes *eo ipso* into the Eidos, is separated from all Nature and physics, and not less from all psychology by veritable abysses; and even this image, being naturalistic, is not strong enough to indicate the difference. (Husserl, *Ideas I* §89)

Husserl makes clear that the noema of the tree is not to be identified with the tree *simpliciter*. Furthermore, the noema cannot subsist in independence from its corresponding intentional act, in this case the act of perception.[8] Should we conclude from this that the noema is some ideal meaning? Not quite. Even after bracketing and reducing the phenomenon of the tree, in order to arrive at the noema of the tree, the result is still the experience *of this tree*. And since we know that the image theory of perception is wrong, that the 'thing perceived in perception is the physical thing itself, in its own factual being' (Husserl, *Formal* §§106, 281) and not a copy or an image, *the noema cannot simply be an ideal structure or a meaning-entity*. Therefore, in his revised version of the *Logical Investigations* published in 1913, the same year as *Ideas I*, in the Appendix to §11 and §20 of the fifth investigation, Husserl argues the following:

> It need only be said to be acknowledged that *the intentional object of a presentation is the same as its actual object, and on occasion as its external object, and that it is absurd to distinguish between them*. The transcendent object would not be the object of *this* presentation, if it was not its intentional object. This is plainly a merely analytic proposition. The object of the presentation, of the 'intention', *is* and *means* what is presented, the intentional object. (Husserl, *Logical Investigations II* 127)

---

8. This, of course, implies a certain reading of noema as an individual entity and not as a universal sense. For a closer discussion of these issues, see Bernet.

How can both of these statements, obviously contradictory (and published in the same year), hold?

I think that the respective context gives a clue as to how to reconcile these statements. The first is found in an ontological context comparing noematic statements with statements concerning reality in itself. Here Husserl confronts the idealism/realism issue invoked by his use of noesis and noema. With this investigative aim in mind, the absolute distinction between noema and object is not surprising. The context of the second quote is quite different. In this Appendix Husserl attempts to clarify the issues surrounding the image-theory of perception and the question of immanence. This passage is therefore concerned with the nature of intentionality or consciousness. Considering the differences in context and aim of these accounts of the relation between noema and object, it is not surprising that the same issue shows itself differently and that the results of the investigations differ: a different aspect of the phenomenon investigated shows itself in correlation with a variation in the investigative perspective. It might thus be a fruitful strategy to shift the investigation from asking *what the noema is* to *how the noema shows itself* in different contexts to truly learn more about its nature in a genuinely phenomenological fashion.

It is also an option to shift the question as to the nature of the relation between noema and intentional object: 'for Husserl the distinction to keep unto is not the one between the intentional object and the real object, but the one between the merely intentional object, and the real and intentional object' (Zahavi 298). This interpretation is supported by a quote that follows shortly after the above quote from the Appendix to §11 and §20 of the fifth investigation:

> 'The object is merely intentional' does not, of course, mean that it exists, but only in an intention, of which it is a real [*reelles*] part, or that some shadow of it exists. It means rather that the intention, the reference to an object so qualified, exists, but not that the object does. If the intentional object exists, the intention, the reference, does not exist alone, but

the thing referred to exists also. (Husserl, *Logical Investigations* II 127)

All of the approaches to the noema discussed so far do depart from a certain one-sidedness. They abstract from the context of the concrete experience, within which the intentional act appears as a whole. They also abstract from the flow of experience and the flow of life within which every intentional act is situated. Even considered from within the *epochē* and the phenomenological reductions, intentional acts are not actually static – they are connected, flowing into and shaping each other, as the concepts of horizon or sedimentation that I will discuss later indicate. They are furthermore situated in a context, they appear against a background, and the retention of previous intentional acts and the protection of further intentional acts do affect the present intentional act. Merely looking at one act – to then distinguish within this singular act noesis from noema, as well as the noematic sense from the noematic predicates and thus only focusing on the meaning element of experience, effectively disregarding duration, situatedness and so on – actually involves a lot of abstraction and leads to a result that is somewhat removed from what we actually experience. While these distinctions and differentiations between meaning, situatedness, temporality and so on do attempt to grasp something that is often hidden or lost in other accounts of experience, there is nothing given in experience that makes these distinctions necessary or renders them the most adequate forms of laying out, ordering or simplifying the structure of experience.

Husserl did emphasise the unity of the intentional act, and in his later genetic phenomenology he also began to investigate the fact that intentional acts can be shaped by previous intentional acts. In *The Crisis of European Sciences* Husserl did provide an account of the historicity and the situatedness of intentional consciousness. And it is this engagement with genesis, history and becoming that thoroughly undercuts the idea of a pure transcendental phenomenology. However, while it is true that

Husserl engaged with all of these issues and clearly recognised their problematic potential, neither he nor his interpreters were fully able to come to terms with these genetic, historical and temporal aspects of experience, especially with regard to the noema, as Derrida convincingly argued in his book *The Problem of Genesis in Husserl's Philosophy*. Ultimately, as long as the fundamental nature of the noema (and its variants, such as cogitato and so on) remain underdetermined, it does not suffice simply to refer to these concepts in order to decide whether phenomenology is a form of idealism or not. So it seems appropriate to take a closer look at the matter.

4

Husserl's Philosophy as Correlated Transcendental Realism

In what follows, I will introduce Husserl's philosophy as a *sui generis* stance on the realism/idealism issue that I will refer to as 'correlated transcendental realism'. I do so because Husserl holds that the mind and the world are fundamentally correlated, and that this correlation is given to us, so that experience cannot be reduced either to the ego or the in-itself. Due to the two-sided correlated nature of intentionality, the mind cannot be cut off from what there is. In these paragraphs I will argue that phenomenology is neither an idealism nor a realism, it is a *sui generis* position. In order to make this argument I will engage with a series of interpretations of phenomenology, namely as idealism, as naïve realism and as correlationism. I will furthermore show why Husserl's world-destruction argument in *Ideas I* does not undercut the intentional two-sidedness, and thus show that phenomenology is not a traditional form of idealism. Then I will engage with Sellars's critique of the myth of the given and argue that phenomenology does not lead to a traditional or naïve form of realism. Finally, I will engage with Meillassoux's critique of correlationism, in order to deepen my argument that phenomenology does not need to remain stuck in the correlationist circle. This is the case because Husserl's transcendental idealism simply amounts to the claim that we cannot know anything about the world *without* establishing an experiential relation to it. This, however, does not negate the mind-independent existence of the world or of its objects. Husserl merely claims that *existing* means to be a possible object of experience, *if there is a consciousness present*.

For the sake of clarity, I would like to emphasise that I am merely investigating whether and how Husserl's method can be used as a path towards dynamic realism, and not whether Husserl ultimately was or was not a realist or an idealist.[1]

Husserl's Reinterpretation of Transcendental Idealism and the a priori Correlation

So how does Husserl's transcendental 'idealism' differ from other more traditional forms of idealism? At heart, any idealism is the attempt to answer sceptical worries about objective knowledge and the mind's presumed (in)ability to access an independent external world. Kant, for example, defines idealism in the following way:

> By an **idealist**, therefore, one must understand not someone who denies the existence of external objects of sense, but rather someone who only does not admit that it is cognized through immediate perception and infers from this that we can never be fully certain of their reality from any possible experience. (Kant A368–9)

Kant then pairs this epistemic claim with a metaphysical claim, namely that there is an absolute ontological separation of mind and the thing in itself.

Husserl's insistence on the merely methodological nature of his version of transcendental idealism paints a very different picture. First, for Husserl, no ontological claims can be made on the basis of the phenomenological method alone, since ontological concerns have been bracketed in the *epochē*. Phenomenology is not concerned with the existence of external objects; however, Husserl does hold that what there is appears

---

1. For an overview of the various debates as to whether Husserl ultimately was or was not a realist, one could look at any of the following quite recent studies: Loidolt; De Palma; Jansen.

directly to consciousness. This direct appearance or givenness is, however, not sufficient to fully cognise what there is. Here Kant and Husserl agree.

Subjective and absolute idealists, on the other hand, follow a different strategy. Instead of separating the ultimately unknowable objects from the objects we experience in a Kantian fashion, these thinkers depart from an integration of the world into the sphere of the conscious, a process rooted in the claim that the distinction between immanence and transcendence is merely epistemological, precisely because it is a distinction only conceivable in and through experience and consciousness. In this case too Husserl seems to choose a different path, rejecting 'any version of subjective idealism that treats the objective material world as illusory or as merely a content of consciousness' (Moran 154). Ultimately, Husserl acknowledges that there is a degree of *correlated* difference between immanence and transcendence, but he does not hold this separation to be absolute, contra Kant, nor does he hold that this separation can ultimately be sublated, reduced or dissolved, contra subjective or absolute idealism.

Still, Husserl himself does occasionally refer to his philosophy as a form of transcendental idealism. Furthermore, there are many passages that suggest that he holds the cogito to be foundational in a way that the world is not. In §41 of the *Cartesian Meditations*, for example, he states that 'all that exists for the pure ego becomes constituted in him himself; furthermore, that every kind of being including every kind characterized as, in any sense, "transcendent" has its own particular constitution' (Husserl, *Cartesian Meditations* §41). If this was all Husserl had to say about the matter, a realist reading of phenomenology would be quite impossible. Husserl, however, continues to clarify how the ego and the transcendent universe belong together and how this correlated 'essentially belonging together' is to be understood. Namely not in terms of actuality, but in terms of possibility:

> The attempt to conceive the universe of true being as something lying outside the universe of *possible* consciousness, *possible*

knowledge, *possible* evidence, the two being related to one another merely externally by a rigid law, is nonsensical. They belong together essentially; and, as belonging together essentially, they are also concretely one, one in the only absolute concretion: transcendental subjectivity. If transcendental subjectivity is the universe of possible sense, then an outside is precisely nonsense. But even nonsense is always a mode of sense and has its nonsensicalness within the sphere of possible insight. (Husserl, *Cartesian Meditations* §41, my emphasis)

Consciousness and world are concretely one, without identification of one relatum with the other and without the possibility of sublation. The transcendent aspect and the subjective aspect are necessarily bound by a co-relation in the specific sense introduced before. To talk about transcendental subjectivity implies talking about the structure of intentionality *and* the intentional objects, precisely because consciousness and 'true being' belong together essentially as part of the intentional correlation. 'Transcendental subjectivity' thus conceived already implies, necessitates and presupposes the whole correlated intentional structure, and thus also includes the object aspect, in this case true being. This, however, does not imply that existence is appearance (as *esse est percipii*) or that things only exist as long as they appear;[2] instead they can be considered as existing if the following counterfactual claim holds: If there was a perceiving consciousness present, then they would appear.

> If there are any worlds, any real physical things whatever, then the experienced motivations constituting them must be able to extend into my experience and into that of each Ego [. . .] Obviously, there are physical things and worlds of physical things which do not admit of being definitely demonstrated

---

2. We can furthermore derive conclusions about things that are not presently given by extrapolating from what we are currently experiencing: 'Also mir sind die Dinge, oder sind viele Dinge, diese bestimmten da, gegeben. Ich kann auch von da weitergehen und von den gegebnenen auf nicht gegebene schliessen. Dort hinter den Bergen wohnen auch Leute, breiten sich auch Flüsse aus' (Husserl, *Phänomenologie* 10, Beilage V).

in any human experience; but that has purely factual grounds which lie within the factual limits of such experience. (Husserl, *Ideas I* §48)

In order to claim that something exists from a phenomenological perspective, it suffices to claim that it would appear if there were a perceiving consciousness present. Thus, to exist as a spatiotemporal, physical thing means to be able to extend into experience, should consciousness be present.

To make a more speculative point, this correlational unity grasps the human condition rather well. We as human beings are both conscious subjects and physically living biological beings. We belong both to the realm of consciousness and the physical world, both aspects being unified in our existence, influencing each other in a correlated manner. But this does not enable us to reduce one aspect to the other or to disregard the difference completely. As biological and physical beings we belong with this world of matter; as conscious beings we can reflect on this state, give meaning to phenomena and interpret what we encounter. Furthermore, the physical world enters and belongs to our consciousness in so far as we think and interpret it. And we realise and enact our conscious concepts, ideas and ideals by reordering and structuring the physical world around us. The 'essentially belonging together' of consciousness and what is usually considered transcendent, i.e. the physical and objective world, is embodied in every individual human existence, if not in every living being. To cut off human consciousness from human physicality, to cut our minds from our physical, biological, corporeal worldliness, and vice versa, is to separate something in thought that cannot actually be separated. To confuse these levels of investigation, to confuse what can be done in thought with what can be executed in reality, is to commit the fallacy of misplaced concreteness. The idea of a pure consciousness without givenness, of consciousness without intentional object, is a merely logical possibility, a possibility of thought, but it is not a real or even a phenomenological possibility, as I will argue in what follows.

Husserl's Philosophy

Pure consciousness? *Ideas I* and the world-destruction argument

At this point it seems prudent to discuss Husserl's well-known world-destruction argument in *Ideas I*, which is often considered proof of his idealism. It is usually interpreted along the following lines: 'When Husserl sounds most like a classical idealist (in *Ideas I* §49), he says that the natural world is "relative" to consciousness, that consciousness alone is "absolute", not "relative" to anything else' (Smith 75).

In order to fully appreciate the role of this argument, it is necessary to know the context in which it is presented. This argument appears in the third chapter of *Ideas I*, where Husserl discusses the region of pure consciousness. In the preceding paragraphs Husserl engages with the theoretical and logical possibilities of reimagining the world in a fundamentally different way (§47), whether there could be a world beyond our world and thus beyond givenness (§48), and whether there could be an absolute consciousness (i.e. a givenness) without a world (§49).

In §47 Husserl lays out the essential role of experience and the essential correlation between things and consciousness. Whatever things are – real or imagined, with this or that essence – they are present *as things given in experience*, and as such, they can never be empty logical possibilities:

> An object that has being in itself [*an sich seiender*] is never such as to be out of relation to consciousness and its Ego. The thing is thing of the world about me [*Umwelt*], even the thing that is not seen and the really possible thing, not experienced but experienceable or perhaps-experienceable. *Experienceablity never betokens an empty logical possibility, but one that has its motive in the system of experience.* (Husserl, *Ideas I* §47)

This thought is the basis for Husserl's claim that a merely logical reimagination of what there is (that is not based in experience) does not disclose actual possibilities.

The second paragraph (§48) discusses a specific logical possibility, namely of a reality beyond this world, a world-in-itself so to speak, that is not given in experience and by its very transcendent nature can never be given in experience. And while Husserl admits that the thought of a world beyond this one that is never accessible in experience does not involve a logical contradiction, he does argue that it involves what I would call a phenomenological contradiction. If something is not actually experienced, but is simply thought up through an empty logical possibility (*durch eine leere logische Möglichkeit erdachtes*) and is in no way (even potentially) accessible through experience for any actual ego (*für irgendein aktuelles Ich*), then this merely logical possibility cannot ground any substantial conclusions about the nature of what can appear, neither for nor against the existence of whatever is being investigated. It is, however, possible to exclude such a merely logical possibility as a genuine (or 'real') possibility through a phenomenological investigation. This can be done by looking at the a priori structure and constitution of the world. What conditions need to be fulfilled for world to appear, even if it appears as transcendent, or as a world beyond this world? First and foremost the empirical reasons for us to even think about such a world need to be able to appear (at least potentially):

> If there are worlds or real things at all, the empirical motivations which constitute them must be able to reach into my experience, and that of every single Ego [. . .] Things no doubt exist and worlds of things which cannot be definitely set out in any human experience, but that has its purely factual grounds in the factual limits of this experience. (Husserl, *Ideas I* §48)

Having thus shown that if something is to exist at all it has to have the ability to show up for consciousness, and that mere logical possibility thus does not imply a real possibility, in §49 Husserl moves on to investigate whether there is such a thing as pure consciousness without a world. It is at this stage that Husserl introduces the world-destruction argument.

Husserl begins with a thought experiment. He imagines givenness without the kind of lawfulness or regularity that characterises factual givenness:

> It is conceivable that our experiencing function swarms with oppositions that cannot be evened out either for us or in themselves, that experience shows itself all at once obstinately set against the suggestion that the things it puts together should persist harmoniously to the end and that its connectedness, such as it is, lacks the fixed order-schemes of perspectives, apprehensions, and appearances – that a world in short, exists no longer. (Husserl, *Ideas I* §49)

While the world thus destroyed would cease to exist, Husserl concludes that pure consciousness would persist in a modified form, and therefore consciousness does not presuppose the world, while the world does presuppose consciousness (as he argued in §47). What renders this argument so confounding to me is the unmediated move from a loss of structure to a loss of existence. Even if the world were given without any of the familiar regularities and structures that phenomenologists currently focus on in investigating perceptions, this does not mean that there would be no world. Why would this chaotic, unordered world not simply be given in a different way – not as a world of enduring constituted things?

Let us dig a little deeper. If this chaotic, unordered world could exist as I claim, how would it allow for perception and constitution, which are processes that seem to presuppose ordering? In answering this question, it does need to be said Husserl himself pushes against the boundaries of what can be done within the reductions in his world-destruction argument, so it seems permissible for me to do the same. However, while Husserl pushes the limits of phenomenology towards an a priori logical argument, I will push them towards an ontological one: How are we to understand the chaos that results from the lack of 'the fixed order-schemes of perspectives, apprehensions, and appearances'? Is this chaos that Husserl talks about the *absolute negation of all order*, something that is essentially non-quantifiable, without any form and thus not perceivable? In the first case it seems impossible for there to be a consciousness or a transcendental ego either, since these elements are distinguishable and thus have a form. Or is chaos to be thought as the *strict opposite* to what is determined, a non-differentiated whole that can at least be pictured? It is this undifferentiated mass or chaos that Plato discusses in the *Parmenides* in consequence of the hypothesis that the one is not (*Parmenides* 164c–f). Here chaos is something indifferent, diffuse and can thus not be thought, but it can be holistically and imaginatively perceived. So, this interpretation of chaos too would not lead to a disappearance of givenness or the world.

There is then a third possible interpretation of chaos. It is this interpretation that I see as the one most in line with the ideas developed in this book, as well as much of contemporary science (which, again, does not imply the disappearance of appearance). Here chaos is thought as the potential for various forms of order (Gloy 19). Order and structures do not need to be simply given; they can emerge over time. Present processual chaotic appearance does not imply that the system will be forevermore unordered. Non-linear evolutionary processes are a concrete example of such developments that create order from chaos. These processes are not geared towards an ordering outcome, not governed through an a priori law determining the development and cannot be grasped through any schema (Gloy 157); nonetheless, such processes generated the highly ordered complexity we call life. Chaos theory is another example of a science that uses mathematical formulae to derive ordered structures from a sea of chaos, because every complex chaotic system can be ordered. Chaos thus does not necessarily imply the non-existence or non-appearance of world.

Hence, I can see no necessary reason why a completely different world would not simply constitute a completely different manifestation of the a priori correlation. I can furthermore see no reason why this logical possibility could constitute an argument for the independent existence of consciousness on more than a logical level, i.e. on a phenomenological level. As far as I can tell, Husserl does not engage with any of these issues in this context. All the arguments for the independent existence of consciousness that follow this passage in *Ideas I* seem simply to presuppose the following set of thoughts. Only an enduring structured world can exist; since the world can be thought as unstructured, it can also be thought as non-existent, which logically leaves pure consciousness as the only necessary aspect of reality. This is a combination of thoughts that leaves much to be desired in terms of being a convincing argument. Thus, instead of solving our issue once and for all – one way or the other – the world-destruction argument is again leading us further down the rabbit hole.

Heidegger's critique of Husserl's focus on pure consciousness as a field of phenomenological study echoes my thoughts. Heidegger argues for the inadequacy of this focus, because pure consciousness is not given phenomenologically. We can never actually experience pure consciousness. In fact, we always only experience the coming together of world and consciousness due to the intentional nature of consciousness. The concept of 'pure consciousness' is an empty logical possibility, because it is the result of *thinking the absolute separation* of mind and world in its most extreme form. According to Heidegger, this line of argument in Husserl is rooted in the history of philosophy and logical reflection, not in the phenomena (Heidegger, *History* 107).

*Husserl's correlated transcendental realism
and the constitution of meaning*

As I have argued, Husserl carves out a unique form of transcendental idealism that, according to him, is more concrete and real than any 'realism'. While I will discuss this type of realism in more detail in the last part of this book, there is one final aspect that I would like to address now. If phenomenology is supposed to be a form of realism, then the world or what there is needs to be able to affect givenness. The possibility of a transcendental realism is grounded in the claim that reality and mind are correlated and thus fundamentally intertwined. This way of conceptualising the correlation leads to the idea that in experience, reality can 'bleed' into the mind in the form of hyle and matter. All the processes of synthesis and meaning-giving follow from this and build on this original unity. The constitution of meaning does not imply a construction of the object; instead, it refers to a two-sided process of disclosure driven by the object and responded to by the subject. Ultimately, sensible experience is a combination of intellect and sensibility:

> *The intellect* is a name for constitutive accomplishments of objects that the ego has given to itself through the activities of identification. The self-giving is a creative self-giving. *Sensibility* is the contrary, <it is a name> for constitutive accomplishments without the participation of the active ego; the grasping of such objects is indeed an activity, but it is a mere receiving of a pre-constituted sense, and further explicating, judging already presupposes this sense, the pure reception of an already constituted sense. (Husserl, *Analyses* §58)

Therefore, what is given through the senses is not simply actively constituted by the subject, as is the case in most idealist as well as constructivist positions. It is passively constructed from the meaning presented by sensual content. The *Gegendstandssinn* (object meaning) is not simply determined or produced by the subject, but is developed and unfolded through the act of perception in a balanced combination of active and passive syntheses. This development can now be more or less focused on the *Gegendstandssinn* or it can be more or less focused on the intellectual aspects shaping this process of unfolding. Either way, this process remains essentially two-sided. This means that we have to read the process of 'constitution' as a process of 'letting the entity be seen in its objectivity' and not as a straightforward 'producing in the sense of making and fabricating' (Heidegger, *History* 71). It is in this sense that reality can bleed into consciousness.

The correlation is so fundamental for Husserl's thought that he ultimately considered phenomenology to be nothing but an investigation into the a priori correlation of subjectivity and objectivity (Husserl, *Einleitung* 441). If this correlation is understood as internally and temporally correlated, the correlation is also that aspect of phenomenological thought that allows for a way into phenomenological realism; the correlation that renders phenomenology a science of 'objective subjectivity' (Husserl, *Cartesian Meditations* §13) in looking at the objective structures of consciousness. And it is this correlation that, *mutatis mutandis*, allows for phenomenology to be developed into a science of *subjective objectivity*. But before I develop phenomenology as a science of subjective objectivity with the use of experiential temporal correlations, I engage with some critical perspectives on correlated phenomenological realism from outside the phenomenological tradition.

Phenomenology, Phenomenalism and Naïve Realism: Sellars and the Myth of the Given

I would now like to situate a realist reading of Husserl's phenomenology further, by defending it from the charge of being a form of naïve realism and thus of falling prey to the myth of the given as defined by Sellars. In engaging with this rather specific argument at this point, I am not attempting a thorough analysis or critique of Sellars's arguments. Rather I am merely attempting to show that, while Husserl would agree with many of Sellars's attacks on foundationalism with regard to empirical knowledge and phenomenalism, he establishes a new and substantially different form of foundation, based on the *structure of givenness* or the *how of appearance*. Furthermore, Husserl acknowledges that this knowledge about the structures of givenness cannot immediately ground empirical knowledge. Nonetheless, knowing these law-governed structures of givenness can aid in testing and examining the adequacy of the interpretations and constructions that are involved in generating empirical knowledge. The aim of engaging with these arguments is twofold. Not only have Sellars's and Husserl's views on givenness often been compared, but there is also a well-documented tendency to conflate phenomenalism and phenomenology (Soffer) that I want to counteract through this discussion.

Phenomenalists hold that what is given in the senses can ground knowledge; however, this applies to the perceptual qualities or bundles of sense data, not the objects of experience as such. It is these appearing sense data (or phenomena), the redness, coldness, sweetness, that are experienced directly and used to constitute all of our experiences as well as reality. This position, as presented for example by Ernst Mach, implies that objects are nothing but (logical) constructions of sense data or ideas that exist as pure data before they are (quite arbitrarily) categorised to be either mental or physical data. This position is generally considered a fundamental influence or even a precursor to the logical empiricism of the Vienna Circle. Phenomenalists and many logical empiricists consequently hold that material objects or propositions about material objects can adequately be reduced to the (possible appearance) of sense data or propositions about (possible) sense data.

Both Husserl and Sellars thoroughly critique sense-datum realism as naïve and simplistic. Sellars, for example, attacks phenomenalism because it presupposes 'the given as the immediate'. Husserl's critique, on the other hand, focuses on the implicit presuppositions of phenomenalism and the fact that these presuppositions cannot actually be evidenced in experience. Phenomenologists hold that the intentional object gives itself as itself (not a set of data) with a certain structure (the intentional matter or hyle) that can be passively synthesised or unfolded by conscious engagement, not merely actively constructed. This refusal of the phenomenalists to attribute material or physical reality to what is given in experience is the reason why Husserl, in his *Basic Problems of Phenomenology*, describes Mach's phenomenalism as a sensation-monism and as a precursor to the phenomenological method. (Husserl, *Phänomenologie* 180). According to Husserl, the difference between his and Mach's position is that Mach employed an inadequate concept of sensation, interpreting all forms of givenness as composed sets of sense data instead of variously correlated intentional objects, and that he is therefore not able to avoid psychologism. Finally, both Husserl and Sellars agree that the sense phenomena presupposed by phenomenalism cannot provide direct empirical knowledge, because 'empirical knowledge requires concepts, inferences and language' (Soffer 302), which undercuts phenomenalism's core conviction.

In 'Empiricism and the Philosophy of Mind' Sellars begins his investigation of the myth of the given by stating that 'givenness' is often equated with the Hegelian term 'immediacy' (Sellars, *Science* 127) which, it stands to reason, can easily lead to the combined idea of 'immediate givenness'. Thus, Sellars argues that 'the point of the epistemological category of the given is, presumably, to explicate the idea that empirical knowledge rests on a "foundation" of non-inferential knowledge of matter of fact' (Sellars, *Science* 128). However, traditional sense-datum theories (including phenomenalism) inadequately combine the two ideas concerning knowledge. The first idea is the claim that there are 'inner episodes' that occur 'without any prior process of learning or concept formation, and without which it would – in *some* sense – be impossible to see, for example, that a physical object is triangular and red' (Sellars, *Science* 140). Secondly, there is the idea that some of these 'inner episodes' are non-referential knowings, which 'are the necessary conditions of empirical knowledge as providing the evidence for all other empirical propositions' (Sellars, *Science* 140). Both of these ideas have some truth to them. Combining them in an inadequate way as traditional sense-datum theorists do, however, leads to the conclusion that such inner experiences can immediately ground propositional knowledge. While Sellars admits that there are immediate inner episodes which can be characterised as directly giving, he denies that these inner episodes can ground empirical knowledge. Sellars's argument consists in separating the qualitative givenness of the phenomenon as inner episode, without which it would be – in some sense – impossible to perceive qualities, from the second idea, namely that these inner episodes provide direct and straightforward empirical knowledge of what there is. It is this line of argument that exposes the idea of grounding knowledge in 'the given' as a myth and leads Sellars to coin the term 'myth of the given'. He argues that givenness is a myth precisely because any candidate for such direct knowledge either presupposes other types of knowledge and is thus not basic, or it is impossible to prove how it rests on basic experience (i.e. sense data).

Sellars's main point against grounding knowledge in direct experience is that every experience of something (or of a property) implies having the concept of this something (or property) prior to noticing it, otherwise we would not be able to notice it as this something (or property): 'For we now recognize that instead of coming to have a concept of something because we have noticed that sort of thing, to have the ability to notice a sort of thing is already to have a concept of that sort of thing, and cannot account for it' (Sellars, *Science* 174). In contrast, sense-datum theorists claim that what is sensed are particulars, which, as Sellars points out, seems to undercut the claim that we can know through sensing, since it is (propositionally structured) facts that we know, not particulars: 'It would seem, then, that the sensing of sense contents cannot constitute knowledge, inferential or non-inferential [. . .] For what is known, even in non-inferential knowledge is facts rather than particulars, items of the form *something's being thus-and-so* or *something's standing in a certain relation to something else*' (Sellars, *Science* 128). Sellars offers some options to come to terms with this conundrum concerning knowledge about particulars. He even considers the idea that there might be a different kind of knowledge, whose object is a particular and not a fact. While Sellars is thus open to the possibility that there are distinct types of knowledge, one whose objects are propositions or facts and one whose objects are particulars,[3] he thoroughly criticises the fact that many sense-

---

3. It is this difference that I introduced in the terminological clarifications at the beginning. As I argued, there is a difference between knowledge of facts and knowledge as unconcealment. Knowing *asyntheta* (i.e. what is simple,

datum theorists conflate these types of knowledge and argue as if givenness could give knowledge of (propositionally structured) facts. If we also consider the idea of immediacy in this context, i.e. that such sensing is immediate not learned (or 'acquired' in Sellars's terminology), we end up with an entirely confused understanding of givenness. It is confused because it conflates two kinds of knowledge, and it is confused because it equates any sensing or experience with clarified or presuppositionless experience. It is this double conflation that creates the myth of the given.

Husserl would fundamentally agree with this line of argument, but would, I think, also contest an unqualified application of these arguments to phenomenology. First, phenomenological descriptions are not considered to lead to direct knowledge about facts; they lead to knowledge about how facts are given. In a second step this descriptive knowledge can then be investigated as to its implications about facts. Secondly, Sellars's all-or-nothing distinction between the concept and the real object (or property) it refers to appears far too simplistic from a phenomenological perspective. Husserl, for example, argues that every perceptual judgement can refer to many different phenomena and can involve many degrees of conceptualisation. He thus provides a much more sophisticated account of the interaction between phenomena or givenness and perceptual judgements or facts than Sellars presents. As part of this complex system, Husserl does, however, also argue for pre-predicative experience especially in the posthumously published *Experience and Judgment* (1974). Here he distinguishes pre-predicative experience from predicative judgement, arguing that the structures of predicative judgements are ultimately rooted in quasi-perceptual experiences. The difference between these levels of experience and judgement is

---

non-composed, or particular), for example, is different from knowing what is composed (of substance and predicate or of quantified existence and predicate). *Asyntheta* can only either be known or have to remain unknown (*Metaphysics* IX, 1052a), while facts can be true or false.

the difference between a *'logische Vorform'* (pre-figuring form) given in perception and a *'logische Vollform'* (fully fledged form). He therefore holds that there are rudimentary pre-forms of the categorical objects involved in judgements and knowledge that can be experienced in perception. Husserl does therefore allow (like McDowell for that matter) for categorical (i.e. non-sensory) experiential intuitions, concerning logical relations or values, for example, in addition to perceptual (sensory) intuitions. As long as these categorical experiences are given intuitively, they are a legitimate aspect of any phenomenological investigation. In contrast to phenomenalism, phenomenology can therefore accommodate degrees of conceptualisation.

Nonetheless, this level of experience does not immediately ground or yield empirical knowledge; instead (putting it simply) it furnishes the pre-structure for judgements and knowledge (Staiti). This is a view that Husserl again shares with McDowell:

> In the view I am urging, the conceptual contents that sit closest to the impact of external reality on one's sensibility are not already, qua conceptual, some distance away from that impact. They are not the results of a first step within the space of reasons, a step that would be retraced by the last step in laying out justifications, as that activity is conceived within the dualism of scheme and Given [. . .] But it is not like that: the conceptual contents that are most basic in this sense are already possessed by impressions themselves, impingements by the world on our sensibility. This makes room for a different notion of givenness [. . .]. (McDowell 9)

However, is it not the case that phenomenology does presuppose the direct givenness of meaning or sense, the noema? Does this not constitute a falling prey to the myth of the given? Let me investigate this issue in more detail, by going back to Sellars. Considering the sentence 'X looks red to S at t' Sellars argues that, fundamentally

> the sense of 'red' in which things *look* red is [. . .] the same as that in which things *are* red. When one glimpses an object and

decides that it looks red (to *me, now*, from here) and wonders whether it really is red, one is surely wondering whether the colour – red – which it looks to have is the one it really does have. (Sellars, *Science* 141)

The inner episode of something 'looking red' and the fact of something 'being red' are here said to involve 'red' in the same *sense*. Which implies that either the ontologically existing red is 'the same' as the epistemologically given red, or that both are red 'in the same sense'. How can this be?

Most naturalists or scientific realists would hold that red in its ontological existence is (according to current theories) a surface structure that reflects light in a certain way, while the epistemologically given red is a subject's brain's interpretation of the experience of these light waves as they hit the retina. But this naturalistic description does not actually capture how we experience redness. Such a causal story cannot account for what it feels like to experience red or, to put it in different words, in what 'sense' it is the same red. This is the case because sensations (*Empfindungen*) have a bivalent nature, as Husserl argues, and they can thus be studied in two ways. On the one hand, one can examine sensations as the reactions of the body to causal stimuli of the external world, or one can investigate sensations in their empirical qualitative presence, how it feels to have such an experience, by focusing on *how* they are experienced. However, if sensations are considered merely in their qualitative givenness, subject not to causal or natural laws but to law-governed conscious structures such as givenness, memory, association and so forth, then Sellars's idea that being given as red and being red both involve 'red' in the same *sense* seems quite intuitive. It is the sense of red that is at stake in phenomenology.

According to Husserl, the intentional object of consciousness, in this case the 'sense' of red (as noema or cogitatum), is never simply given in its finished form:

> This sense, the *cogitatum qua cogitatum*, is never present to actual consciousness [*vorstellig*] as a finished datum; it becomes

'clarified' only through explication of the given horizon and the new horizons continuously awakened [. . .] [It . . .] is at all times imperfect; yet, with its *indeterminateness*, it has a *determinate structure*. (Husserl, *Cartesian Meditations* §19)

The given senses (the noemata or cogitata) are never 'fully present' or 'finished'; they are continuously unfolding, always to be further explicated, to be investigated further. It is the lawful structure governing both the unfolding of the horizons as well as the correlation between the acts of consciousness and the objects of consciousness that remains stable. It is this insight into the lawful structure governing the unfolding of the phenomena and the correlated stability that grounds phenomenological realism, as opposed to the direct insight into objective reality of naïve realism. But this shift from sense data to the correlation as a ground for knowledge has a price: the law-governed structures of intentional consciousness merely allow for investigations of the how of givenness (and not what is given) and thus, strictly speaking, only allow for knowledge about the structures of givenness, not about *what* there is. This is the case precisely because Husserl agrees with Sellars in that the 'inner episodes' as such cannot straightforwardly ground knowledge about *what* things are. They can only ground knowledge about *how things are given, how they are correlated*. This is the reason why the phenomenological method is not and never can be considered a form of straightforward realism.

The next question to tackle is whether this correlation itself constitutes a version of the myth of the given. Let me investigate this by beginning with a generous reading of the myth of the given. In the first of his Carus Lectures, Sellars states that to 'reject the Myth of the Given is to reject the idea that the categorial structure of the world – if it has a categorial structure – imposes itself on the mind as a seal on melted wax'; or formulated positively: 'If a person is directly aware of an item which has categorial status C, then the person is aware of it as having categorial status C' (Sellars, 'Lever' 11). Taking this general formulation of the myth of the given, Carl Sachs argues that in fact phenomenology does succumb to this very general rendering of the myth, because of the correlation:

> Only in this fully general sense of the Myth can we understand why Sellars says that versions of the Myth occur in 'dogmatic rationalism' as in 'sceptical empiricism,' let alone that there are 'Kantian' and even 'Hegelian' versions of the Myth. Likewise, there is, I suggest, a specifically phenomenological version of the Myth, one in which what is 'given' is precisely 'givenness itself,' or as Husserl calls it, the noesis–noema correlation. (Sachs 161)

With Sellars, Sachs argues that it is the correlation itself that imposes itself on the mind, and this imposing is the reason why phenomenology too succumbs to the myth of the given, the only difference from sensualist positions being the fact that it is not some specific content that is simply given, but the correlation itself. At first glance this seems a plausible position, so let us investigate it in a bit more detail.

According to McDowell, the allure of the myth of the given 'expresses a craving for rational constraint from outside the realm of thought and judgement' (McDowell 18). The myth of the given is alluring because we want our thoughts and judgements to be limited by what there is, so that they do not depend on subjective interpretation alone. And phenomenology does find these constraints in the a priori law-governed structures of intentional consciousness and the phenomenal matter, not in the 'given' sense data. Since phenomenal matter and passive constitution alone do not yield a graspable or understandable given in Sellar's sense, this aspect is not problematic; thus I will turn to the a priori law-governed structures of intentionality.

Phenomenologists hold the correlation to be fundamental, and in a certain sense it does ground knowledge. However, this cannot be quite the entire story. First and foremost, this correlation is not itself simply given immediately; it is thus not 'a given', but the result of intense cognitive work employing the reductions and a restriction to description. These conceptual tools are necessary in order to discover this phenomenon, because we tend to overlook this correlation, thus not registering this givenness. Only if a phenomenological stance is taken up and experience is thoroughly investigated does this correlation even show itself, so it cannot be considered to be simply 'given' in a straightforward sense. In the natural attitude this correlation is hidden, even for trained phenomenologists. While the correlation is present in the natural attitude, it only becomes present to mind after it is uncovered from a phenomenological perspective. It is always present but not always noticed, and thus cannot be considered as 'a given' that would ground knowledge in the sense of the naïve realist. So, every givenness of the correlation is the result of taking up a philosophical, i.e. a phenomenological, stance and thus cannot be considered 'given' in the sense introduced by Sellars.

Beside this aspect of unmediated givenness, there is also the aspect of foundationalism that plays a part in the critique of the given as a grounding of knowledge. Even if the correlation is not simply given, it is in a sense foundational and could therefore still be considered problematic. Here again phenomenology does not quite fit the charge. It is not the case that the correlation grounds knowledge in a foundational sense; on the contrary, it is the condition of possibility of givenness, because consciousness (i.e. intentional givenness) is a constitutive part of the correlation. To be conscious is to be intentionally directed; thus there would be no consciousness (and therefore no knowledge) without intentionality, without an intentional object it is correlated with. The correlation is thus grounding in the sense that the Kantian categories are a transcendental grounding of knowledge. The correlation does not exist without intentional consciousness and therefore it does not ground in a naïve realist sense. If the correlation was a simple givenness that impresses itself on the passive mind, which is how a naïve realist would characterise knowledge as arising from givenness, this would imply that the mind (as intentionality) impresses itself on itself (as consciousness) in the givenness of the correlation, thus being both active and passive at the same time. This, in turn, undercuts the idea that phenomenology falls prey to the myth of the given, the idea that phenomenology grounds knowledge on simple, naïve and unreflected givenness.

Speculative Realism and the Critique of Phenomenology as Correlationism

Having shown that correlation does not lead phenomenology to fall prey to the myth of the given, I will now take a closer look at another critique of correlation as idealistic, by focusing on the charge implied by 'correlationism' as proposed by new realists in general and Quentin Meillassoux in particular.

In his book *The End of Phenomenology*, Tom Sparrow provides a very harsh critique of phenomenology. He sees it as an open-ended search that can never achieve any positive outcome. Using Husserl's drive to constantly improve on descriptions, not only with regard to the objects of investigation but also with regard to the phenomenological method and its central terms, he argues that phenomenology is neither a well-defined school nor a well-defined method. In fact Sparrow points out that the argument could be made that 'phenomenology never really existed' (Sparrow 204). As his investigation continues, Sparrow does, however, discover a common thread to phenomenological research, namely its adherence to the transcendental method (Sparrow 14) in the form of the correlation, which according to Sparrow renders phenomenology fundamentally committed to some form of idealism. He clarifies that when his 'book proclaims the end of phenomenology, it means that phenomenology *as a method for realists* has worn itself out' (Sparrow 13). Sparrow continues to argue that any genuine realism (from a post-Kantian continental perspective) can only be achieved by going beyond any form of correlationism, because any position that presupposes correlationism is unable to reach the real, the *great outdoors*:

> By 'correlation' we mean the idea according to which we only ever have access to the correlation between thinking and being, and never to either term considered apart from the other. We will henceforth call correlationism any current of thought which maintains the unsurpassable character of the correlation so defined. (Meillassoux, *After Finitude* 5)

Philosophers who are critical of a correlational approach to knowledge do not criticise the relationality of knowledge as such, since all theories of knowledge are based on a subject–object relation of some sort. But these thinkers are very critical of what they conceive to be the anti-realist core of any correlationist position, namely that 1) what we can know is true only for us, because 2) we have no 'access to the "Absolute" – that is the real as independent from human thought and interest' (Dukic und Morin 4). While it is true that phenomenologists do hold that there is no such thing as an objective view from nowhere – and that even if there were such a thing as an objective, i.e. a subject-independent, view on the world, it would still be a view, and thus would still imply a consciousness that holds this view – this for a phenomenologist does not imply that what we know is true only for us.

While it is furthermore adequate to claim that in correlationist positions one can only have access to the correlation between thinking and being, never being privy to either thinking or being in absolute separation, in the case of phenomenology it is not quite fair to claim that, that is all that we have. At least in Husserl's conception of a correlational philosophy, we also have indirect access to the whole correlated system and the way it develops through time. This is an insight that makes it possible to push the investigation of the correlation in various directions, for example towards the limits of the correlation, as I have argued above. Doing so shifts the investigation from the system to its nodes, while still retaining the temporal and correlated aspects. Whether I focus my attention on the structure of the phenomenon (in realist phenomenology), or on the structures of the ego (in transcendental phenomenology), or even on the constitution of (potentially) either (in genetic phenomenology), or the correlated changes over time, the a priori correlation itself remains unchanged, while the focus of the investigation changes and with it the aspects of the correlation that are revealed.

While the basic critique proposed by the new realists that we cannot leave the correlational circle thus holds, it is simply not the case that the correlational circle is robust, static or unaffected by what there is. It is a circle that de facto is perilously held in place by the a priori structure of intentionality, and that is affected by any influence, as long as these influences are not excluded from the investigation. Only if we stabilise this circle by ignoring the further temporal and relational impact on it does the correlation seem to exclude the world. Only if we cut the circle off from its embedded, temporal and relational existence, by not allowing further investigations, for example, or further descriptions, further adaptations, thus turning the circle from an ongoing, evolving and responding process to something static – only then does the correlation turn into a prison that separates the mind from the world.

Meillassoux's argument from ancestrality as it is presented in *After Finitude* provides an additional point of critique, namely the claim that phenomenologists cannot accept the literal truth of scientific statements, since phenomenologists cannot simply accept statements such as 'The accretion of the Earth happened 4.6 billion years ago' as true. Instead, a phenomenologist can only accept these kinds of statement as true 'for us', thus de facto undermining the concept of truth as well as the idea of objectivity. What phenomenologists thus cannot acknowledge, according to Meillassoux, is the fact that science can grant us access to the great outdoors, to a reality that is not situated in or contained by the correlationist circle (Meillassoux, *After Finitude* 26). And he introduces the argument of the 'arche-fossil' to make this point. Meillassoux considers 'any reality anterior to the emergence of the human species – or even anterior to every recognized form of life on earth' to be ancestral. And he takes arche-fossils to be 'materials indicating the traces of past life' as well as the 'materials indicating the existence of an ancestral reality or event; one that is anterior to terrestrial life' (Meillassoux, *After Finitude* 10). He claims that correlationist philosophies cannot cope with the (falsifiable) objective validity of scientific statements about ancestral reality and arche-fossils, because the correlationist is forced to add a 'for us humans' to any such scientific statement. Meillassoux takes care to distinguish his argument from similar arguments that refer to the unobserved. The example of the arche-fossil references a time before consciousness and thus before the existence of givenness itself. 'So the challenge is therefore the following: to understand how science can think a world wherein spatiotemporal givenness itself came into being within a time and a space which preceded every variety of givenness' (Meillassoux, *After Finitude* 22).

At this point, the relevant question seems to be the following: 'Would I, if I had a time machine and travelled back to a time before the existence of consciousness and thus before givenness, be able to experience the accretion of the earth?' If so, then it seems to me that it is possible to experience this state of affairs, if a consciousness is present, and it is therefore a possible object of experience. Since the phenomenological criterion for existence is to be potentially experienceable, this does not seem to pose a problem. As I argued above, Husserl merely claims that for something to exist means for it to be a possible object of experience – *if there were a consciousness present*. Thus, even the arche-fossil seems to stand in relation – in the potential relation of being experienceable.

> An object existing in itself is never one with which consciousness or the Ego pertaining to consciousness has nothing to do. The physical thing is a thing belonging to the *surrounding world* even if it be an unseen physical thing, even if it be a really possible, unexperienced but experienceable, or perhaps experienceable, physical thing. (Husserl, *Ideas I* §47)

If the event of the accretion of the earth is an event of possible experience, even if it was not actually experienced by anyone (before my time-travelling adventure), then I cannot see the problem. If, however, Meillassoux is arguing that even if I were to travel back in time, I would still not be able to experience that ancestral event at that ancestral time (i.e. before the factual advent of consciousness), then I simply do not understand the argument.

One might counter my argument by pointing out that Husserl considered the 'attempt to conceive the universe of true being as something lying outside the universe of *possible* consciousness, *possible* knowledge, *possible* evidence' (Husserl, *Cartesian Meditations* §41) to be nonsensical. This claim could pose a problem for my attempt to defend phenomenology against the charge of a simple correlationism and thus for a realist reading of phenomenology – if it is not interpreted carefully. Husserl does not claim that we cannot conceive of an independent universe that is outside of actual knowledge, of actual experience and thus evidence. He merely states that to claim that true being lies outside of any possible consciousness while *simultaneously thinking and talking about it* is nonsensical. This argument also holds with regard to the reality of time and temporal dimensions, which I will address in what follows. Staying with the example of the ancestral event for now, Husserl's quote simply means that this event's existence (before the rise of consciousness) is accessible to us, known to us only through the direct and indirect scientific data suggesting such an ancestral event. If we lacked this data, we would not have any experience or evidence of this event, and it would be nonsensical to think we could talk about something that is not given to us in any way.

One last point; in *After Finitude* Meillassoux distinguishes between *strong correlationism*, the position that the in-itself can neither be known nor thought, and *weak correlationism*, which holds that the in-itself can be thought (but not known). Phenomenology, I would claim, is a unique variation of weak correlationism. While the in-itself can neither be thought nor known, it can be experienced. This variation of weak correlationism is possible, as I argued with regard to Sellars, because phenomenological experience is not to be identified with propositional knowledge. Thus, a more genuinely phenomenological answer to the charge of correlationism is that while we cannot come to know reality in itself through the phenomenological method, because 'empirical knowledge requires concepts, inferences and language' (Soffer 302), we can experience it. We can *experience* the world in itself through our bodily existence, if we are careful not to overly distort these experiences through our thoughts, concepts and interpretations.

While Tom Sparrow is thus right to claim that realist commitments are not a direct *product* of the phenomenological method (Sparrow 3), the phenomenological method does have the capacity to provide a path towards realism, because, as Husserl argues, experience transcends itself towards the object (it has the character of a '*über sich hinausweisen*') (Husserl, *Logical Investigations II* V §11). Husserl thus insists on the reality of things, not because of any a priori necessity, but because this is the only rational option from looking at the a posteriori data that we are given:

> All in all, the world – in its existence and in what it is – is an irrational fact, and its facticity resides uniquely and exclusively in the strictness of the motivational nexuses – which actually permit all the examined possibilities to appear as fallow possibilities, as baseless, purely fabricated possibilities. On the other hand, the existence of a world in which not only do individual realities come together in general, but to which ultimately each and every occurring datum makes its contribution is the only rational possibility, one which is indeed not given *a priori* but founded *a posteriori*. (Husserl, *Thing* §84)

While phenomenology cannot claim to provide access to a mind-independent world directly or to provide absolute or certain knowledge about it, I hope to have shown that it can provide experiential, a posteriori indications of the structure of reality, just as it can provide a posteriori, experiential insight into the correlational a priori.

5

Phenomenological Realism: The Argument from Temporality

In this chapter I will finally provide a systematic argument for phenomenological realism using our experience of temporality.[1] Husserl's main innovation with regard to a philosophical account of temporality is the claim that temporality or change can be experienced directly. Many modern thinkers, including Husserl's teacher, Brentano, argued that time, succession and change can never be experienced directly. On the contrary, such experiences of temporal change were considered the result of constructions, of memory, of productive and reproductive phantasy.[2] Husserl's insistence that flow and change can be experienced directly thus turned temporality into a phenomenon, transforming it into a possible object of phenomenological investigation,[3] and in keeping with Husserl's general style he continued to develop his stance on the issue of time throughout his career.

The early Husserl bases his investigations of time on the distinction between two major aspects of temporal experience,

---

1. In engaging with temporality, I mainly focus on Husserl's lectures on time-consciousness (*Internal Time*), and because of the focus on spatiotemporal objects or things I will also engage with time as presented in the *Thing and Space* lectures.
2. Compare the discussion in Bernet, Kern and Eduard 101, or in Kortooms 28.
3. How integral temporality is to intentionality remains a matter of debate. It is unclear whether Husserl considered the intentional structure of time-consciousness to be a *sui generis* type of intentionality, next to perception, imagination and so on, or whether he held that time-consciousness is a moment present in each and every intentional act, so that it has to be considered a moment of intentionality as such.

namely the subjective sensation of duration and the objective duration of sensation.[4] The subjective dimension focuses on the fact that consciousness and conscious experience are temporally extended. These investigations are concerned with the flow of consciousness and the temporality of experience itself. It takes time to experience. In investigating the objective duration of sensation, the focus is on the duration characterising the given phenomenon, for example temporal objects such as melodies. What renders temporal phenomena such as melodies such excellent objects with which to investigate objective temporality is the fact that these sorts of phenomena are inherently temporally distributed. Evidently, a melody could not be what it is if it did not endure. Husserl thus considered these to be the best phenomena to understand objective time, precisely because such objects were not merely in time but necessarily contained an extension of time (Husserl, *Internal Time* §7). And while this objective temporality is situated within the temporal extension of experience, these temporalities are not identical.

However, this leaves us with the question as to where the everyday things of the world, the spatiotemporal objects, would fit into this division; are they as temporal as *temporal objects* such as melodies? I would argue that this is the case. If we investigate any thing (i.e. spatiotemporal object) closely enough and over a sufficient period of time, there can be no doubt that they prove themselves temporally extended. Simply because they do not exhibit all their qualities at one point in time, they are like melodies. While something is being created or in the process of becoming, its properties change and not all its properties are present. The same, I would argue, holds for the process of decay as well as for the period of existence between becoming and perishing. So, temporality is as integral to melodies as it is to spatiotemporal objects, with the difference that while the temporal changes characterising melodies are easily perceptible and unfold with a speed that makes them impossible to ignore,

---

4. See Bernet's introduction to Husserl, *Internal Time*.

the temporal changes characterising spatiotemporal objects can be so minute and slow that the objects can seem immutable. Consider the shifts in tectonic plates that generate and move mountains, for example.

In what follows, I presuppose that all spatiotemporal objects are in fact genuinely temporal, that they have not only a location in space and time, but also an extension in space as well as temporality, a qualitatively changing extension in the temporal dimension (a duration) that is integral or essential to every spatiotemporal object. I furthermore presuppose the speculative metaphysical argument introduced at the beginning, namely that in actuality there is no temporality without change. Time without change can be conceptualised, can be thought, but it cannot be experienced. Thus, I take time without change to be a possibility of thought but not a real possibility.

Time and Temporality in Phenomenology

When it comes to the phenomenology of time, Husserl's lectures on internal time, *On the Phenomenology of the Consciousness of Internal Time, 1893–1917*, is a central text. However, as the title indicates, these investigations are mainly concerned with internal time-consciousness and temporal objects, while the current investigation is focused on the temporality of spatio-temporal things. Thus, I will use these lectures as background in what follows, but I will supplement them with reflections from the *Thing and Space* lectures and *Ideas II*, as these lectures focus on spatiotemporal objects and objective nature. However, as the title *Thing and Space* suggests, these investigations too do not focus on the temporal dimension of spatiotemporal things or change. In fact, less than thirty pages are dedicated to the issues of time and change in this investigation of the thing. But at least these lectures do focus on the kinds of objects that are relevant for this investigation and there are some preliminary reflections that are relevant for us.

In *Thing and Space* Husserl distinguishes the following ways of temporal givenness:

1. *objective temporality* of physical time (clock time)
2. *conscious temporality* of memory, of expectation, the experience of a continuous flow of nows and of a temporal horizon
3. *pre-phenomenological temporality* (as given in the temporal extension of perception and in the temporal character of perceived phenomena), an extension which is analogous to its spatial extension. (Husserl, *Thing* §19)

But there is a fourth form of temporality indicated in the last chapter of the *Thing and Space* lectures, namely:

4. the temporality of the changing phenomenon itself is distinct from objective time but still given within the temporal extension of perception and the continuous flow of now. I propose to define this temporality as the *temporality of the changing phenomenon itself* (thus excluding the case of merely apparent changes that are the result of things like bodily movements or other kinesthesis,[5] a change of the environment and so on).

The first layer, namely worldly or 'objective time', is the measurable time of the appearing objects, i.e. what constitutes itself as a thing like time (*dingliche Zeit*) (Husserl, *Thing* §19). Even though this layer seems to indicate a mind-independent temporality, we should not forget that it *appears* as objective time, and since the main characteristic of objective time (or clock

---

5. Husserl does look at the possibility of perceiving movement in objects, while it is actually the bodily subject that is moving, as an extreme form of kinesthesis (*Thing* §83). To exclude this problem, we will only look at changes in the phenomena while the subject is as stable as possible, discounting temporalities 1 and 2 as well as bodily movement for the purposes of this investigation. Just as with the *epochē* and the reductions, there remains the question as to whether we can ever fully achieve this ideal position. While this remains questionable it is obvious that we can try to approach such a position.

time) is measurability, it presupposes a measuring mind. Thus, this layer of objective time is still very much correlated with conscious structures.

The second layer is subjective time experience or personal time; this is the immanent or pre-empirical time of intentional acts, sensa and appearances, i.e. what it feels like to experience duration or time. Thus, in any conscious process in which

> a worldly Object appears as cogitatum [. . .] we have to distinguish the *Objective temporality that appears* (for example: the temporality of this die) from the *'internal' temporality of the appearing* (for example: that of the die-perceiving). This appearing 'flows away' with its temporal extents and phases, which, for their part, are continually changing appearances of the one identical die.
> However, these changes in 'what it feels like to experience time' are also not to be confused with an experience of change in the object of perception. (Husserl, *Cartesian Meditations* §18)

Finally, the third layer of temporality that Husserl mentions in the *Thing and Space* lectures is pre-phenomenological temporality. Husserl considers this to be the temporal extension of the thing, a stretching of the thing and all of its components through time (Husserl, *Thing* §19). This temporal extension is 'a sibling of the spatial' extension (*verschwistert mit der Räumlichen*, §20). In the investigations on inner time-consciousness, this pre-phenomenological layer of temporality is interpreted more generally as the ground for all temporality and defined as the unchanging flow of now moments; thus, it is transformed into the pre-phenomenal flow of time-constituting consciousness (Husserl, *Internal Time* §34) Thus, this layer of temporality does not characterise the temporality allowing for the duration or location in time of spatiotemporal objects, but refers to the flow of consciousness and is thus transformed from a grounding layer that relates to objects and their space-time to an inner grounding layer that relates to the flow of temporality.[6] Husserl

---

6. This shift in the pre-phenomenological temporality is partially possible due to a structural analogy. There is a parallel between the fundamental stratum

furthermore argues that we are only able to measure objective time because of the succession of mental states (subjective time). And the unity of the succession of various subjective mental states as well as the temporal extension of things given in experience is founded in the conscious pre-phenomenal flow of now moments, in our consciousness of succession.[7] Husserl insists that even though these layers are foundationally related, they are not to be confused.

In what follows, I refer to these three layers in sum (objective, subjective and pre-phenomenal flow) as the *layers of inner temporality*, in order to distinguish them from the fourth form of temporality introduced above, namely, the temporality constituted by changing things, which is closely intertwined with the reading of the pre-phenomenal flow as a temporal extension akin to spatial extensions proposed in the *Thing and Space* lectures. Before I introduce this additional layer of temporality in more detail, I want to provide some reasons for the adequacy of this distinction between the inner layers of temporality and the outer layer of the temporality constituted by changing (i.e. temporally distributed) things.

To be precise, this distinction between inner temporality and the temporality constituted by the changing object is not the

---

of givenness that cannot be reduced to acts of synthesis that Husserl explores in the idea of ur-hyle and the ur-element of time constitution from which all temporality flows. See, for example, the manuscript from 1921, E III 2/24b.

7. In Husserl's lectures on internal time-consciousness we do find much more detail on these various levels and on the close interrelation between them. Looking at the pre-phenomenal flow of time-constituting consciousness, for example, we can see an unchanging passage of now moments that characterises the living present. It is a two-sided time-constituting phenomenon: the living present is at the same time non-temporal as well as the continuous progression of now moments, a standing stream (Husserl, *Internal Time* §§39, 50, 54). This dual nature of the pre-phenomenal flow of time-constituting consciousness as timeless allows accounting for the unity of temporal experiences, while the fact that it is at the same time also continually changing in the form of a stream of now moments allows for the constitution of the other levels of temporality.

distinction introduced above between the subjective sensation of duration and the objective duration of sensation, since both these layers are part of the group of inner layers. Thus, there are two distinct layers of 'objective' temporality; one belongs to the inner layers of temporality (namely the objective temporality of measurable physical time), while the status of the second is as yet unclear. The first layer is measurable time or clock time, i.e. a translated or standardised temporality of change. Physical time is a 'translation' or a standardised version of the temporality of change, because physical time is the standard against which every change or flow is measured. Every change is compared to and measured by the number of repetitions of a highly stable and repetitive oscillating movement (i.e., a very stable and repetitive form of change). These kinds of repetitive changes, for example the swing of a pendulum, the movement of the earth around the sun, or the vibrations of the caesium atom, provide a standard for measuring all other forms of change and thus a standard for translating all other temporalities into the intervals of the chosen repetitive oscillation or stable change. This is why Aristotle can claim that time and change are different, because change is only connected to a specific object, while time is a generalised standard of temporal duration that can be applied to any change, and secondly, change occurs at different speeds, while time does not (*Physics* 218b10). The reasoning behind both claims is that one form of change (for example, the movement of planets in space) has been separated from its object, thus standardised and then generalised and used as the regular 'time' against which all other changes and their temporalities are measured.

This 'translated' time is useful for many practical purposes, but it is not the same as actual temporality. It is the temporality of a single (objective) change that provides the standard used to measure every temporality. This process presents temporality and flow as a standardised repetitive movement that is so uniform that we almost forget that the movements of the pendulum of a clock (or the oscillation of the caesium atom) are actually nothing but a standard of change against which we measure all other changes. Objective time is simply a specific understanding and measuring of every temporality against one specific kind of repetitive change, and we commit a *fallacy of misplaced concreteness* if we think that this standardised and idealised change is the nature of temporality.

The second layer of objective time, and the layer that I am interested in, is the temporality constituted by changing things themselves irrespective of this standard, and that is made visible by considering the pre-phenomenological temporality of spatio-temporal objects. That such a difference between the layers of inner temporality and the temporality of the changing things holds is a direct consequence of the injunction introduced in §13 of *Thing and Space*. This paragraph is concerned with the flux and articulation of the giving consciousness and contrasts it with the flux and articulation of the given object. Husserl emphasises that these sets of temporal flows are not to be identified: 'The flux and articulation of absolutely giving consciousness is not the flux and articulation of the given object [. . .] The "phenomenon" alters' (Husserl, *Thing* §13).[8] Husserl states that 'we must not mingle together what concerns the consciousness which constitutes the givenness and what concerns the object itself. Thus, we must not interpret into the object the flux, the changing, and the articulation of the giving consciousness' (Husserl, *Thing* §13). There is thus a distinction to be made between the flux, changes and articulations of the giving consciousness and the characteristics of the thing. So, the flow and structure of the giving consciousness is not the flow and structure of the object given in consciousness. This statement, so far, might only apply to the layers of inner temporality, i.e. to the difference between subjective and inner objective temporality. However, since Husserl did not explicitly introduce the layer of temporality of the changing thing (i.e. outer objective temporality), it is not surprising that he would not account for it. Still, since there is a difference to be

---

8. 'Abweisung eines Missverständnisses: Gliederung des gebenden Bewusstseins ist nicht die Gliederung des Gegenstandes [. . .]'.

made between the flow and structure of the giving consciousness and the flow and structure of the object given in consciousness, this should also hold for the layer of temporality of the changing thing (should it exist, which I will argue for in what follows). At least, I cannot see any reason why this distinction should not apply in this case too. Therefore, the temporality constituted by the changes characterising the object cannot be reduced to either one or all flows of inner temporality; it is a *sui generis* form of temporality.

Change and Temporality in the *Thing and Space* Lectures

I argue that Husserl ultimately failed to see fully one fundamental aspect of spatiotemporal things, namely that things change and that this change (like other layers of temporality) is continuous as well as fundamental and thus cannot be reduced to law-governed structures of consciousness without substantially distorting the phenomenon. In making these arguments I will mainly refer to the *Thing and Space* lectures and supplement this material with discussions from *Ideas II*, an investigation into the relation between the sciences and philosophy, material nature and objective constitution, thus about phenomena similar to the ones in question in *Thing and Space* and in this book.

Even though Husserl did investigate time-consciousness in quite some depth, in investigating *sense perception* and what is *given in sense perception*, his main focus here was on investigating phenomena in an unchanging presence, thus effectively hiding from sight the changeable temporal aspects of what is given. There are many reasons for such a focus on presence, spatial extension and a corresponding lack of interest in the ongoing changes of the temporal extension of spatiotemporal objects. Ignoring changes (that are often imperceptibly small or so slow as not to register easily) renders any investigation infinitely less complex and allows for a clear account of self-identity or essence, and thus for the appearance of certainty and knowledge.

Husserl argues that in order to 'grasp the essence of the thing and determine it conceptually', we need to perform an act of presenting that excludes any and all changes in the object:

> The task is to presentify to oneself (if need be, by free fiction) series of perceptions connecting up together in a continuous way in which the perceived object is one and the same and thereby shows, in the progression of the perceptions, in an ever more perfect way, what lies in it, what belongs to its essence. (Husserl, *Ideas II* §15a)

Phenomenological knowledge about the nature of things or categories of things, grounded in the concept of 'essence' and the method of eidetic variation, would simply be impossible if things (i.e. spatiotemporal objects) were considered in their inherently changeable nature. The idea of unchanging presence at the heart of things is rooted in the old Aristotelian claim that there is no change without a thing that undergoes that change. In Husserl's words: 'the possibilities of motion and rest, of qualitative change and qualitative permanence, are based in principle on the essence of the material thing in general' (Husserl, *Ideas II* §15b). But again, this is a presupposition that is not grounded in experience, if we examine the phenomena closely enough and over a sufficient period of time.

This focus or unchanging presence shapes the investigations in *Thing and Space*. Husserl acknowledges this explicitly: 'the object stands in perception as there in the flesh, it stands, to speak still more precisely, as actually present, as self-given there in the current now' (Husserl, *Thing* §4).[9] Change is not considered a fundamental factor when investigating spatiotemporal objects. Husserl only discusses change and thus this form of objective outer temporality on the five pages of §19 and on the last twenty pages of *Thing and Space*, but instead of truly accounting for the

---

9. 'Der Gegenstand steht in der Wahrnehmung als leibhafter da, er steht, genauer noch gesprochen, als aktuell gegenwärtiger, als selbstgegebener im aktuellen Jetzt da.'

phenomenon of change as outer temporality, he simply discusses the regularities underlying our perception of change.[10] And even though in *Ideas II* Husserl treats the problem of change in a more substantial way, the focus is still on explaining change as a regularity that does not truly affect the nature of the perceived phenomenon as standing, as being present, being in the now, because ultimately the 'physical or material thing is *res extensa* [. . . with] its essential attribute, *extensio*' (Husserl, *Ideas II* §15), and not a genuinely temporal or changeable thing. The objective thing 'remains what it is even if changes occur in my subjectivity and, dependent on it, in the "appearances" of the thing' (Husserl, *Ideas II* §18e). The objective thing is objective precisely because it shows itself in the mode of (continuing) fulfilment, irrespective of our perception of changes; its changing (if it changes at all) is merely a secondary aspect that does not affect the essence or identity of the thing.

Nonetheless, Husserl is well aware that spatiotemporal objects are not only fundamentally spatial, but also fundamentally temporal. In order to account for this fact, without having to account for genuine (substantial) change in the phenomena, he introduces two distinctions. He distinguishes genuinely temporal things that are characterised by changes (i.e. melodies), from temporal things that are not characterised by changes, i.e. for which their extension in time is a constitutive moment, but whose temporality is one of constancy and not of change. And he also distinguishes these types of temporal things from genuinely atemporal objects (Husserl, *Internal Time* 228, no. 29).

---

10. In these pages Husserl focuses on describing the laws governing the experience of continuous and regular change, while using a quite reduced understanding of change as the shift in (accidental) properties or movement, thereby ignoring more fundamental changes. He does not look into changes that involve various forms of qualitative change such as fireworks, football matches or a rising cake. He also does not investigate temporally extended changes that make the diachronic identification of the thing quite problematic. Possible examples of such genuine or substantial changes are explosions, growth or death.

Temporal things that are not characterised by changes are thus unchanging, not because they are timeless, like abstract objects, but because their temporality simply has no effect on their determinations, i.e. on what they are. Kortooms sums up Husserl's view succinctly:

> The difference between abstract, timeless objects and temporal objects that are not characterised by changes is that, in the case of the latter, no abstraction is performed from the temporal determinations that belong to them. Rather, their temporal extension may be left unspecified, because these objects are sufficiently determined without their temporal characteristics having been ascertained. (Kortooms 56)

In treating spatiotemporal things as unchanging Husserl implies that there are temporal objects whose temporality is not essential or not truly relevant. Husserl explains that we 'can also speak of objects that fill their time with constantly identical material and of temporal objects that fill it with changing material' (Husserl, *Internal Time* 228, no. 29). My counter-argument would again be that there is no such thing as a temporal object that only fills its time with constantly identical material. If investigated thoroughly enough and over a long enough time, things change materially. In treating concrete spatiotemporal objects as effectively non-temporal, they are taken as (and thus transformed into) abstract objects; the distinction between temporal and timeless objects can be manipulated through the process of abstraction. This distinction between concrete, self-sufficient temporal objects and abstract, non-self-sufficient ideal objects is not absolute, since one can turn a concrete, self-sufficient object into an abstract, non-self-sufficient object by abstracting from its temporality: 'It is possible to disregard all temporal determinations that belong to an object. What then results is an abstract, non self-sufficient object. In contrast, temporal determinations belong to every concrete, self-sufficient object' (Kortooms 55). This abstraction manipulates the phenomena in ways that lead investigations (especially when they focus on the change and becoming of spatiotemporal objects) astray. When phenomenological investigations treat spatiotemporal objects as de facto non-temporal (by disregarding their temporality and thus their changing nature), these objects are by that very course of action taken as abstract-ideal objects, effectively violating the phenomenological rules of remaining only with what is given and of always moving towards the things themselves.

In §19 of *Thing and Space* Husserl acknowledges the fictive nature of this procedure of taking things as unchanging, but he claims that this does not affect the investigation:

> Our previous analysis privileged certain of the most simple cases. It did not relate purely and simply to all perceptions but was restricted to perceptions of unchanged objects, whereby these perceptions were taken in turn as completely unchanged in themselves. That might be an abstract fiction,[11] but it could not shake the evidence of our analyses, insofar as this evidence adhered to moments which remain unaffected by possible factual variations of perception. (Husserl, *Thing* §19)

By bringing things to mind as unchanging, we can *conceptually* 'perceive' them as unchanging and thus investigate them as unchanging, which is, as Husserl admits, an abstract fiction. This view, namely that one can disregard the temporal qualities of some temporal objects, leads one to treat spatiotemporal objects as fundamentally spatial (as *res extensa*) and to treat change as accidental, as subtractable.

Let us now look at instances where Husserl actually engages with the issue of change in things, even if it just takes the form of an investigation of the regularities underlying our perception of change in *Thing and Space* (under the title 'The Constitution

---

11. The German is clearer in stating that the expression 'fiction' mainly applies to the fact that perception is never fully static; the term 'fiction' does not seem to apply to the thing itself: 'wobei diese Wahrnehmungen selbst als in sich völlig unverändert angenommen wurden. Das letzte mochte eine abstraktive Fiktion sein.' See also 'Wir haben bisher eine absolut ruhende Dingwelt fingiert' (Husserl, *Thing* §78).

of Objective Change') and in *Ideas II* §15. In these paragraphs Husserl attempts to come to terms with change by introducing schemata and regularities that characterise qualitative change, and thus attempts to introduce law-governed correlated structures to which qualitative change could be reduced:

> In this way the duration of the being of the thing, with respect to any property, disperses itself into segments. But the overriding unity of the thing is still there; each first-degree property is changeable, yet the changes of the properties are again subject to rules of dependence in regard to circumstances. (Husserl, *Ideas II* §16)

Effectively, qualitative changes are treated as discrete, segmented and governed by lawful regularities, whose flow does not constitute an actual temporality. Husserl's argument is that there is an underlying law-governed unified structure that determines all change, whose discovery allows us to reduce the perceptible changes to these structures without any relevant loss of information. This is not the case with the other layers of temporality he discusses. While the flow of now moments in pre-phenomenological givenness, or the ceaseless continuity of subjective or objective temporality, cannot be reduced in such a simplistic way, Husserl proposes to handle the temporality of qualitative change in this manner. Qualitative change is then simply reconstructed as not taking up an actual (indivisible), continuous duration, like the other layers of temporality. I would remark that this does not seem to describe the actual phenomenon of qualitative change, which is not given as discrete, but as a continuous duration (if the object is investigated closely enough and over a sufficient period of time). But Husserl does not treat change like other layers of temporality. Instead, he treats the temporality of qualitative change like a quality that can either be present or absent in spatiotemporal objects.

Thus, if the flow of temporality constituted by change could be reduced to a law-governed structure, it becomes clear why spatiotemporal things can be treated as if they were unchanging.

Time and again Husserl explicitly advises his readers to do just that: 'consider some outer perception, e.g. that of a house, and let us specifically take up perceptions which contain no change whatsoever' (Husserl, *Thing* §14).[12] He urges us to focus on an object of perception that is free of change, in order to investigate other moments such as its qualities and its identity more easily. But when Husserl talks about choosing a perception that is free of change, he is simply referring to the exclusion of qualitative changes in the phenomenon, while the ongoing change of temporal flow of the inner layers of temporality are not considered subtractable. Nowhere does he suggest that it is possible to disregard the temporality or change involved in the pre-phenomenological flow, the subjective flow of experience and the objective flow of time. These layers cannot be taken as unchanging. So why can it be done for the temporality of change?

Even though Husserl argued for the fact that change is a real phenomenon that can be experienced directly, change in things is still treated as secondary, as reducible. I suppose this is the case mainly because objective change in things causes various epistemic problems in relation to identity as well as knowledge, and thus cannot be a fundamental aspect of things.[13] And, I would argue, it might be precisely this traditional philosophical presupposition, that change is not substantial or essential to what there is, that made it impossible for Husserl to fully account for and come to terms with the layers of temporality constituted by changing objects, and that led to the difficulties he tried to solve through genetic phenomenology.

---

12. 'Betrachten wir irgendeine äußere Wahrnehmung, z.B. die eines Hauses, und zwar können wir Wahrnehmungen nehmen, die in sich nichts von Veränderung enthalten.'
13. 'Die [. . .] „neue Grundfrage ist: Wie konstituiert sich das Ding als Identisches der Veränderung und näher der qualitativen Veränderung? [. . .] wir nehmen auch wahr, dass Dinge sich qualitativ und nur qualitativ ändern. [. . .] Die Dinge bleiben also dieselben. Sie ruhen noch immer' (Husserl, *Thing* §78).

Temporality and Genetic Phenomenology

Even though genesis and temporality, becoming and change are thus at the heart of many phenomena, conceptually investigating these aspects of what is given does invite a host of problems, especially if one wants to generate fundamental knowledge in departing from this realm of genesis, change and temporality. Until the 1920s Husserl's answer to this problem was to conceive of a lawfully structured domain that is so originary that it could ground lived experience as well as objective knowledge; a domain so fundamental that it could ground psychology as well as logic, so 'that the constituting lived experience in its very temporality' is 'neither psychological nor logical' (Derrida 53), but phenomenological. As a result, Husserl bracketed the objective temporal dimension of change, focusing on individual intentional acts, idealised unchanging things, and he devised an almost 'static' understanding of constitution. Still, the problem remains: how can we bring together the call for an immanent fundament for science, an indubitable ground of knowledge rooted in lived experience, with the fact that such experience is fundamentally temporal and inundated by changes? The issue of temporality had to be addressed and Husserl chose to confront it in the form of genesis. This shift from transcendental to genetic phenomenology is an unavoidable effort to address the issues caused by the internal contradictions hidden in a static understanding of phenomenology.

When investigations are based on the direct experience of what there is, change cannot be disregarded; at the same time, however, this undercuts the idea of an ultimate, ideal, transcendental structure that is not subject to change, because 'a historical dimension might jeopardize the transcendental character of phenomenology. The debate has been narrowed down to two options: either a phenomenology in the strict sense, or its reformulation in terms of hermeneutics. Heidegger took the second path, followed by a host of philosophers' (Ricœur, *Key* 9). And if this temporal and historical dimension inherent to what there is, that is given as a phenomenon, does indeed undercut the transcendental character of Husserl's phenomenology, then on the one hand phenomenology might turn out not be as strict a science as Husserl would have liked; but on the other hand, a realist reading of phenomenology becomes even more plausible.

Part III Process Thought

In the last part I engaged with experience and temporality from the perspective of phenomenology; I will now proceed to investigate the ontological aspects of both experience and temporality through the lens of process thought. This transition presents us with a host of problems, the first of which is the fact that process ontology is probably less familiar to many readers; thus, I will be less technical in my account than I was in my account of phenomenology. Furthermore, I will not focus on one thinker only, but present two main perspectives or approaches. Many of my reflections will be based on Bergson's thought, because his account of a processual reality can be grasped relatively easily and intuitively. His approach is less technical and more metaphorical than Whitehead's or Deleuze's, for example. He can provide us with a first insight as to how to think a dynamic reality without also having to contend with its relationality explicitly. This is not to say that Bergson's thought allows for an unrelated (or atomic) view of what there is. It is simply the case that Bergson's vision of a processual reality can be made intelligible without also discussing relationality explicitly, while Whitehead's or Deleuze's thought make an explicitly relational engagement necessary from the outset. In addition, Bergson's concept of *durée* (duration, existing as process) is prima facie not as closely intertwined with experience as existing as process is in Whitehead.

In a second step I will introduce Whitehead's system, which does ask more of the reader. In order to not overburden the reader with too many conceptual frameworks, I will mainly use

Deleuze's thought to illustrate and further deepen the understanding of Bergson and Whitehead, instead of also introducing his rendering of process philosophy. I have chosen to do this because Deleuze's account goes far beyond a focus on temporality and relationality. His rich account focuses on difference, repetition and multiplicity, thus fundamentally incorporating differential issues involving society, conceptual development, politics and much more into the ontological framework, an approach that goes beyond the scope of the present book.

As mentioned above, this third part of my investigation focuses on the ontological aspects of experience as well as temporality. It has as its *Leitfaden* a temporal understanding of being, i.e. the idea that being (or beings) cannot be adequately understood if what there is as given in direct experience is conceptually separated or divorced from temporality. I will begin my discussion of temporal existence by looking at ways of conceptualising temporality in a little more detail, to then move on to investigate temporality from an ontological perspective by engaging with Aristotle as well as process perspectives. I will end this part by engaging with the role of ontological temporality in radicalised experience, as it is conceptualised in process thought. Here I will argue that experience is not necessarily the personal experience of a (transcendental) subject but instead can be understood more broadly as a mode of being that also generates and brings forth what there is. It is this understanding of experience that accounts for the relational unity of what there is. Here especially Whitehead's concept of 'prehension' or 'feeling' will help to open up the investigation towards what there is. The central argument goes as follows. We do in fact experience what there is and we have direct access to what there is, because we as physical and biological beings are part of what there is: we are an integrated, interrelated element of what there is and thus fundamentally connected to it. This leads to an understanding of experience that is 'more emotional than intellectual, more active involvement than passive observance. We are not receptive, private subjects that mirror external objects; we can perceive only because we are always in the midst of those perceivable events' (Cooper 11). It is simply our ability to reflect and conceptualise that creates the impression of a fundamental distinction between our bodily existence and the world we dwell in.

6

The Nature of Time: Time, Temporality and Being

> Time was what in being, or what mixing with being, had resisted reduction [. . .] (Derrida 3)

The nature of time is one of those topics that have fundamentally shaped twentieth-century thought.[1] Time, its reality and its relation to being have been investigated in fundamentally new and divergent ways, by thinkers in every tradition, from Bergson and McTaggart to Husserl and Heidegger. At the same time revolutionary developments in the field of physics allowed for a new relative understanding of objective time and for a reframing of the nature of time as space-time. Much has been said about the issue, and the question of the nature of time has become more confounding for all the approaches and interpretations available. Since this is a study focused on dynamic realism, which is connected to the question of time but not limited to it, I decided to forego an in-depth discussion of the nature of time and instead to focus on a specific aspect of the investigations of the nature of time, namely the relation between time and being.

There are two ways to think about the connection between time and ontology. We can focus on the ontological status of time, i.e. the question whether time is real or not. Or we can investigate the connection between ontology and time by looking at the temporality of ontological beings, investigating the temporal nature of being, ontological temporality. With regard

---

1. Parts of this section are based on Röck, 'Time'.

to the first question, I simply presuppose the reality of time, since within experience the actuality, relevance and effectivity of time is indubitable. In line with the outlook of this book, it is the second question that I focus on. The theoretical background that allows me to investigate this ontological dimension of time is shaped by phenomenology, process thought and pragmatism. All three schools of thought explicitly recognise the fundamental ontological role and relevance of time, and this acknowledgement contributes to their respective development of radically new ways of doing philosophy and of understanding what is. In sum, many thinkers in these traditions hold time itself to be 'the deepest ground of ontological inquiry', a recognition that created new systems 'of fundamental philosophical concepts' (Chernyakov 11).

The common ground shared by phenomenology and process thought is precisely this insight into the fundamental relevance of temporality as it is experienced for our ability to understand what there is. Both Heidegger and Whitehead, for example, consider temporality an essential element for understanding being as such:

> Both thinkers find this temporal kinesis that flows thought the very heart of Being displayed most vividly in human experience, which thereby becomes, as Husserl would say, a *Leitfaden* or transcendental clue for an interpretation of Being as such. (Cooper 11)

This intimate connection between being and temporality is even more evident if we consider Heidegger's *Being and Time* and Whitehead's *Process and Reality*:

> The fundamental agreement between the two works is explicit in the titles: the authors share a basic intuition that all of reality is essentially temporal. Whitehead did not write of process on the one hand and reality on the other, nor did Heidegger mean to distinguish Being and time as separate domains of study. It is creative process that makes reality possible for Whitehead, just as time is the disclosive ground of Being for Heidegger. Moreover, it is their nonlinear characterization of time by which real

entities are better understood as events than substantial objects that allies the two philosophers against nearly the whole of the modern philosophical tradition. (Cooper 11)

What is this non-linear understanding of time that is supposed to capture the way we actually experience it? It corresponds to what I have referred to as 'ontological temporality'. This ontological temporality can be spelled out in different ways, depending on the conceptual background, for example as *epochal time* (Whitehead), *ekstatic temporality* (Heidegger) or as *duration* (Bergson).

What rendered this insight into the temporality of the ontological realm revolutionary and fruitful, when it comes to developing new conceptual frameworks, is the fact that throughout the history of Western philosophy this connection between time, being and change had been downplayed because of its epistemic implications. According to traditional ways of conceptualising being, there is a tension between being (or existence) and temporality (or change). This tension is best expressed in Fragment 8 of Parmenides' famous poem. He argues that being (τὸ ἐόν) has not ever been and will not be, since it is now, all together, one, indivisible (DK 8, 5f). He claims that there can be no temporal dimension or change connected to being; being simply is and it is fully what it is with no room for becoming or change. Thus, from the outset of Western philosophy, time was either to be considered a mere appearance, and thus excluded from true being, or a property of consciousness or the human soul.

However, when it came to the natural sciences, or to philosophical investigations of φύσις (nature, physical reality), natural beings, time and change were obviously intimately connected. This shift towards an acceptance of the temporal nature of reality in the investigation of the natural beings (that we encounter in everyday life) is beautifully exemplified in Plato's *Timaios*. The *Timaios*, which focuses on the becoming of the natural world, is the only Platonic dialogue in which he discusses the temporality and change of beings in depth. The other dialogues tend to focus on the unchanging and atemporal ideals that are the cause of temporal being. In the fourth book of the *Physics* Aristotle argues that time is nothing but the measure of movement, or as he puts it, time is the 'number of movement in relation to the before and after' (*Physics* 219b1f). In Aristotle, 'time' is thus conceptualised as the measuring rod or a measuring tool ('the measure of movement') that we use to measure the changes and movements that we observe in natural beings. Aristotle furthermore defines nature through change, by claiming that nature is actually an inner principle of change (*Physics* 192b20–3). This leads Aristotle – in the investigations concerned with physical and biological nature – to an understanding of time that connects it back to the changes or movements (natural) beings are involved in.

While some philosophers and physicists have argued for the unreality of time, there are contemporary cosmologists and physicists who seem to agree with Aristotle's idea that nature should be thought as fundamentally temporal. As the philosopher Unger and the physicist Smolin put it:

> Time is real. Indeed, it is the most real feature of the world, by which we mean that it is the aspect of nature of which we have most reason to say that it does not emerge from any other aspect. Time does not emerge from space, although space may emerge from time. That time is inclusive as well as real means that nothing in nature lasts forever. Everything changes sooner or later, including change itself. The laws of nature are not exempt from this impermanence. (Unger and Smolin xi)

This opposition between a purely theoretical understanding of being that is divorced from time and change, in the case of Parmenides, and a definition of (natural) being that is based on an engagement with and observation of phenomena and connected to change, in the case of the *Timaios* and of Aristotle, has shaped our ambivalence in understanding the connection between being, change and time until today. Thinking, conceptualising and reflecting on being, change and time usually leads to a separation of these aspects. A focus on the actual experiential givenness of these phenomena, on the other hand, seems to lead to a more unified understanding of how being, change and time relate.

This, of course, leads us back to the question of how we should investigate time. Is time best understood as an inner (subjective) phenomenon and thus investigated through introspection, or should it be considered an (objective) natural phenomenon?[2] Ricœur refers to this conundrum, namely that time seems to have a seemingly irreducible phenomenological as well as a seemingly irreducible cosmological dimension, as the first aporia of time (Ricœur, *Temps* 12). In order to engage with this tension between cosmological (objective) and phenomenological (subjective) time from a somewhat different perspective, and look at various intuitions around the nature of time, I will begin my investigation by taking a look at the way that we metaphorically describe or visualise time. I will use this starting point to investigate three conceptualisations of time that are relevant for our purposes, namely time as objective, as subjective and as ontological. Next to cosmological and phenomenological time, I will thus also introduce a third understanding of time, namely ontological temporality that is connected to the temporality of the changing thing.

The Nature of Time: Approaching the Essence of Time through Metaphors

As far as I can see there are at least three fundamental intuitions shaping the way we think time, namely 1) time as (objective) succession or as a location in time, 2) time as (the experience of) flow and passing and 3) time as (ontological) becoming. There are also three corresponding metaphors used to capture these intuitions:

---

2. This, of course, should not imply the question whether or not time is real. I am simply using this question in its epistemic dimension, i.e. questioning what would be the best way to study and understand what time is.

the timeline (or the container), the flow of the timestream and time as unfurling and growth. Let me outline these correlations, before I discuss them in more detail below. The first view of time considers time through geometrical and spatial metaphors. This view either excludes genuine change completely (if time is considered a container within which events are ordered in time) or merely allows for change in the attributes of pastness, presentness or futurity (as a progression on the timeline). But such geometrical intuitions do not allow for actual changes of what there is. This intuition, as I will argue below, shapes both the A- as well as the B-series of time as developed by McTaggart. The second intuition focuses on our experience of the flow of consciousness and the temporal dimensions of experience. While there is an experience of change that is taken seriously, these changes are merely regarded as temporal modifications constituted by the experiencing subject and not considered on an ontological level, as I argued in the second chapter. The third view considers time as ontological growth (i.e. the process of unfolding, becoming or perishing). Change here is fundamental to *what is*. In this view, change is not restricted to a change of temporal attributes, a continuous flow or a temporal modification, but describes ontological reality.

In what follows, I will discuss these intuitions in more detail and argue that these three intuitions and their metaphors can be correlated with certain modes of investigation and certain investigative aims. Depending on what aspects of temporality the investigation is focused on, and the practical results that are pursued in an investigation, different views of time are more adequate. If I need to measure and standardise time, for example, in order to allow people to catch a train or to calculate the velocity of a moving object, then time as a linear progression is a highly advantageous concept. If, however, our experience of time is in question, the psychology of memory and anticipation, then focusing on our experience of time seems to be a more natural fit. These first two basic intuitions about the nature of time can be combined fruitfully, generating more elaborate stances on the nature of time, but the stances cannot be fully harmonised. If we finally want to focus on accounting for our concretely lived, bodily existence, if the questions at hand concern the changes involved in the growth of cells, in the becoming of habits and traits, time appears as a progressive unfolding and a process of generation through and with us, as we become in time. This concrete temporality of becoming can neither be reduced to the way we think or measure, nor to the way we experience the world, and thus constitutes a third intuition about the nature of time, that is rooted in the way we exist in the world.

Measurable Time: The Metaphor of the Timeline

The first understanding of time as succession or ordered location (situatedness) rests on a spatial metaphor, the line (or the container). Thinking time through a geometrical metaphor allows for a transference of order. Just as space provides an ultimate spatial order irrespective of the perspective of the viewer, thinking time through a spatial metaphor provides the temporal order for objects or events to be situated on a timeline or within a temporal dimension. Understanding time through the metaphor of the timeline is most familiar to us in the form of clock time, as the linear progression from one hour to the next, one day to the next, one month to the next, and so on. The metaphor of time as a container (or a dimension) is most familiar to us in the form of space-time. Space-time is conceived as a four-dimensional extension within which every temporal point is ordered and ultimately located, just as every point in space is ultimately located in the conventional understanding of space. This view of time is defended by 4D theorists, for example, who consider time to be a set of points, as argued by D. C. Williams in 'The Myth of Passage'. Thus, measurable time, thought through the metaphor of geometric space, turns time into an analogue of space, which allows for the application of spatial qualities to time. This concept of time is problematic for the present investigation, because time and space are fundamentally different when it comes to movement, change and flow. Space (geometrically conceived) does not involve any change or movement.

It is not surprising that it is difficult to situate change or flow, i.e. the quality of temporality, in such a geometrical view of time, which in turn led many philosophers to conclude that change, flow or time does not exist at all (or that some dimension of time does not exist), even though change, flow and temporality are everyday experiences. Aristotle, for example, argues that any extension of time is either 1) in the past, 2) in the future or 3) connects past and future (the moment of now). But, he argues further, the past does not exist any more and the future does not yet exist, so neither of them can be genuinely real. Finally, the moment of 'now' is nothing but the ever-changing point dividing the past from the future and thus cannot be said to exist independently from past and future (*Physics* 217b29–218a30).[3]

One reason for these difficulties in combining our experience of time with this geometrical view of time is that this view turns temporality into an extrinsic quality, which leads to the impression that events and things are merely accidentally in a time, that they could be at any other point in time without losing their identity. This means that if an event were to take a different place in this order, this exchange would not affect the identity of the event. Just as the spatial location of my pen has no impact on the identity of my pen, the temporal location of an event is not considered to be a factor that contributes to its identity. In a certain sense 'this time' and its 'now' as well as 'before' and 'after' are transcendent to the events taking place or the things

---

3. Aristotle looks at the nature of this 'now' again and again in these passages, with different results (for example, *Physics* 218a3seq), but he ends chapter 11 with the claim that 'now' is not time, but an attribute of time (*Physics* 220a21). So if all of the components that constitute time do not exist independently (now) or simply do not exist (past, future), we have to conclude that the sum of these components, including the attribute 'now', does not exist either (*Physics* 217b33–218b30).

located in time. This mode of conceptualising time sees it as an ordered extension that itself is not temporal, neither changing, nor flowing nor growing.

One might now argue that there is a difference that I seem to be disregarding, and that is accounted for by the British Idealist McTaggart, namely the difference between the A-series and the B-series, which are two ways of understanding time that McTaggart introduced to ultimately prove the irreality of time. He analyses time in terms of temporal events and their relation to other events. Events can be thought as either earlier or later relative to other events; this constitutes the B-series of time and involves no change, since these temporal relations of being before or after never change. On the other hand, events can be thought of as changing their position in regard to past, present or future. An event is first in the future, then it is present and then past, depending on the now point. This is the A-series, and McTaggart claims that this series accounts for the changes we experience.

I would agree with McTaggart that time thus conceived is not real. While either description is perfectly adequate for various conceptual accounts or logical inferences, both descriptions are insufficiently adequate conceptualisations when it comes to grasping the actual phenomenon of time. Both the A- and B-series describe time in a 'spatialised' manner, with the A-series evoking the image of the timeline and the B-series the image of the container. While the B-series understands time as a static sum of past, present and future, turning time into an atemporal container, eliminating change and flow altogether, the A-series seems to account for some form of change, a movement along the timeline. But there is a fundamental difference. McTaggart famously translates change or flow into a specific movement of the A-series, namely into a modification of the temporal attributes associated with an event on the timeline at different points in time. The argument here is that the temporal flow can be translated into the attribution of a relative before and after, without any relevant loss of information. This way of conceptualising time does involve change, but only concerning the fact that some event first has the quality of being in the future, then of being present, and finally of being in the past. The only change truly accounted for is the relative before and after. It remains unclear how tensing events in this way is supposed to explain, account for or even simply adequately portray the actual flow given in experience or the evolutionary unfolding present on the level of ontology.

The A-series remains an abstract and 'spatialised' understanding of time that rests on the image of atemporal points that are lined up like individual pearls on a timeline that connects and unifies them. None of these points is privileged, they are all the same. There is, however, the 'now' index, i.e. the moment where a future point transforms into a point in the past. This 'now' is generally considered the effect of a living consciousness moving along the timeline. Thus being 'tensed', i.e. possessing the property of pastness, presentness or futurity, is often considered a subjective phenomenon or the effect of perception by an observer. Without such a perceiving subject determining the present and thus situating the relative past and the relative future, there would be no way to determine whether an event or a being is in the future, the present or the past. This is why pastness, presentness or futurity become characterisations that can be attributed to an event and removed from the event without changing the event itself.

There are different attempts to grasp this idea of the flow of now that attempt to exclude the conscious dimension, for example, the moving spotlight theory. Another metaphor is the description of the flow of nows as a sequence of still-frame after still-frame that constitutes the moving image we experience. These ways of explaining temporality through a non-conscious experience of flow do so by ignoring actual change in what is given as changing. Instead of accounting for genuine passing, a genuine becoming or transforming, this way of conceptualising time only provides us with distinct (atemporal) instances that need to be connected by some invisible, transcendent, ideal timeline (or time container), plus an observer, a spotlight or a movie reel. And while the resulting conceptual rendering of temporal succession can be connected closely to the way we use tense and does explain these uses quite well (Tegtmeier), it cannot provide us with an adequate metaphor or explanation of our experience of the temporally extended, continuous passage of time and the experience of ontological change that shapes our daily lives.

The Experience of Time: The Metaphor of Flow

In contrast to our investigation of time as a spatial concept, our experience suggests that temporality and duration are fundamental and ubiquitous. Whether we close our eyes and just focus on emptiness or trace the events before our open eyes, the stream of consciousness is always present, and with it an experience of flow, of time passing. Although temporality is a natural part of experience, problems seem to arise as soon as we attempt to account for this part of experience in a conceptual fashion. The most famous expression of this dilemma is Augustine's dictum that, of course, we know what time is, until we have to explain what it is (Augustine XI, 22). Most philosophers agree that, when it comes to experience, time seems to be woven into the fabric of reality. The experience of time is indubitable and quite unproblematic, but any attempt to conceptually grasp it leads to aporias and contradictions.

The shift in understanding time proposed by phenomenologists resolves these conflicts by simply prioritising our experience of time over our conceptual understanding. This methodological step allows for insights such as the fact that we do not actually experience temporal succession. We do not experience one event following another; instead, we experience an extended transformation, without a clear cut or distinction separating these states. Yuval Dolev puts it very succinctly when he states that '[t]he experience of motion does not consist of a perception of succession nor is it derived from a succession of perceptions.

Succession plays no role in the perception of motion, or, for that matter, in motion itself' (Dolev 41). Motion is simply not experienced as a succession of events, or as a set of events one after the other; it is an ongoing event, one single movement. As Bergson put it,

> let us imagine an infinitely small piece of elastic, contracted, if that were possible, to a mathematical point. Let us draw it out gradually in such a way as to bring out of the point a line which will grow progressively longer. Let us fix our attention not on the line as line, but on the action which traces it. Let us consider that this action, in spite of its duration, is indivisible if one supposes that it goes on without stopping; that, if we intercalate a stop in it, we make two actions of it instead of one and that each of these actions will then be the indivisible of which we speak [. . .] (Bergson, *Creative Mind* 164–5)

Only in retrospect can any continuous movement be dissected into parts, intervals or successions, by focusing, for example, on the geometric space it traversed; but these kinds of divisions are the result of conceptual engagement. They are not an adequate description of what is given in experience. We also do not actually experience the relations of before and after. Tenses are concepts that are the result of a reflection on the order of events after the fact. Actual sensory and conscious experience of time and temporal relations, if we exclude the experiences of memory or dreaming and the like, is restricted to now, albeit a temporally extended now.

The main focus of a phenomenological view on temporality as it is perceptually experienced is thus the temporally extended present, with its protentional and retentional dimensions. In accounting for time-consciousness, Husserl emphasises the essential distinction between 'objective time' and time-consciousness:

> Someone may find it of interest to determine the objective time of an experience [. . .] It might also make an interesting investigation to ascertain how the time that is posited as objective in an episode of time-consciousness is related to actual objective

time [. . .] But these are not tasks for phenomenology. (Husserl, *Internal Time* §1)

Not only do these different approaches yield different results, but conceptual objective time is not even a possible object of a genuine phenomenological investigation and vice versa for certain phenomena. We cannot even experience objective time. A phenomenological approach to time can, however, engage with the temporal aspects of phenomena such as memory or projection, that neither ontological time nor objective time can adequately come to terms with. In acknowledging these differences, we discover the limits of phenomenological investigations. They also show us, *mutatis mutandis*, the limits of a purely scientific 'objective' account of time.

Ontological Time: The Metaphor of Growth and Becoming

Most thinkers working on the philosophy of time during the twentieth century tended to focus on either a geometric and thus scientific understanding of time, or on the subjective, conscious experience, and thus on the phenomenology of time. The question at stake in this book, namely the temporality of changing beings, i.e. the correlation between being and time, has been addressed by relatively few Western thinkers. These include process thinkers, Friedrich Nietzsche and Martin Heidegger. Heidegger, for example, explains why time is fundamental to an adequate understanding of being in the following words:

> But why time, precisely? Because in the inception of Western philosophy, the *perspective that guides* the opening up of Being is time, but *in such a way* that this perspective *as such* still remained and had to remain concealed. If what finally becomes the fundamental concept of Being is *ousia*, and this means constant presence, then what lies unexposed as the ground of the essence of stability and the essence of presence, other than time? But

> *this* 'time' still has not been unfolded in its essence, nor can it be unfolded (on the basis and within the purview of 'physics'). For as soon as meditation on the essence of time begins, at the *end* of Greek philosophy with Aristotle, time itself must be taken as something that is somehow coming to presence, *ousia tis*. This is expressed in the fact that time is conceived on the basis of the 'now;' that which is in each case uniquely present. The past is the 'no-*longer*-now;' the future is the 'not-*yet*-now?' Being in the sense of presence at hand (presence) becomes the perspective for the determination of time. But time does not become the perspective that is especially selected for the interpretation of Being. (Heidegger, *Metaphysics* 220)

So, from the inception of Western philosophy, 'being' or 'existence' was thought with and through a temporal dimension. Temporality was, however, reduced to the dimension of presentness and was thus investigated in such a way as to ignore or exclude the dynamicity and creative openness and duration that characterise genuine temporality. This acknowledgement allows for new ways of engaging with both temporality and being. Whitehead and Heidegger, for example, both went so far as to propose different, non-linear ways of understanding time in order to develop a more adequate understanding of being: 'Heidegger's ecstatic temporality of Dasein and Whitehead's epochal concrescence of the actual occasion provide the basis for an interpretation of reality in which the past is absorbed into the real constitution of things as projected futurally for a dynamic unity' (Cooper 11).

Let me now begin my account of ontological time, without reducing it to presence and by arguing that the dynamic and creative ontological time cannot be reduced to either subjective or objective time. What there is moves and changes independently of the flow of either consciousness or the temporal extension of experience. In examining experience, it seems indubitable that the temporal flow created by the bird flying past my window is not the temporality of the stream of consciousness, nor is it the temporal extension of experience. Ontological temporality is also distinct from objective time. It is impossible to reduce the temporality of changing things to the objective temporality of succession, since this way of thinking time, especially in its form as clock time or space-time, presupposes one of these ontological temporalities (for example, the movement of the sun around the earth, the movement of grains of sand through a passage, or the duration of an oscillation of a specific atom) as a standard against which all other temporalities are measured. Thus, objective time is a standardised and generalised form of ontological temporality.

Heidegger argues that the traditional distinction between phenomenological time-consciousness and objective time ignores a more fundamental relation we have to time: we *dwell* in time. Traditional concepts of time presuppose that any point of time is first situated in the future, somehow flows towards the present, becomes present and then fades into the past. Every now in the succession of present nows is born in a shadowy future and perishes in a dead past. And while it does feel quite natural to conceptualise the passage of time from the future towards the present into the past, this is not how ontological growth and unfolding actually happen; this does not describe how we dwell in time.

Taking a concrete ontological being, for example the process of a growing tree, it feels inadequate to begin the account of its temporality with the tree's blossoming in the future, to move to its becoming real now as the sapling breaks through the soil, and end with its fading into having been planted in the past. If we want to describe actual ontological becoming, if we attempt to describe the unfolding of nature, to describe changes that go beyond merely the changing of tense, it seems rather counterintuitive to begin with a future endpoint, to move to the becoming now and to imagine it fading into the past. We are much more likely to begin a theoretical-descriptive account of the tree's becoming with the present as the starting point that leads us to the investigation in the first place. From there we would move to the planted seed in the past, moving to its present effect or result and then projecting towards its future development, which is likely to occur if the process is not influenced or stopped. In contrast to the other metaphors that look towards the future as the origin from which becoming flows, a future that becomes present and vanishes into the past, the metaphor of growth is only accessible in the present but rooted in the past. The ground and basis for all becoming is the past and in a sense the past is what is the fundament, the ground of what there is. This shift, from a focus on the future to a focus on the present as a result of the past is correlated with a shift from an abstract, conceptual understanding of time to a concrete, embodied, physically lived way of understanding time. Actual processes and becoming beings that are present now have their roots in the past. The present is the fruit or result of these past processes and developments. This past becomes active and creative in the present with a look towards the future and the aims that are to be realised. Any concrete process has a trajectory that ties the past to the future via the present. The direction of the flow of ontological time from the past towards the future reverses traditional objective as well as subjective conceptualisations of the direction of time, and it does not privilege the present over the past or the future.

In this ontological view of time the past provides the source, material or framework for the changes unfolding in the present. In observing these present unfolding changes, a certain direction of the process becomes evident that points towards a likely future, given that the process continues to unfold unhampered and without unforeseen influences. At any moment any of these unfolding changes that are pointing towards one future can be manipulated, can be influenced by external factors or can be self-regulated (in humans, for example, by taking a conscious decision to behave differently) in order to point towards a different future outcome. This openness of processes with regard to the future that they are evolving towards allows for a certain degree of freedom and the option to 'choose' or 'shift' between different futures to be realised. This openness of the future, inherent in the understanding of temporality as growth, is the reason why it can accommodate the human experience of freedom and genuine novelty. This ontological sedimentation or accumulation guarantees a certain longevity of the past, a continuance of the past, not as a dimension of time, but as a part of physical facticity.

Deleuze described these open and creative ways of reordering time in his three syntheses of time in *Difference and Repetition*. Of course, Deleuze went much further than I do here, addressing many different issues in the context of these syntheses regarding freedom and action, the revolutionary or differential potential of time for us and so on, but since this investigation is focused on an account that marries phenomenology and process ontology in order to arrive at dynamic realism, I cannot address these issues here.[4] This lack of engagement with social, political – simply human – issues should not be interpreted as a judgement on the value of these questions or applications; it is simply beyond my ability to address these issues without losing the coherence of the argument.

One last point before I move on. I do wonder whether it is not the case that all three aspects, objective, subjective and ontological time, are integral to a balanced understanding of time and that we need all three to be able to engage with what there is in the most fruitful way. I end this investigation by going back to Augustine. Shortly after he admits in the *Confessions* that he cannot explain what time is, he states what he does know and can explain: 'I state firmly that I know this: if nothing were to pass away, there would be no past time; and if nothing were impending, there would be no future time; and if nothing existed there would be no present time' (Augustine XI, 22). Without conceptualisation, without thinking about what will be, there is no idea of the future right now, as there would be no past without the experience of passage, of things passing us and our leaving them behind. There would also be no present without becoming being. This shows a path towards a unified

---

4. For an excellent introduction to and discussion of these syntheses of time, see J. Williams.

understanding of time, weaving together aspects of all three ways of understanding it: a way that combines the passing away that we experience, the future we conceptualise and the being that we are living now, to produce a much deeper and more subtle understanding of time than the sole focus on just one or two of these aspects could allow.

Digression I: Epochal Time. Whitehead's Understanding of Ontological Time

At this point it seems opportune to address one reconceptualisation of time that has been mentioned, namely Whitehead's understanding of time and becoming, since it is entirely adequate to read Whitehead's philosophy through the lens of the issue of temporality (Vanzago, *L'Evento* 11). The issue of time was one of *the* philosophical problems *par excellence* that shaped Whitehead's thought, and it was through a rethinking and restructuring of our understanding of time that Whitehead was able to generate a radically new, and I would claim adequate, access to what there is. While I will introduce Whitehead's position with regard to time here, I will attempt to introduce as little specific terminology as possible, so as not to detract from the general line of argument. In the discussions following this digression I will continue to use an unspecified understanding of ontological time, as I have done up until now. This generality is by design and its aim is to leave room for different ways of spelling out ontological temporality that suit different ontological frameworks.

It is still the case today, as it was at the time of Whitehead's writing, that our physical theories about the large-scale dimensions, the cosmos and its spatiotemporal structure are not fully compatible with our understanding of the small scale, i.e. quantum phenomena. One fundamental obstacle to the unification of modern physics is the role that time plays in the different theoretical environments. 'Whereas general relativity is most naturally interpreted in terms of a four-dimensional view in which time is inseparable from space-time, orthodox quantum theory assumes the independence of time to the quantum system' (McHenry, *Event* 9–10). Whitehead developed his process philosophy as an ontological framework that could do justice both to astrophysics and quantum physics and support the process of unification of all sciences by providing a general ontology, a basis for all the sciences (McHenry, *Event* 10). Whitehead's revolutionary understanding of time formed a central axis of this attempt.

Whitehead proposes a unique way of understanding becoming in a relational, dynamic as well as atomistic fashion, which in turn makes it necessary for him to develop a unique understanding of time. Actual occasions (the fundamental entities in Whitehead's ontology) are atomic quanta of becoming that do not have a simple location in either space or time.

> The conclusion is that in every act of becoming there is the becoming of something with temporal extension; but that the act itself is not extensive, in the sense that it is divisible into earlier and later acts of becoming which correspond to the extensive divisibility of what has become.
>
> In this section, the doctrine is enunciated that the creature is extensive, but that its act of becoming is not extensive. (Whitehead, *Process* 69)

Whitehead famously argued that 'there is a becoming of continuity, but no continuity of becoming. The actual occasions are the creatures which become, and they constitute a continuously extensive world. In other words, extensiveness becomes, but "becoming" is not itself extensive. Thus, the ultimate metaphysical truth is atomism' (Whitehead, *Process* 35). The becoming beings are temporally and spatially extended but atomic durations of space-time that are internally connected to each other as well as to their relative past through prehensions (i.e. feeling or experience). The fact that these actual occasions are extensive and thus not simply located (i.e. internally related in both the dimensions of space and time) allows Whitehead to account for the particle-wave dualism that characterises quantum phenomena: 'Nature is comprised of atomic, unit events that are more wave-like [. . . than particle-like]. The wave concept is more fundamental in the sense that the quantum entity is not an object that is simply located but rather occurs as a slab or duration of space and time' (McHenry, *Event* 46). Since there are numerous studies on the subject,[5] I will not provide a detailed account of the reasons why Whitehead held that becoming was not extensive (i.e. not continuous), but they range from Zeno's paradox to (as already mentioned) developments in physics. However, this conviction makes it necessary for Whitehead to develop an understanding of time that accounts for the becoming of continuity without presupposing a continuity of becoming. He thus developed his understanding of 'epochal time', which describes not temporally extended atoms of time that in conjunction constitute temporal extension, and it is this temporal extension that we usually refer to as linear time or physical time.

The term 'epoch' designates a temporal extension that is conceived as a leap, by analogy with quantum leaps. An epoch is a temporally extended happening that cannot be actually subdivided, so an event that has the duration of half an epoch or any other fraction of an epoch is not a real possibility, it is merely a logical one. It is this character that allows Whitehead to account for the discontinuity presupposed by the quantum physics of his time (Whitehead, *Science* 138).[6] However, these epochs are also asynchronous; not all becoming is aligned in its temporal location or in its duration; there is not one single objective (clock) time, but a multiplicity of ontological temporalities constituted by becoming beings. These variations allow Whitehead to account for the temporal relativity presupposed by relativity theory.

Whitehead considers the classical notion of time to imply or presuppose a linear, serial development, along the lines of what

---

5. See, for example, Vanzago, *L'evento*; McHenry, *Event*.
6. This should not be taken to imply that Whitehead identifies the particles presupposed by physics with event entities (i.e. actual occasions). This is not the case. See Whitehead, *Adventures* 239.

I have introduced here as objective or linear time. To him this view implies that '"becoming" involves the notion of a unique seriality for its advance'. Whitehead rejects this view in stating that

> physical science has abandoned this notion. Accordingly, we should now purge cosmology of a point of view which it ought never to have adopted as an ultimate metaphysical principle. In these lectures the term 'creative advance' [i.e. temporal becoming] is not to be construed in the sense of a uniquely serial advance. (Whitehead, *Process* 35)

The problem with such a serial understanding of time is that it presupposes that 'two actual entities define the same actual world' (Whitehead, *Process* 65), which, following relativity theory, cannot be the case. There is no contemporaneity, as implied by relativity, since temporality and duration are a matter of perspective.

Digression II: Dynamic Event Ontologies and Static Event Ontologies

At this point I would like to spell out in a bit more detail what the term 'becoming beings' refers to on an ontological level, by distinguishing (static) event ontologies from dynamic event ontologies or process ontologies. This distinction is a little tricky because the terms 'event' and 'process' are neither clearly defined nor are they consistently applied.

Thinkers such as Alfred North Whitehead, Bertrand Russell, C. D. Broad and W. V. O. Quine have developed dynamic event ontologies. This shift towards dynamic events or processes was made either to account for our actual experiences, the fact that temporality is a fundamental aspect of reality; to be able to account for the complex, dynamic interrelatedness of reality; or in order to provide a conceptual scheme that would be compatible with quantum and relativity theory (or for a combination of these reasons).[7] Russell, for example, argues that what there is are events, conceived as particulars, not only because what we actually perceive are events and not entities, but also because this framework better suits the insights of physics – both quantum theory and relativity:

> From all this it seems to follow that events, not particles, must be the 'stuff' of physics. What has been thought of as a particle will have to be thought of as a series of events. The series of events that replaces a particle has certain important physical properties, and therefore demands our attention; but it has no more substantiality than any other series of events that we might arbitrarily single out. (Russell, *History* 832)

Other attempts to account for events that are generally proposed by contemporary analytic metaphysicians tend to remain more faithful to traditional atemporal conceptual frameworks, by considering events to be one category among others, or by considering events to be higher-level phenomena that can ultimately only be understood if they are reduced to (or explained through reference to) stable objects. Genuine change and becoming, as might be obvious from this characterisation, play very different roles in these different kinds of accounts of events, and thus not all event ontologies can be considered genuinely dynamic ontologies or process ontologies.

Traditionally, the ontological question of *what there is* is interpreted as a question concerned with the fundamental building blocks of reality. This interpretation of the ontological project presupposes that the basic constituents of reality are well-defined and essentially unchanging entities or elements that make up what we call reality. These types of ontologies are best characterised as *building-block ontologies*, i.e. ontologies that presuppose the constitutive elements of reality to be unchanging building blocks. What unifies all varieties of building-block ontologies, including event ontologies of this kind, is the presupposition that temporality has no intrinsic relation to the fundamental entities

---

7. See, for example, McHenry, *Event* 2.

that exist. Many philosophers who engage with events on an ontological level treat them either simply as such (temporally extended) building blocks, or as complex (i.e. not fundamental) phenomena that ultimately presuppose such substantial building blocks. The paradigmatic examples used to discuss events are evental entities such as weddings, football matches or birthday parties, and the main concern seems to be the question of how to fit such events into the respective ontological framework. Davidson's theory of events is just such an example. He takes events to be spatiotemporal particulars, i.e. entities that are located and extended in space as well as time, that are individuated and thus identifiable. The early Davidson proposed this individuation as causal, by holding that no two events can have the exact same causes; later he shifted to the claim that events are individuated by the fact that no two events can occupy the exact same spatiotemporal extension. Either strategy leads him to conceptualise events as temporal entities.

Ontologies that include such evental entities in their conceptual scheme, not as complex apparent phenomena but as *sui generis* entities, generally consider events to be temporally extended building blocks, i.e. building blocks that endure for a certain period of time. In analytic philosophy this understanding of event ontology is quite prominent and has been defended by, for example, Hacker and Cresswell. Another strategy is to consider events to be complex phenomena that ultimately rest on stable substances or other stable entities. In this case events are not fundamental and do not have much explanatory power, which means that reality ultimately is not temporally dynamic. In his book *Individuals* Strawson treats events in just such a manner by arguing that in order to report or describe events a reference to material bodies and persons is indispensable, and that events are thus dependent on more fundamental entities, namely spatiotemporally located individuals.[8] This view is a result

---

8. A descriptive approach does not necessarily lead to a stable, building-block ontology. Any truly *dynamic ontology* is based on a close description of actual

of Strawson's aim of developing a descriptive metaphysics that focuses on the macroscopic entities that are easily available and registered through the human senses, and these objects appear to be involved in events while remaining stable. While it is thus intuitively plausible to consider events to be dependent on more fundamental stable entities (McHenry, *Event* 1), this is a consequence of focusing on specific scales of investigation and thus on specific types of events. Enlarging our scales and timeframes allows for quite different phenomena; '[f]or example, in the case of the cosmic microwave background, the microwave "glow" that fills the sky is a remnant of the radiation that was present in the early universe that has now cooled to 2.7K. Where is the physical object of which this radiation is a property?' (McHenry, *Event* 21). Similar issues arise with regard to weather patterns, for example.

The reason why Western philosophy has so far tended to overemphasise stability is thus also connected to the scales and timeframes immediately available to individual human experience:

> In all discussions of nature we must remember the differences of scale, and in particular the differences of time-span. We are apt to take modes of observable functioning of the human body as setting an absolute scale. It is extremely rash to extend conclusions derived from observation far beyond the scale of magnitude to which observation was confined. For example, to exhibit apparent absence of change within a second of time tells nothing as to the change within a thousand years. Also, no apparent change within a thousand years tells anything as to a million years; and no apparent change within a million years tells anything about a million million years. (Whitehead, *Modes* 141)

Such evental ontological systems tend to be less concerned with an attempt to account for the dynamicity, temporality or change that *dynamic event ontologies* are concerned with explaining, and

---

experience, temporality and becoming; these aspects have to characterise the beings themselves.

thus are not helpful for present purposes. In order to distinguish the two ways of understanding events, I will refer to processual positions as *dynamic event ontologies* and to the more static positions as *event ontologies*. While, at first glance, one might be tempted to conflate dynamic event ontologies (i.e. all forms of process ontology from Heraclitus to Deleuze) and event ontologies (i.e. the position that considers at least some of the building blocks that constitute reality to be temporally extended events), there are fundamental differences.

Most event ontologies consider events to be some form of re-identifiable individual. This characterisation might apply to past events but will not grasp present events readily. Furthermore, the limits of such an event entity are highly porous. Consider a football match, for example, as a complex extended event entity, consisting of substances (the players, the football, the pitch, the goals, the spectators and so on) that are integral parts of the event entity 'this football match' and that interact over a specific amount of time in specific, relatively regulated ways. All of these interactions that fall within the context and the temporal duration of the event 'this football match' constitute the event. When this event starts – with the players arriving in the stadium, them running on to the field, the starting whistle, when the tickets go on sale – is relatively random. The same uncertainty holds with regard to what such an event includes and what it excludes. Are the people watching it part of the game or not? If they aren't then all the financial incentives that drive the sport should also be excluded from its definition, which seems rather inadequate. But if the spectators are part of the game, when exactly do they become part of it? When they buy the ticket? When they arrive at the stadium and so on? So even if it looks as though the event 'this football match' is a well-defined event entity, in reality the limits that separate this event from other events are rather porous.

The problems that event ontologies have to contend with in attempting to account for events, without allowing for fundamental dynamicity, do not end here. The constituent elements of 'this football match' can now themselves be considered as events; for example, the event of player A scoring a goal is an event that is part of the event 'this football match'. Thus, the event entity 'player A scoring a goal' is being established, which might begin when he is passed the ball and might end when the ball crosses the goal line. Again, these starting and ending points are relatively arbitrary and porous, but they are necessary to preserve the various identities of the events. This kind of strategy will quite obviously lead to an infinite regress, if fundamental non-eventual entities are not introduced.

The biggest issue from a process perspective is, however, that the event 'this football match' (and all of its sub-events) itself does not change. While change might happen within the event, the event itself takes up the role of a stable entity overarching, framing or carrying these changes. Our preference for unchanging stability thus again leads us to conceive of events by analogy with objects. From this perspective an event becomes a temporally extended object, with a distinct beginning and end. The event becomes an interval, an entity bound by two points in time, its actual progressive and unfolding temporality frozen into place. The event thus conceived cannot unfold any more, it has always already unfolded. Thus, the events themselves are thought through extension again, as an unchanging interval that is clearly limited and generates re-identifiable entities. These event entities do not exhibit the properties of genuine temporality (i.e. creative ongoing and unfolding) or internal relatedness. Within this interval there might be thought to be further event intervals, but these do not affect the structure of the larger event interval itself; its limits and identity remain fixed. Events are then understood as thing-like or as a state of affairs, where the event [s, P, t] is either described as a temporally extended 'thing' s that has P at t, or as the state of affairs of s having P at t. Sometimes, events are even considered to be tropes, 'so that an event is the instantiation of a property at a spatiotemporal region' (Simons, 'Events' 366). In the latter case, there is no correlation between changes and events at all.

The paradigmatic type of event that these considerations generally depart from are 'static events', and even though an event thus conceived 'includes' temporality and changes, it itself is not changeable, but is transformed into an unchanging bearer of change. So, with regard to change, these types of event ontologies are nothing but a variation of substance ontology. These types of events retain the building-block structure of classical ontology.

There are, furthermore, authors who use the term 'process' in a similar atemporal or unchanging fashion as introduced above, thus considering processes as self-identical building blocks that make up reality (or at least a region of it). Compare, for example, Quentin Meillassoux's claim that processes are determined entities that can be exchanged for each other:

> From my perspective, to conflate time with becoming is to obscure the very meaning of chaos. This might have the air of a paradox, but it is in truth immediately evident: if time can produce everything that is noncontradictory, it is not a process. For a process is always determined; it is always a process such that in relation to it I can think without contradiction that another process might replace it. (Meillassoux, 'Contingency' 326)

While Meillassoux is right that it is thinkable (without contradiction) that one process might replace another, this way of thinking presupposes that processes are limited, determined, self-identical. It implies that processes can be treated like any other form of building block, thus stripping processes of what distinguishes them from other entities.

Dynamic ontologies as presupposed in this book, on the other hand, are unified by the claim that the *unfolding flow of becoming being*, i.e. temporality, cannot be divorced from being without oversimplification. In a dynamic understanding of reality, temporality becomes a genuine ontological feature; there is no ontological 'basis' or 'substrate' (or superstructure like an unchanging 'event') that is not fundamentally temporal. No thing (or process) can be exchanged for another, because such an exchange would impact, distort or at least shift the temporal region constituted by the process in question. Each process can only exist in its time, in connection with the precise becoming temporalities surrounding it. It is impossible to take one process out of its temporality – it fundamentally is its temporality.

7

Experience and Temporal Being

In line with the dual structure of the book I will now move from ontological considerations to some of the epistemic issues involved in process thought. Just like phenomenologists, process thinkers tend to distinguish between everyday (unexamined) ways of experiencing and a radicalised or clarified form of experience. However, in process thought the way to achieve such experience is not guided by the methodological steps of *epochē* and reduction. While different authors propose different approaches as to how we can access this form of experience within process thought, I will limit my discussion of how to achieve this radicalisation or clarification of experience to Bergson's method of experience as intuition and to Whitehead's understanding of experience as feeling and prehension. Deleuze's empiricism, which presents an innovative and creative synthesis and broadening of Bergson's and Whitehead's positions, can provide an accessible entry point. Deleuze considers himself an empiricist, whose empiricism 'is derived from the two characteristics by which Whitehead defined empiricism'. These characteristics are that 'the abstract does not explain but must itself be explained; and [that] the aim [of philosophy] is not to rediscover the eternal or the universal, but to find the conditions under which something new is produced (creativeness)' (Deleuze, *Dialogues* vii). Just like Whitehead, Deleuze thus emphasises the immanent nature of reality. This means that there is nothing beyond experience or underlying experience that in principle cannot be accessed through experience. It might be the case that something is never experienced, but there is nothing that is in principle unexperienceable.

Along similar lines, Whitehead argues that the 'aim of philosophy is sheer disclosure' (Whitehead, *Modes* 49) of what is given in experience, because

> [o]ur datum is the actual world, including ourselves; and this actual world spreads itself for observation in the guise of the topic of our immediate experience. The elucidation of immediate experience is the sole justification for any thought; and the starting-point for thought is the analytic observation of components of this experience. (Whitehead, *Process* 4)

However, just as the phenomenological focus on the descriptions of givenness does not imply a naïve realism, this emphasis on disclosure through immediate experience (and its ontological interpretation) is also not a naïve taking as real what is given. There is a certain attitude to be taken when engaging with immediate experience, namely one of infinite attention and care: there is no aspect, no moment, no element of experience that can be safely ignored or abstracted from. Furthermore, we have to take care not to over-interpret what we experience, not to reshape experience in order to match our thoughts. On the contrary, Whitehead's focus on experience is supposed to lead us to reshape our modes of thought so that they match immediate experience in all its complexity, not vice versa.

Furthermore, the processual ontologies built on givenness are not dogmatic. Just as there is no ultimate phenomenological description, there is no final 'clear cut, complete analysis of immediate experience' (Whitehead, *Process* 4). This is due to the creative, processual and open-ended nature of reality. So, the reason why '[p]hilosophers can never hope finally to formulate these metaphysical first principles' is not simply due to a '[w]eakness of insight and deficiencies of language' (Whitehead, *Process* 4), even though these aspects contribute to the difficulties we are encountering; it is also due to the creative and open nature of reality. Accordingly, process thinkers argue that our metaphysical and speculative investigation of the data of experience (i.e. the phenomena), if it is to be adequate, has to be open-ended and needs to leave room for doubt, improvement and creative change. 'There remains the final reflection, how shallow, puny, and imperfect are efforts to sound the depths in the nature of things. In philosophical discussion, the merest hint of dogmatic certainty as to finality of statement is an exhibition of folly' (Whitehead, *Process* xiv).

From a process perspective, experience is more than an epistemic tool to get at what there is; experience shapes what there is on an ontological level. Any creative becoming is fundamentally internally related to every other creative becoming through experience. The term 'experience' covers all forms of internal relatedness, it includes all forms of ontological relations, from causation to feeling. So, in this terminology a causal relation can be expressed in terms of perception, feeling, sympathy or experience, as I will explain in more detail in what follows. Thus, just as the term 'experience' does not imply consciousness, the term 'feeling' does not imply emotionality or a conscious subjectivity. This, in turn, implies that to talk about experience, at least in the case of Bergson and Whitehead, is to also talk about objective existence.

It is at this point that Deleuze diverges from Whitehead in his account of experience. While for Deleuze, empiricism is fundamentally connected to creativity and becoming, just as experience is for Whitehead, it is less directly connected to experience as internal ontological relation and the creation or becoming of being. For Deleuze, especially in the case of philosophy, empiricism is about the creation of concepts, about a creation through thought. Becoming in an ontological sense is the ground for difference and multiplicity, an openness that allows for the creativity of empiricism, but empiricism (or better, experience) is itself not a constitutive aspect of the multiplicity itself. For Whitehead as well as Bergson, however, experience, feeling or sympathy is an essential, an integral aspect of creative ontological becoming. This difference in accounting for the root of creativity between Bergson and Whitehead on the one hand, and Deleuze on the other, is expressed in the shift from using the sensually connotated terms 'sympathy' or 'intuition' in Bergson and 'experience' or 'prehension' in Whitehead, to the more conceptually connoted term 'empiricism' in Deleuze.

The Method of Intuition in Bergson

According to Bergson, temporality, change and becoming are fundamental, but generally not accounted for in systematic philosophy. In order to account for this aspect of reality, Bergson developed the concept of *durée* (duration), which names the duration or ontological temporality that characterises our reality.[1] Bergson uses this term to refer to the actual flow, the undivided and indivisible movement of actual change. The reason we cannot see this fundamental durational nature of reality when examining our experiences is that we are so focused on our conceptual understandings, on the constant elements, that we cannot actually see what is given (Bergson, *Creative Mind* 131). One such conception that hinders our seeing of what there is is the long-standing philosophical conviction that there can be no knowledge of that which is truly dynamic. Ultimately, philosophy thus tended to disregard direct experience and instead focused on the abstract, the conceptual and the ideal as a guide for philosophical investigations. This is the dilemma we somehow seem still to be facing. Do we try to investigate changing reality as it is and thus give up the aim of absolute knowledge? Or, do we abstract, catalogue and categorise in such a way as to fashion a reasonably adequate and often very useful reconstruction of reality that we can actually know? It is no wonder that

---

1. This reading of *durée*, however, implies the ontological understanding of duration of later works such as *Creative Evolution*, which I presuppose without critically examining it or comparing it to the status of *duration* in earlier works.

most philosophers still choose the latter option. The problem with this path, however, is that what we get to know is not actually what there is. Only if we manage to put aside the 'artificial schema we interpose unknowingly between reality and us' (Bergson, *Creative Mind* 142) will we be able to actually discover and disclose the creativity of changing reality.

Bergson argues that the best way to reach actual experience, to reach beyond the veil of conceptual prejudice, is to plunge into this seeing, to plunge into perception instead of trying to rise above it through intellectual engagement and abstraction. The aim of such a plunge is to deepen and widen perception so that ultimately nothing that is given in experience is eliminated or disregarded. Only such a deepened perception, that is not deformed by any conceptual embellishments, can lead to a true grasping of what there actually is. It is this line of thought that both process thinkers and phenomenologists share. Bergson's plunging into experience mirrors Husserl's attempt to reduce and/or bracket our preconceptions. For Bergson, this requirement of shifting from a natural attitude, which for him is the habitual interpretation through intelligence towards intuition is, however, not achieved through a well-thought-out methodological *epochē*, but by beginning his investigations with a specific attitude that nonetheless mirrors the phenomenological method to a surprising degree:

> We will assume for the moment that we know nothing of theories of matter and theories of spirit, nothing of the discussions as to the reality or ideality of the external world. Here I am in the presence of images, in the vaguest sense of the word, images perceived when my senses are opened to them, unperceived when they are closed. All these images act and react upon one another in all their elementary parts according to constant laws which I call laws of nature [. . .] (Bergson, *Matter* 17)

The reason for taking up this attitude, however, is not the construction of a science of the absolute structures of consciousness, as it is for Husserl. Instead, it constitutes an attempt to gain insight into what there is, independently of mind and consciousness, to construct a genuine metaphysics as 'true empiricism'. Thinking about the concrete and dynamic world using intuition is thus not merely an epistemic endeavour, it is at the same time a metaphysical project:

> Either metaphysics is only this play of ideas, or else, if it is a serious occupation of the mind, if it is a science and not simply an exercise, it must transcend concepts in order to reach intuition. To be sure, concepts are indispensable to it, for all the other sciences ordinarily work with concepts, and metaphysics cannot get along without the other sciences. But it is strictly itself only when it goes beyond the concept, or at least when it frees itself from the inflexible and ready-made concepts and creates others very different from those which we usually handle; I mean flexible, mobile, and almost fluid representations, always ready to mould themselves on the fleeting forms of intuition. (Bergson, *Creative Mind* 168)

Thus, the connection between metaphysics and intuition is an immediate one. Intuition leads to a knowledge about what there is immanently, concretely as well as temporally, and thus leads to a metaphysics that 'has nothing in common with a generalization of experience, and yet it could be defined as the whole of experience' (Bergson, *Creative Mind* 200). Thus, metaphysics 'must transcend concepts to arrive at intuition' (Bergson, *Creative Mind* 168). It must arrive at the direct presence of the object in its givenness, as it is experienced without any (or at least minimal) conceptual mediation.

In order to see, to perceive and experience what there actually is, we do have to distance ourselves somewhat from our practical involvement with the world. We have to detach our investigations from attempting to achieve some practical goal – be it political impact or objective knowledge. This attempt at 'disinterestedness' is a reflective break with the world and our direct involvement with it. However, this distancing and reflecting is not to be understood as the Platonic attempt to transport 'oneself immediately into a world different from the one we inhabit, in developing other faculties of perception than the senses and consciousness' (Bergson, *Creative Mind* 139). Bergson's suggested break from practical life does not imply turning one's back upon it, but simply implies a break from the necessities and restrictions of practical life in order to free oneself to see what there is actually given in experience. It is this aimless and thus genuinely open engagement with perception that allows us to grasp change and duration in their original givenness. It is precisely this *aimless* plunging into perception that Bergson refers to as 'intuition'. Only such useless and aimless investigations of experience can disclose the dynamic nature of reality, and allow us to grasp change and duration in its original mobility – but *it can do nothing further*. This way of engaging with experience only allows access to what there is as it is, but as such would not be an adequate starting point for most other philosophical, scientific or political projects.

Is Bergson an idealist?

Considering that Bergson puts such an emphasis on the term 'intuition', one might wonder whether he is actually an idealist. Bergson does acknowledge that the term 'intuition' might be misleading since it has various idealistic connotations. But none of the traditional uses of the term quite reflect the meaning that Bergson envisions:

> Of all the terms, which designate a mode of knowing, it [intuition] is still the most appropriate; and yet it leads to a certain confusion. Because a Schelling, a Schopenhauer and others have already called upon intuition, because they have more or less set up intuition in opposition to intelligence, one might think that I was using the same method. But of course, their intuition was an immediate search for the eternal! Whereas, on the contrary, for me it was a question, above all, of finding true duration. (Bergson, *Creative Mind* 30)

If this is the case, why does Bergson insist on using the term? The concept 'intuition' is generally used to describe the ability to grasp an object in its sensual and/or essential form passively, i.e. without any mental activity, and thus to grasp the object of experience as it is, completely untouched by the act of grasping it. The term is derived from the Latin *intueri*, which means 'admire', 'consider', 'regard' or 'look at'. Intuition is therefore a 'mental but still sensual-unmediated (*anschaulich-unvermitteltes*) grasping of the essence of an object, a form of visual thinking'[2] that leads to unmediated knowledge. It is a form of non-discursive knowledge gained through immediate consideration or contemplation, and thus a form of knowledge that cannot be proven or disproven by logical means alone, nor can it be attained fully through dialectical reasoning. There are two main forms of framing intuition according to the kinds of objects that can be grasped through it, namely 1) a rationalist and 2) a sensualist understanding of intuition.[3]

A rationalist understanding of intuition presupposes that we gain true knowledge by immediately grasping reasons, propositional knowledge, geometrical or mathematical truths. This understanding of intuition shapes Plato's epistemology, for example. It is also present in Spinoza's *scientia intuitiva*, which considers intuition to be a direct grasping of the most general intelligible essence. It is this understanding of intuition that Kant refers to when he claims that *intellectual intuition (intellektuelle Anschauung)* is impossible. The second, sensualist understanding of intuition will be somewhat familiar to English speakers, since it is used to translate Kant's *Anschauung*, which in Kant refers to the unordered sense data provided by the senses and the 'material' for categorisation. This second understanding of intuition also refers to a direct, unmediated and passive attaining, but this

---

2. My translation of 'Eine geistige, aber doch anschaulich-unmittelbare Erfassung des Wesens eines Objektes; ein schauendes Denken' (Eisler).
3. Husserl's categorial intuition, however, does not fit easily in either camp. It combines elements of the sensual intuition, as categorial intuition has to be grounded in givenness to be phenomenologically relevant, with intellectual intuition, as its objects are not directly given forms of categorial relations. For more detail, see Lohmar.

time of empirical, i.e. sensible objects. Bergson's understanding of intuition belongs to this category of sensual intuition; this is also the reason why Bergson considers his philosophy to be true empiricism. What is thus given, however, does not need to be manipulated to lead to insight. The object gives itself sensibly and it gives certain structures and limitations that can then be conceptualised in various ways, but these conceptualisations, if they are to be adequate, can only spell out what is given.

For Bergson 'intuition' is an epistemic method, which takes the form of an entering into the object to be known, or the form of sympathy. It is a method that can lead to the metaphysical insight that duration[4] is essential to what there is, and it allows us to access and learn about concrete reality in its temporality or its ongoing duration. Thus, for Bergson, the aim of intuition is not a rationalist one, namely a direct insight into eternal truths, but instead constitutes a form of direct grasping of what there is, in its duration. To Bergson, intuition still 'signifies first of all consciousness, but immediate consciousness, a vision which is scarcely distinguishable from the object seen, a knowledge which is contact and even coincidence' (Bergson, *Creative Mind* 32). For Bergson, intuition is thus not directed towards attaining absolute objective knowledge about necessary laws, abstract or atemporal essences, as in traditional forms of idealism. It describes an aimless plunge into the world we experience – the world we live in.

At this point, it is important to distinguish the term's usage in analytic philosophy from Bergson's understanding. In the analytic tradition the term 'intuition' is mostly used to refer to a simple prejudice or a conviction that stems from a certain education, cultural environment or language use, and that is not rationally or reflectively achieved, but simply present. This form of intuition simply refers to an implicit bias that is shared by a large part of society. To Bergson, intuitions do not correspond to the unreflected mental state that I have, if I have a conviction

---

4. Duration is Bergson's *terminus technicus* to describe the temporal (processual) and evolutionary character of every becoming entity and being as such.

about the truth of a proposition. The reason why, according to Bergson, the intellect alone does not suffice to attain intuition is that reason and intellect are specialised in attaining the kind of knowledge that is geared towards practical and useful ends. This is a kind of knowledge that renders our engagement with the material, conceptual and law-governed world more effective and more efficient. Reason and intellect, as they have been developed throughout Western philosophy, are tools that cannot be used in a disinterested way and thus are always geared towards goals and not towards attaining disinterested knowledge about the nature of reality as it is given in experience.

Whitehead agrees with Bergson's assessment that we tend to abstract and stabilise what is given in our thinking; we tend to think what there is by analogy with space, because this renders our engagement with the world more efficient. But he disagrees with Bergson's analysis of the role of the intellect in this:

> [T]he history of philosophy supports Bergson's charge that the human intellect 'spatializes the universe'; that is to say, that it tends to ignore the fluency, and to analyse the world in terms of static categories. Indeed Bergson went further and conceived this tendency as an inherent necessity of the intellect. I do not believe this accusation; but I do hold that 'spatialization' is the shortest route to a clear-cut philosophy expressed in reasonably familiar language. Descartes gave an almost perfect example of such a system of thought. The difficulties of Cartesianism with its three clear-cut substances, and with its 'duration' and 'measured time' well in the background, illustrate the result of the subordination of fluency. (Whitehead, *Process* 209)

And to be fair, Bergson would insist that intuition could not ensue without intellectual engagement or reasoning. We have to engage rationally with the world before intuition can be achieved. Just as one usually has to turn a mathematical problem over in one's mind again and again, before a flash of insight and understanding emerges, we have to investigate the world thoroughly by means of reason and rationality before we are able to intuitively see its durational character. The claim is merely that rational engagement alone does not suffice to fully know duration or to enter into intuition.

Intuition, analysis and knowledge

In my discussion of phenomenology, I argued that for Husserl, immediate givenness is not to be identified with immediate propositional knowledge about what things are; instead givenness provides insight into how things are given. In contrast to this position, Bergson does hold that intuition can give us absolute knowledge, but he argues that moments of intuition are not readily available and can generally only occur after thorough and prolonged intellectual engagement. To Bergson, true knowledge is thus the result of an adequate or successful mixture of analysis and intuition. Thus, true knowledge combines analysis or conceptual engagement, which is an intellectual engagement that amounts to a grasping of the object 'from the outside' by going around it, and intuition, which implies an understanding from within, a metaphorical entering into the object in order to fully grasp it. Both of these characterisations are metaphorical descriptions of a certain quality of engagement. Which of these investigative qualities is present in any given investigation depends not only on the method used, but also on other factors, such as the object investigated and the investigative aim.[5]

What precisely do these metaphors bring to light? In the first case, the process of intellectually 'going around' the object and describing it from each of the perspectives that are accessible one after the other implies a quality of discreteness or distinctness. There are various singular impressions characterising the object that can be added up to form a unified account. There is no internal structure or order posed by the object that would

---

5. Just to provide one example, the difference in accounting for actual temporality as either clock time or as duration is the result of applying these different qualities in the investigation of the same phenomenon.

determine in any way which of these perspectives is the starting point, how this summative account should proceed, which perspectives should be taken to be relevant and which are to be considered irrelevant for the investigation in question. All of these decisions flow or follow from the initially chosen perspective, the direction of the investigation, as well as the practical and intellectual interests that gave rise to the investigation in the first place, and not from the object. From this starting point, we begin to reconstruct the whole by adding those perspectival impressions considered relevant to the perspectival impression we began the investigation with. Thus, we build up the whole for our knowledge by adding constitutive part on to constitutive part.

The problem with this additive approach to knowledge is that these singular impressions are not genuine parts or elements, which would allow for such a reconstruction, but merely partial and perspectival expressions of the one unified, single object. This kind of analysis leads to more and more abstraction, fragmentation and specialisation. It is not conducive to grasping a whole as such. One simply cannot gain insight into a whole by analysing its partial expressions; this process alone does not suffice. By the very nature of analysis the resulting knowledge is furthermore relative: relative to the starting point of the analysis, relative to the principles and practical goals that guide the reconstruction, relative to what is being considered relevant and what can be disregarded in the reconstruction, and thus relative to the interests that we follow in generating this conceptual reconstruction of the simple and undivided original that we actually wish to know. Bergson provides us with a very good image of the problems that such an approach implies:

> If I wish to explain to someone who did not know Greek the simple impression that a line of Homer leaves upon me, I shall give the translation of the line, then comment on my translation, then I shall develop my commentary, and from explanation on explanation I shall get closer to what I wish to express; but I shall never quite reach it. (Bergson, *Creative Mind* 161)

Intuition, on the other hand, is the simple sympathetic impression that allows for knowledge of the simple and undivided original – it is a grasping of the whole, not as a sum of parts or perspectives but *as a whole*. It implies a sort of 'entering into the object' that can only be attained after thorough analysis, and if, in addition to this analysis, in a second step, one manages to let go of the perspectives, the preconceptions and the interests, and just let the object guide the investigation. In this way the whole can show up as a unity of 'composite parts', i.e. internally related parts, that cannot be clearly separated or distinguished like constitutive parts. These composite parts, accessible in intuition, are fully integrated singularities, they fit only one whole, and since composite parts are singular, they can only be combined in one specific way with other composite parts to create one specific object. A good example to illustrate the nature of composite parts is an event. A moment or an aspect of any concrete event can fit into the rest of the event in just one specific way. On a practical level, looking at a specific concrete event, it does not even make sense to consider whether any process constituting this event could be added at a later point in time or inserted in a different event. The later time would not exist without this factually present event, and if it were inserted into a different event, it would cease to be this event. Composite parts cannot be exchanged or removed from their whole without destroying the whole, or at least transforming it into something essentially different.

To sum up, the main difference between the qualitative modes of knowing that Bergson introduces is the following: intuition is able to grasp a single and concrete being in its temporal becoming in a single and undivided instant of experience, while knowing through analysis has to abstract from the dynamic dimension the relatedness of concrete being and its singularity, splitting it into perspectives that are shaped by practical interests, aims and preconceptions. The analogies to the phenomenological methods of continuous perspectival description, eidetic variation and insight into essence are obvious. However, while phenomenological experience and description can only disclose phenomena and their how of givenness with certainty, intuition can disclose the in-itself, but only in an unsystematic and non-discursive manner. Intuition is, according to Bergson, a simple and indivisible experience of sympathy that allows us to grasp an object from within, by moving us into that object to understand its unique singularity. Both the phenomenological method and Bergson's intuition emphasise a focus on the object as given in immediate experience and a letting go of perspectives and preconceptions. Both share the aim of letting the object guide the investigation; these approaches differ merely in what they consider to be the nature of possible objects of investigation, whether they are entities in their worldly 'enterable' dimensionality or phenomena.

What can we learn from intuition?

While any analysis provides us with merely relative knowledge, intuition, if used adequately and rigorously, can lead to an absolute way of knowing the actual ontological being in its temporal, interrelated and singular becoming – what there is in its duration. This absolute knowledge is therefore an absolute knowledge of the becoming concrete and creative singular – of that which is continuously and creatively changing. This means that this form of absolute knowing has nothing in common with a traditional understanding of absolute certainty or absolute knowing. Intuition can grasp what there is wholly or absolutely, but not in an atemporal, eternal or transcendent sense. It is absolute in the sense that it can bring to consciousness what there is in concrete duration beyond perspective, as it is – in, with and through its essential changes. Such a knowledge cannot simply be translated into a propositional or an abstract symbolic form, or treated adequately with the traditional tools of logical or conceptual analyses. It does not stand in direct competition with propositional or conceptual knowledge.

This leads to the main difficulty with the kind of knowledge that results from intuition — how can or should this knowledge be shared, made intersubjectively accessible? How can we share intuitions, if analysis, general concepts and abstract symbols are inadequate? Bergson proposes the use of images or metaphors in order to communicate the knowledge that has been gained through intuition. While he admits that these tools will not be able to communicate intuitions directly, he argues that they can prepare or enable the reader or listener to have intuitions themselves. In the words of Bergson: 'No image will replace the intuition of duration, but many different images, taken from quite different orders of things, will be able, through the convergence of their action, to direct the consciousness to the precise point where there is a certain intuition to seize on' (Bergson, *Creative Mind* 166).

So why should we even bother with intuition, if it only leads to images or metaphors about the world we live in? This kind of philosophical knowledge truly is quite useless, when it comes to more conceptual or more practical concerns. The kind of knowledge gained through intuition appears especially useless if it is directly compared to the apparently unending usefulness of the kind of scientific and reflective knowledge we gain through the intellect and rationality. We should, however, keep in mind that the usefulness or uselessness of knowledge does depend on the investigative aim shaping the respective investigation. If an adequate understanding of the actual nature of the concrete world surrounding us is the aim of an investigation, the argument could be made that all the useful knowledge gained in scientific and abstract analysis is actually quite useless, since it remains partial and perspectival, while intuition can at least account for the durational wholeness that we experience in the world. I would like to end this discussion with a mode of thinking about the usefulness of philosophy proposed by Heidegger that shapes much of my thinking. Heidegger asks us to consider whether the uselessness of intuitive philosophical knowledge could not point towards the heart of what it means to be actually engaged with philosophy:

It is entirely correct and completely in order to say, 'You can't do anything with philosophy?' The only mistake is to believe that with this, the judgment concerning philosophy is at an end. For a little epilogue arises in the form of a counterquestion: even if *we* can't do anything with it, may not philosophy in the end do something *with us*, provided that we engage ourselves with it? (Heidegger, *Metaphysics* 13)

Whitehead: Ontological Experience as Bodily Feeling

For Whitehead, the connection between experience and being is so fundamental that it is adequate to claim that everything in existence actually is the result of experience. What there is, including physical nature, is thought as a network of experiences and a result of experiences. According to Whitehead, experiences create and connect everything. The easiest way to conceptualise this thought is to consider experiences to be a form of internal relation. An experience is not external to the experiencing entity or process, but effects it internally and thus co-creates what this entity or process is becoming.

In order to convey this ontological status of experience and the fact that it is a kind of experience that is not connected to consciousness or sense organs,[6] Whitehead coins the term 'prehension' (derived from apprehension) or 'feeling'. Whitehead's understanding of sensory perception as prehension or feeling is inspired by the following passage in Descartes' second *Meditation*:

> Lastly, it is also the same 'I' who has sensory perceptions, or is aware of bodily things as it were through the senses. For example, I am now seeing light, hearing a noise, feeling heat. But I am asleep, so all this is false. Yet I certainly seem to see, to hear, and to be warmed. This cannot be false; what is called 'having a

---

6. 'Prehensions of actual entities – i.e., prehensions whose data involve actual entities – are termed "physical prehensions"; and prehensions of eternal objects are termed "conceptual prehensions." Consciousness is not necessarily involved in [. . .] either type of prehension' (Whitehead, *Process* 23).

sensory perception' is strictly just this, and in this restricted sense of the term it is simply thinking. (Descartes vol. II, 19)

Using this connection or identification between perceptions or feelings (in a specific sense) and thinking, Whitehead concludes that in 'Cartesian language, the essence of an actual entity consists solely in the fact that it is a prehending thing (i.e., a substance whose whole essence or nature is to prehend)' (Whitehead, *Process* 41). According to Whitehead, to interpret the *res cogitans* merely as an intellectual *res* is to minimise this larger understanding of thinking that also includes feeling and perceptions. Whether Descartes intended such an enlarged understanding of the cogito or not, the structural analogies between thinking and feeling that he points towards cannot be ignored. Just as I cannot doubt that I am engaged in intellectual exercises, that I am thinking in the propositional sense, I also cannot doubt that I am feeling, that I am perceiving. None of these acts themselves can be an illusion, even if what is given in any of them can be misunderstood, misinterpreted, misapplied or misread in many ways. We might mistake the cause or the reasons why we experience certain feelings, but

> the act of feeling is incontestable, real for itself, it needs no other justification than its activity. [. . .] The important point of this unexpected affiliation [of feeling and reality] is that it allows Whitehead to establish feeling as a constant activity, which involves all aspects of a subject, and whose reality is in the activity itself. (Debaise, *Nature* 44)

Using this understanding of feeling, the process of becoming itself can therefore be explained through experience as prehension or feeling, because prehension both explains how any actual occasion is connected to its past and its environment (i.e. not simply located) and provides the mechanism that allows for the transition from one actual occasion to the next. In any act of prehension or feeling of the present actual occasion, the 'present subject absorbs [i.e. prehends and integrates] the data of the immediate past or the objects, and the many past occasions become a novel one' (McHenry, *Event* 56). This process of becoming of a novel actual occasion is one of growing together, which Whitehead refers to as 'concrescence'. This process of concrescence is the

> emergence of the present from the past [and it] is an asymmetrical relation. The past is internal or contained in the present, but the present is external to the past. That is, the present actual occasion is understood to be a process of self-creation by prehending the past, but the past does not prehend the present [. . .] (McHenry, *Event* 56)

So, what there is are many processes that taken together grow into what we refer to as specific entities.

Whether a process is a subject or an object of experience therefore depends on whether a process is actually becoming or whether it has become the past. If it is currently becoming, then it is the subject having and integrating experiences. The subject experiences the past processes that have become before it and thus are the objects of experience. For Whitehead, any relation between process-objects and process-subjects (or more precisely *superjects*) is an experience that connects every participating process. This process of processes growing together to form larger process-subjects and process-objects that seem relatively stable is 'concrescence' (*con-crescere* – growing together), and it describes the fundamental way that ongoing becoming and existence take place.

The processes that are the results of such integrations of feelings or experiences are called 'actual occasions' or 'actual entities', to emphasise both the processual as well as the atomic structure of Whitehead's process ontology. Actual occasions are the result of integration (or exclusion, which is a form of experience that Whitehead calls 'negative prehension') of experiences into a process and thus constitute what we experience as part of lived reality.

> The actual entity terminates its becoming in one complex feeling involving a completely determinate bond with every

item in the universe, the bond being either a positive or a negative prehension. This termination is the 'satisfaction' of the actual entity. (Whitehead, *Process* 44)

As soon as the actual entity completes this process of becoming, as soon as it is fully present, it becomes an object, it becomes part of the past and thus a possible object of perception for future actual occasions. Thus, every actual occasion is both a subject and an object. It has been a subject during its process of becoming, and turns into a determinate, public object for perception as soon as it has fulfilled this process of becoming. To exist is either to experience other actual occasions or to be the object of experience for other actual occasions. Thus, processes do not exist independently from experience, they are the results of experience.[7]

Prehension (or feeling) is conceptualised as a process of ontological unification and actual creation. Every experience (or feeling) is integrated into the becoming being and thus shapes the ongoing creation of this being. Feeling is a *present activity* of integrating the past. To clarify his point, Whitehead uses a technical term: prehension. There is no real difference in nature between the terms 'feeling' and 'prehension', but the latter outlines an important element of the activity of feeling. The term's primary origin is that of cognitive activity, an operation of knowledge, the act of 'the intelligence seizing something' (Debaise, *Nature* 48).

Using a first analogy, we can say that as human beings our experiences make us what we are, even on a physical level. The food we experience changes our biochemistry, the air we experience affects our lung capacity, the noise pollution we experience affects our ability to concentrate and so on. This integrational

---

7. 'Tutto è esperienza: dal trasferimento di energia all'astrazione ideante. Questa prospettiva spiega così anche perché Whitehead parli delle entità attuali come di "gocce di esperienza". L'attuarsi è un sentire che produce un'esperienza, la quale si struttura in esperiente ed esperito. Ma l'esperiente e l'esperito, cioè il soggetto e l'oggetto, non preesistono all'esperire, anzi ne sono un effetto' (Vanzago, 'Introduzione' 24).

view of experience is more fundamental than the way we traditionally interpret the apperception of a quality, a sense datum or a phenomenon, which remains on quite a superficial level. These sensible and superficial inputs are usually considered to be simple objects of experience, which are not internally related to the experiencing subject. These experiences connect the object with the subject, but this connection does not affect either relatum internally. Traditionally, experience is understood in a distanced manner, without truly affecting what is, simply because the ontological effects of experiencing are generally not accounted for. If experience is only investigated in its epistemic dimension and is furthermore reduced to conscious experience, as tends to be the case, it is rather easy to overlook the ontological impact that experiences have on experiencing entities. The terms 'feeling' or 'prehension' underline the fact that experiences do have ontological effects. What is felt or prehended is integrated on all levels, including physical, biological, visceral and (potentially) conscious. Thus, to prehend means to dwell in (as being-in) and to interact with (i.e. being-with or being internally related) the surrounding world. This leads to the claim that everything that exists as part of physical nature, by virtue of existing, is both subject and object of experience. Thus, all of nature, all of reality is fundamentally situated on the same level of 'realness', connected through and via experience.

So Whitehead, like Bergson, asks us to rethink reality as fundamentally creative, open and dynamic (or durational), but he also asks us to think of everything through the lens of experience. For Whitehead, there is no going beyond experience. There is no great outdoors that we are barred from, simply because we are consciously experiencing beings. On the contrary, experience is what shapes our existence, the existence of everything around us, and it is what connects us to what there is – experience connects us to the great outdoors:

> For natural philosophy everything perceived is nature. We may not pick and choose. For us the red glow of the sunset should

be as much part of nature as are the molecules and the electric waves by which men of science would explain the phenomenon. It is for natural philosophy to analyse how these various elements are connected. (Whitehead, *Concept* 29)

Experience between epistemology and ontology

In the above description of the ontological dimension of experience as prehension, the difference between phenomenology and process thought becomes clear. Phenomenology is a post-Kantian form of epistemology, while most process ontologies tend to take the form of pre-Kantian ontology. It is this difference between epistemology and ontology, between post-Kantian and pre-Kantian, that leads many interpreters to conclude that there are entirely different conceptions of experience at work in phenomenology and process ontology. As Ron L. Cooper puts it in his book *Heidegger and Whitehead*:

> Whitehead's and Heidegger's analyses of experience are perhaps most readily contrasted in the view that Whitehead interprets human experience as an instance of his causal theory of nature (which some readers see as old-fashioned metaphysics), while Heidegger offers a transcendental description of human existence (which strikes some readers as too subjectivistic). (Cooper 1)

This account can be generalised to apply to both traditions. This assessment does suggest that phenomenological experience and process philosophical experience are fundamentally incompatible. This initial assessment can only stand, however, if a shared conviction is not considered, namely that the traditional subject–object distinction is an obsolete remnant of an outdated way of thought and not an adequate rendering of what there is. Phenomenological descriptions in general are not intended to provide merely subjective descriptions; the aim is to provide lasting knowledge, but to do so by beginning with experience. Similarly, Bergson and Whitehead are not interested in constructing a traditional, objectivistic metaphysics. Causation does play a fundamental role in their respective ontologies, but the basis of causation is creativity, evolution or experience, i.e. a process usually considered to be subjective: 'Whitehead shows that we come to an understanding of causality not through a scientific inquiry into efficient causes but through an analysis that reveals the primordial *Ereignis* of causality to be a structure of originative experience itself' (Cooper 2).

The causality Whitehead is interested in is therefore not an abstract or theoretical rendering of causality, but experiential causality. And in this sense Whitehead's engagement with causality is not as un-phenomenological as it might seem at first. In order to discover experiential causality, one has to begin by closely describing the kinds of regular/structured influences that show themselves in investigations of our everyday experiences, if we examine them closely enough and without preconceptions. A rock, for example, could be said to 'experience' the sun when it is heated up by the sun's rays. The rock is thus *causally affected* by the sun, which relates to a specific aspect of experience that Whitehead termed causal efficacy. If causation is thus investigated as causal efficacy (i.e. as an aspect of perception), in its epistemic as well as its ontological dimension, we have an understanding of causation that in principle can be investigated by phenomenology. Whitehead also argues that such an investigation not only leads to a better understanding of experience, but also to a better way of understanding causation. Thus, according to Whitehead, experience can be couched both in the metaphysical language of causation as well as the reflective language of epistemology or phenomenology. The gap between a phenomenological and process ontological understanding of experience shrinks further:

> This direct perception, characterized by mere subjective responsiveness and by lack of origination in the higher phases, [can be accounted for as follows:] In the language of causation, it describes the efficient causation operative in the actual world. In the language of epistemology, as framed by Locke, it describes

how the ideas of particular existents are absorbed into the subjectivity of the percipient and are the datum for its experience of the external world. (Whitehead, *Process* 117)

In what follows, I will first introduce Whitehead's understanding of conscious experience as a complex interaction of causal efficacy and presentational immediacy. Then I will move on to explain the impact that understanding aspects of experience as causal efficacy has on Whitehead's understanding of causality.

Causal efficacy and presentational immediacy

On an epistemic level of analysis, what we generally call 'experience' on a conscious level, according to Whitehead, actually shows itself to be a complex interaction of various levels of engagement. What we commonly think of as (conscious) perception is actually a symbolic activity that is the result of the fusion of two ways of experiencing, namely *causal efficacy* and *presentational immediacy*. Everyday (conscious) perception is composed of two basic experiential aspects, namely a visual aspect (presentational immediacy) and a felt aspect (causal efficacy). Causal efficacy, which describes the mode of experience that characterises every prehension (not only conscious experience), is the more fundamental and the more basic of the two modes. It provides the ontological and experiential ground on which the higher level of presentational immediacy is grounded. Causal efficacy provides a diffuse and unclear, corporeal or visceral feeling, a diffuse affecting and being affected, in the form of a sense or a mood. Presentational immediacy, on the other hand, provides its object with much more clarity and is the aspect of experience that can be connected to sight and vision. Vision (presentational immediacy) creates the impression of an objective datum and thus the impression of some distance between the observer and the observed, while causal efficacy discloses an immediate connection to and integration with the world.

> For example, in touch there is a reference to the stone in contact with the hand, and a reference to the hand [. . .] Thus [the subject] M, which has some analytic consciousness of its datum, is conscious of the feeling in its hand as the hand touches the stone. According to this account, perception in its primary form is consciousness of the causal efficacy of the external world by reason of which the percipient is a concrescence from a definitely constituted datum. The vector character of the datum is this causal efficacy. (Whitehead, *Process* 120)

In feeling what there is in this way, perceiver and perceived grow together (concrescence) and create a new datum, the perception.

Causal efficacy describes a type of physical or bodily givenness of the world that is experienced as visceral feeling. It is the sense that we have of the world before we have made sense of it. It is neither rational nor logical. 'It is evident that "perception in the mode of causal efficacy" is not that sort of perception which has received chief attention in the philosophical tradition. Philosophers have disdained the information about the universe obtained through their visceral feelings and have concentrated on visual feelings' (Whitehead, *Process* 121). Western philosophy thus has a tendency to 'equate human perception with the clear and distinct ideas found in the mode of presentational immediacy' (Cooper 100), and tends to give precedence to a more abstract and visual level of experience, while ignoring the most basic sensing of causal efficacy. Which is to say that Western philosophy tends to focus on the presenting visual aspects of perception, which appear to be clear and distinct, so that 'epistemological theory' could focus 'upon the immediate, conscious experience while ignoring the more immediate, vague feelings of the world' (Cooper 100). These vague feelings or prehensions of causal efficacy are, however, the threads that internally relate and thus bind all of reality together, that allow for causality and a unified understanding of what there is. Only if the level of causal efficacy is disregarded can *what there is* be conceived as a set of distinct, individual, substantial entities that in a second step need to be related to each other, to which, in reality, they are always already connected, and which, in a third step, need to be connected to the surrounding world that they, in reality, always already dwell in.

So how does the term 'causal efficacy' relate to causality? Whitehead argues that causal efficacy grounds causality in experience and thus provides a way to undermine Hume's sceptical arguments against causality:

> Hume's polemic respecting causation is, in fact, one prolonged, convincing argument that pure presentational immediacy does not disclose any causal influence, either whereby one actual entity is constitutive of the percipient actual entity, or whereby one perceived actual entity is constitutive of another perceived actual entity. The conclusion is that, in so far as concerns their disclosure by presentational immediacy, actual entities in the contemporary universe are causally independent of each other. (Whitehead, *Process* 123)

It is the focus on the clear, visual elements of experience, i.e. presentational immediacy, so prevalent in Western philosophy, that leads to the kinds of sceptical arguments proposed by Hume. A focus on causal efficacy can be deployed to understand causality as an actual interaction on an ontological level. Whitehead would concede that Hume is right in claiming that we cannot actually see the causal effect or the causal interaction, but Whitehead adds that we can feel or prehend it in the form of causal efficacy.

In this respect causal efficacy can be compared to the concept of 'proprioception' of external influences, as it is employed in analytic metaphysics to undermine Hume's sceptical arguments. Proprioception or bodily awareness is used to argue that we can in fact experience causality, namely when we are bodily affected and experience the effect of the causal action through our own bodies. These proposals are quite similar to Whitehead's arguments around causal efficacy and emphasise that we can experience being causally acted upon, that we can experience causality. The advantage of Whitehead's concept of causal efficacy to these discussions, however, is that he does not presuppose a strict ontological separation between subject and object, which renders this argument against Hume even more powerful than arguments based on proprioception. The explanation of causality through proprioception necessitates an additional argumentative step, namely explaining how any objective (causal) influence can affect or effect a change in the subject's experience and how these two spheres connect. Whitehead's answer to this problem is simple: it is the nature of experience to be such a causal influence. It is also simply the nature of experience to transcend the subject–object dichotomy.

According to Whitehead, Hume was correct in claiming that all our ideas stem from immediate sensations; however, he failed to truly account for actual perception and instead focused on presentational immediacy only. If we include our bodily experiences available through our physical and bodily being-in-the-world and being with the world, a different picture emerges. It is the sole focus on presentational immediacy that clouds our judgement when it comes to understanding actual experience. This one-sided focus is part of the reason why the common-sense understanding of experience criticised by Husserl, Bergson and Whitehead cannot adequately account for concrete givenness or concrete experience. Immediate experience as causal efficacy is by its very nature vague, and thus not very efficient or easily mathematisable, but it gives the world in its concrete interconnected, becoming, temporal relationality. If this is the case, what steps could be taken in order to fully account for all of experience?

Whitehead advises us that in order to do this, we would need to abandon some philosophical and theoretical preconceptions that have fundamentally shaped philosophy as well as science. In the preface to *Process and Reality* Whitehead provides a list of the kinds of myths and philosophical preconceptions that would need to be rejected in order to experience what there is as it is, and while there is a clear overlap with the phenomenological approach, when it comes to the issue of speculation, metaphysics and the Kantian revolution the assessment is, predictably, quite different:

> These lectures will be best understood by noting the following list of prevalent habits of thought, which are repudiated, in so far as concerns their influence on philosophy:
> 1. The distrust of speculative philosophy.
> 2. The trust in language as an adequate expression of propositions.
> 3. The mode of philosophical thought which implies, and is implied by, the faculty-psychology.
> 4. The subject–predicate form of expression.
> 5. The sensationalist doctrine of perception.
> 6. The doctrine of vacuous actuality.
> 7. The Kantian doctrine of the objective world as a theoretical construct from purely subjective experience.
> 8. Arbitrary deductions in ex absurdo arguments.
> 9. Belief that logical inconsistencies can indicate anything else than some antecedent errors.
>
> By reason of its ready acceptance of some, or all, of these nine myths and fallacious procedures, much nineteenth-century philosophy excludes itself from relevance to the ordinary stubborn facts of daily life. (Whitehead, *Process* viii)

Part IV Dynamic Realism

> It would be foolish to try to prove that nature exists;
> for obviously many such things exist. To prove
> the obvious through the non-obvious is to show
> lack of judgement, and involves one in talk about
> words, to which no thought corresponds.
> Aristotle, *Physics* 193a3–6

In what follows, I will be using the correlation between phenomenology and process thought as manifest in the ambiguous nature of experience that was discovered in Parts II and III to argue that combining these traditions is the most adequate strategy to learn about actual reality. I do so by investigating various ways in which my two basic accounts of realism – namely that 1) reality is that which, when you (or, to be more precise, *we*) stop believing in it (or thinking it), doesn't go away, as well as 2) reality is that which resists – can be aligned with both phenomenological description as well as processual accounts of what there is. Then I will provide a full-fledged account of engaged experience as the final epistemic tool that allows for a dynamic and realistic understanding of what there is. I will apply these tools to various concepts of reality. This progression of thought will lead me from naturalism and materialism, via scientific realism to phenomenology, and a relational as well as processual understanding of what there is in terms of life and nature as dynamic realism.

8

What There Is:
The Dynamic 'Object' of Experience

A quick aside before I move on to discuss the problems involved in thinking, conceptualising and speaking an object that is truly dynamic. When using the English language, it is almost impossible, or at least highly cumbersome, to avoid terms that seem to imply static beings. If, for example, I wanted to refer to some processes, even the general term 'something' seems to indicate a fundamental entity, a 'thing'. However, within the framework of dynamic ontology the use of the terms 'thing' or 'object' merely conforms to established language use and should not be taken to imply an atemporal *thing*, in the same way that the use of the expression 'sunrise' should not be taken to imply that the person speaking actually assumes that the sun is rotating around the earth and is thus literally rising in the east. The use of this term is a simple conforming to established ways of speaking.

At first glance it is the case that the world seems to be given in a way that is just as compatible with the claim that everything is constantly changing, as it is with the claim that in experience some things remain (fairly) stable. We do experience change as well as stability. The question we have to face at this point is the following: what are the advantages and disadvantages of considering reality stable and change secondary, versus considering reality changeable and stability to be a result or effect of continuous changes? Just as observable changes can be explained as a form of apparent but not essential change, apparent stability can be understood as the result of continuous, stable and ongoing movement. While either explanatory route is open to us, the path chosen should ideally create a balance between stability and change, between continuity and change, without simply ignoring one aspect or reducing one aspect to the other.

While, theoretically, it is just as viable to presuppose ontological stability that appears to change in some instances as it is to presuppose ontological dynamism that appears stable for certain periods, when it comes to understanding concrete reality this book is an attempt to argue for the adequacy of the latter position. So far, I have been arguing that the structure of reality as it appears in experience (and as it is described in particle physics and relativity) demands an ontology that can cope with genuine (substantial) change as well as continuity and stability. I have referred to ontologies that are able to come to terms with the contradictions involved in becoming and change without considering change as merely accidental as *dynamic ontologies*. Generally speaking, such ontologies presuppose a 'concept of being' that accounts for existence in terms of being processual (becoming) and being relational (organic). The concept of being that shapes dynamic ontologies is 'becoming existence'. In what follows, I will first introduce the Heideggerian idea of a 'concept of being', and then explore the ontological background against which I develop the concept of being of 'becoming existence'.[1]

What is a Concept of Being?

When we talk about 'being' (or 'existence'), we can talk about two things. Either we focus on entities that are 'doing' the being, or we can inquire about what conditions need to obtain for something to have existence. In the first case, we are looking at beings; in the second case, we are looking at the causes and conditions that all these beings share. The first question is focused on the qualities characterising 'being' or 'existence', the second is

---

1. For a detailed introduction to this concept, see Röck, *Physis*.

focused on the common cause or reason of being. This structure reflects a somewhat analogous division between ontology and metaphysics that I introduced at the beginning, as well as the Heideggerian distinction between *beings* and *Being/Beying*, and the ambiguous Aristotelian understanding of the aims of the *prote philosophia*, the first philosophy. Aristotle argues, on the one hand, that the first science is about investigating *on he on*, beings as beings and their attributes in general (*katholou*, Metaphysics 1003a2 –5). On the other hand, he also claims that the *prote philosophia* is the science investigating the first and highest being (*Metaphysics* 10026a13–16), and thus the science investigating the common cause or reason for all being or existence.

These dichotomies, separating individual beings and their properties from principles, laws or structures, indicate a certain ambiguity at the heart of our understanding of being that needs to be united through a conceptual rendering of Being/being. It does seem intuitively plausible to say that various entities have different ways of being in the world, a different form of existence: stones, for example, seem to exist in quite a different way from properties (if we grant them both existence for now), just as it seems quite natural to claim that dreams exist in a way that is different to the way money or swimming pools exist. All these differences of existence can still be subsumed under one understanding of Being, since they have to have something in common that allows us to consider them to exist. This common nature or common structure can now be thought in two ways. Either it is or is not identical in every entity. If it is identical in every entity, then this univocal concept of being applies to everything there is. If it is not identical in every entity, then the various ways beings exist are analogical. All beings then exist in analogy to genuine Being, a principle, first cause or ur-being shaping and ordering all the ways different beings exist differently. If this common nature of everything that exists is conceived as identically different in every being, then this too constitutes a univocal understanding of being, which is the notable exception to this strategy of accounting for existence.

From the perspective of univocity, everything that has existence has the exact same form of being, the same existence. This holds for Deleuze's understanding of this univocal nature as difference as well. Deleuze was the philosopher who reintroduced the idea of univocity as a genuine way of thinking 'being' to continental philosophers, by defining its nature not as the mere existence implied by the existential quantifier, but as Difference:

> With univocity, however, it is not the differences which are and must be: it is being which is Difference, in the sense that it is said of difference. Moreover, it is not we who are univocal in a Being which is not; it is we and our individuality which remains equivocal in and for a univocal Being. (Deleuze, *Difference* 39)

The hallmark feature of all there is, for Deleuze, is thus Difference. This is a position very close to Heidegger's claim that what there is has the nature of Event, or Whitehead's claim that what there is is processual. What unifies these thinkers is the fact that they conceive of what there is not through identity or stability, but through difference, disruption or change. This univocal understanding of being, first developed by Duns Scotus, is a position that appeals to contemporary sensibilities and has many contemporary advocates. The notion of mere existence, as expressed by the existential quantifier, is an example of such a univocal understanding of Being. This, of course, makes things terminologically complex, as 'mere existence' is simply another *concept of being*, a concept of being that equates existence with pure presence, to the exclusion of any further determination(s).

Similarly, there are various ways to think the concept of being as analogous. Being can be conceptualised as the *genus maximum*, i.e. the most general term in one's categorical structure, which is not quite the same thing as thinking being as *being in general*, nor is it the same thing as thinking the *summum ens*, the highest being. Since the existence of all beings is considered analogous to the kind of ur-being presupposed in the respective ontology/metaphysics, how this Being is understood affects our understanding of every object, entity and event that exists. Understanding being in any of these ways is, however, itself merely an analogy, and according to Heidegger it is an analogy that is entirely inadequate to truly think the temporal or epochal nature of Being. While thinking of Being as the highest genus, as *summum ens* or being in general is quite helpful for many purposes, these are not the only ways to think 'being' analogously, and all the different analogical renderings of 'being' bring their own advantages and disadvantages.

Whether one now is of the view that existence is analogical or univocal, what cannot be denied is that there are various ways of understanding being, that there are various concepts of being that can be discussed and investigated.

Becoming Existence and Temporal Being

Traditionally, ontologies tended to allow for qualitative differences in existence or being – there 'is' the existence of substances and the existence of attributes, the existence of ideas and the existence of copies, the existence of God and the existence of material entities, and so forth. All these forms of being are characterised by different qualities and not by whether they exist or not – they all do exist (even though not all of them necessarily exist within any given ontological system). Still, most ontological systems were based on the presupposition that the primary type of being is the kind of being stones, things and objects have. Every*thing* that one could encounter in reality, so it was thought, is best explained with reference to this type of existence. The resulting forms of ontology, while allowing for a variation in being, do emphasise identity, re-identification, ontological independence and generally imply some form of essentially static fundament that is not subject to change.

More contemporary attempts at developing adequate ontologies include powers-ontologies, the ontologies of possible worlds or ontologies of fictional objects. Over the course of the last century ontologies have become less and less focused on describing the way material objects, i.e. three-dimensional physical entities (or Aristotelian primary substances), exist, and have begun to consider more and more exotic objects as genuine ontological objects. These variations of the paradigmatic entities that shape our understanding of being are making it much easier to think processuality or becoming as a concept of being. Given that becoming and perishing are fundamental aspects of the world in which we live and which we experience, the concept of being employed in our investigation of precisely this reality should be able to accommodate these characteristics. I therefore propose 'becoming existence' as a concept of being that is able to embrace these fundamental features of concrete reality. Becoming existence can be defined as the processes of becoming, being and perishing, and I hold that it is much more adequate as a tool to come to terms with concrete reality, as it is given in experience, than other concepts of being.

My approach to the question as to the nature of existing objects is rooted in the thought of Aristotle, who defined them as primary substances. Aristotle used at least four distinct terms to distinguish between different ways of investigating and understanding these primary substances. We generally use the term 'substance' for all four. Aristotle distinguishes 1) the *tode ti* (this there – the object of ostensive definition, i.e. the object that can be pointed out), 2) the *hypokeimenon* ('what has been thrown underneath', the substrate, the unchanging carrier of properties), 3) the *synholon* ('what together forms a whole', the hylemorphic compositum) and 4) the *ousia* (mostly translated as form or essence). Most classical ontological renderings of becoming (or change in general) attempt to dissolve the problem of becoming by explaining how the *hypokeimenon* or the *ousia* remain immutable through the process of becoming, so that the hylemorphic compositum can be considered to persist through all changes in its identity or essence. The *tode ti*, on the other hand, is usually not considered a viable point of departure when explaining becoming or change, since it does not allow for a distinction between changing and unchanging aspects. In contrast to most traditional ontological systems, dynamic ontologies do precisely depart from the experience of the *tode ti* (this there), as it is given.

The fundamental category of existence in dynamic ontologies that characterises the *tode ti* is becoming existence (or, in short, 'being' as defined at the beginning). Already on a linguistic level the term expresses an attempt to balance change ('becoming') and stability ('existence'). It refers to a way of being that is fundamentally processual or dynamic, but in such a way that this becoming creates continuity and stability. This way of thinking takes its cues from modern biology. Becoming beings are thought as patterns, structures and regularities, and not as absolutes that either exist or don't. Processes and the objects they constitute can be considered as either being more or less stable and robust or as more or less unstable and variable. Thus, from a process perspective, the objects that result from processes should not be considered either existent or non-existent. They are more or less stable singularities, more or less robust intersections of processes. Just as surface tension is the result of the tendency of water molecules to form weak bonds when in contact with air, processes form semi-stable objects in favourable circumstances. Thus, the substantial, apparently stable nature of reality that we also experience is a type of emergent phenomenon (very loosely defined). It does, however, emerge in such a way as to include the phenomenon of becoming, if investigated closely enough and for a sufficient amount of time.

From a traditional perspective, becoming existence appears to be a somewhat self-contradictory concept of being that attempts to unite processual becoming and stable existence. Hence such being does not exist in the full sense of the word, since a becoming or developing being does not yet fully exist, but does have some form of existence, and thus has to be thought as (at least somewhat) non-existent. This stands in clear contrast to the univocal understanding of being that characterises contemporary analytic philosophy, at least for those thinkers who take quantification to be fundamental. Here 'existence', especially in the modern reading of mere existence in the form of the existential quantifier, is generally used as an all-or-nothing sort of second-order predicate, which leaves no room for genuine becoming, or a form of being that is neither existing nor not existing. Mere existence, as expressed through the existential quantifier, implies that something either exists or does not exist, *tertium non datur*. Philosophers who refer back to Parmenides in their account of existence claim that there are some qualities (i.e. further predicates) implied by existence. These qualities implied by attributing or predicating existence as a univocal concept of being are, for example, the possession of diachronic self-identity, or unchangeableness, and so on. Most modern accounts, however, dispute even these minimal ascriptions (Tegtmeier 34), precisely because existence should not be considered a property or first-order predicate at all. The result of this understanding of existence as a second-order predicate *only* is an ideal understanding of mere (i.e. unqualified) existence, which is to be understood in purely functional terms. This functional understanding of existence as mere existence is the basis for the use of existential quantification in modern logic as well as much of contemporary ontology.

Mere existence as a concept of being is defined in such a way as not to imply any qualities whatsoever. Existence is to be understood as mere existence and nothing further, which makes any qualitative account of existence (including processual accounts) impossible. Thus, this account of existence cannot even capture the qualitative differences between existing as a becoming being, existing as a perishing being, or just existing as being present. If we remain in the realm of actual experience, there is, however, no doubt about it: the becoming x is not in quite the same way as the present x is, or the perishing x is. But mere existence has never been the only possible concept of being available to describe the way things are, nor does it need not be the only possible choice. *Mere existence* and *becoming existence* could be two (not necessarily competing) concepts of being, both adequate for certain investigations and inadequate for others. While mere existence is probably one of the most adequate ways to understand and analyse the concept of being we have in mind when we investigate meaning, or investigate the way we talk, reflect and reason about reality, I would argue that becoming existence is the most adequate concept of being if we want to describe and understand what there actually is, and thus the most adequate fundament for developing a dynamic realism.

There are two relevant aspects that separate the (generalised and simplified) analytic view presented above from my proposal on the level of philosophical logic, philosophy of language as well as metaphysics. From such an analytic view, it is the case 1) that existence (if 'existence' can be considered a predicate at all and not merely a copula or similar) is a second-order predicate and can therefore only be predicated of a property (i.e. a concept) and not an individual, and 2) that existence cannot be (functionally) defined through other terms, because it indicates 'mere existence' and thus cannot be grasped through reference to another property or quality. These central differences between this view and my view hinge on the Kantian idea that predicating existence does not add any information when predicated of an individual. This, as I hope to have convincingly argued, is not necessarily the case, or better, does not need to hold in all cases. While this Kantian stance is certainly logically consistent, and solves many conceptual problems in logical languages, it does not seem to provide the best heuristic to come to terms with actual, experiential reality and the way it is.

So, the question is as follows: do individuals instantiate a property or quality of being that can be called 'existence', and are various ways of defining 'existence' available, so that attributing existence to an individual does convey some information? My claim is that concrete individuals (i.e. processes) can and do in fact exist in a way that is best characterised by the hallmark features of reality described in this book. What is given through the senses tends to exist in the form of becoming being. This quality of being is situated towards one end of the spectrum. On the other end of the spectrum we have ideal logical structures, ideal numbers and so on. These thought-entities exist differently. My instinct would be to claim that they exist in the form of mere existence as described above, but I ultimately leave this to logicians who are much better equipped to answer this question than I am. In any case, much of what concerns the average philosopher exists between these extremes and tends to present as neither purely processual nor purely static or atemporal.

9

Being between Ontology and Epistemology

The Ontological Dimension

Every investigation begins with a question, but questions do not simply offer a new start. Questions are shaped not only by the experiences and thoughts that gave rise to them, but also by the preconceptions implicit in the terms used to phrase them. So, asking about the nature of what is real is, for example, not quite the same as asking for the nature of spatiotemporal reality. The first mode of asking after what there is allows for the reality of ideas, at least in a certain sense, while the second doesn't. In this way, minute aspects, ways of wording a question, preferring one phrase over other phrases can substantially change a question and ultimately lead to a very different investigation. Nonetheless, it is the question investigated in any given intellectual engagement that will provide the point of departure for the investigation in question. Being thus aware that the question one begins with has a conceptual history, I have chosen to frame my question in a way that should at the very least make its presuppositions explicit. So, the precise question that will ground and guide my investigation in this book is, as already mentioned in the first part, the following:

If this everyday world that we live in is to be taken to be what is real, as our actual, direct experience would suggest, what would the hallmark properties of this reality be? How would we characterise what there is as we encounter it in our everyday lives? This question focuses the flow of arguments on the most fundamental *properties*, *characteristics* or *ways of being* of what there is. So, instead of simply asking what there is, or what the basic constitutive elements of existence or being are, I am asking *how* reality exists, and thus focusing the investigation on qualitative ways of being. I am asking how we can adequately characterise what there is. Furthermore, I consider 'real' to refer to *the world we actually live in, the everyday reality surrounding us*, and I consider 'actual, direct experience' to be *a form of radicalised and clarified experience*. Both of these definitions are rooted in the preceding investigations, but I will provide a summary characterisation in what follows.

Real is the world that resists us

My favourite definition of what the term 'real' is, is offered by Philip K. Dick: 'Reality is that which, when you stop believing in it, doesn't go away.' According to this understanding, what there *is* are the train doors that are closing as I rush down the stairs of the station. What is real is the desk against which I regularly bang my shin. What there *is* is the tree that provides shade as I read my book while sitting underneath it. Whether I believe that trains and timetables are social constructions or not, I will not be on that train on the way to my appointment if the doors close just before I can board. Whether I feel the pain in my shin or not, whenever I try to take up the space currently occupied by my desk with my shin, my desk will stop my attempts to do so – every single time. Whether I appreciate the shade or not, it is there. All of these things stubbornly remain, whether or not I personally happen to perceive them or believe in them. There might be many more – and quite different – things that are also real, or that are real in a different sense, but at the least these things are real.

This stubborn resistance of the real is my main criterion for characterising what there is. There is something to reality that limits our intellectual as well as physical incorporation, adoption, construction or interpretation. As Maurizio Ferraris puts it:

'Strong, independent, stubborn: that's the world of objects surrounding us [. . .] We cannot change the world [. . .] at will [. . .]' (Ferraris, *Positive Realism* vii). It is this persisting and indomitable aspect of reality that is the only possible guideline for the development of a realistic stance. It is this aspect of reality that is not amenable to intellectual manipulation, and is thus the only aspect that can provide a standard against which we can measure the adequacy of our thoughts, interpretations and judgements.

This presupposition suggests that the resistance of what there is and our experience of it can be a tribunal for our thinking, as McDowell argues in *Mind and World*. He calls this stance 'minimal empiricism', and to him it simply entails that it is in the experience of an indomitable world, in the experience of a reality that does not conform to our thoughts, that we become aware of whether our thoughts actually respond to the world as it is given in experience, or whether they do not actually account for what is experienced:

> A belief or judgement to the effect that things are thus and so – a belief or judgement whose content (as we say) is that things are thus and so – must be a posture or stance that is correctly or incorrectly adopted according to whether or not things are indeed thus and so [. . .] Now how should we elaborate the idea that our thinking is thus answerable to the world? In addressing this question, we might restrict our attention, at least tacitly, to thinking that is answerable to the empirical world; that is, answerable to how things are in so far as how things are is empirically accessible [. . .] And now, how can we understand the idea that our thinking is answerable to the empirical world, if not by way of the idea that our thinking is answerable to experience? How could a verdict from the empirical world – to which empirical thinking must be answerable if it is to be thinking at all – be delivered, if not by way of a verdict from (as W. V. Quine puts it) 'the tribunal of experience'? (McDowell xi)[1]

---

1. This is possible for McDowell because he too holds that experience is neither pure passivity nor pure activity. With Kant he argues that experience is a collaboration between spontaneity and receptivity. In experience 'conceptual capacities are drawn on in receptivity' (McDowell 9). In effect

But what about all the idealistic and speculative forms of realism? What about the reality of numbers and laws? Do they not conform to exactly the same criteria as described above? Do the laws of nature not stubbornly remain, whether we believe in them (or think them) or not? Do they not resist us and thus limit our attempts at conceptually manipulating reality? Quentin Meillassoux, a 'Pythagorean' realist, is a realist in this sense. He believes that the primary qualities of things, i.e. what is mind-independent, are not uncovered through senses or through experience, but through mathematics. Thus, according to Meillassoux, only rational intuition or rational speculation can disclose actual reality. And while there are no a priori reasons that could ultimately justify why I begin my discussion of realism with experience/phenomenology and not with a form of rationalist idealism, I can provide some intuitions and a posteriori explanations for my inclination to consider experience a better basis for (speculative) dynamic realism than logical or conceptual investigations and pure speculation.

While the question of what is really real – either the rational order or law-governed structure that shapes and orders what there is, or the sensible qualitative givenness of what there is – is an eminent philosophical problem, in ordinary life and ordinary language use things seem to be a lot clearer. We distinguish easily and relatively clearly between what is real and what is ideal: real is what can be touched and experienced through the senses and ideal what can be grasped with the mind. And this is the use I would like to stick with. While both realms are 'real' in the sense that they can have effects, that they are able to affect our senses and influence our thinking, we tend to have no difficulties in distinguishing the concept of pain from actually feeling pain, or the ideal of love from the actual sensation of being loved. We furthermore unerringly label only one of them as

---

McDowell is thus reinterpreting the same inner-outer distinction that phenomenologists and process thinkers are attempting to navigate in new and fruitful ways.

actually real while considering the other merely conceptual or rooted in thought. I do admit that these are simple examples that favour my reading. The issue becomes more complex when we begin to investigate numbers and laws, social constructs or political parties. Ordinary language or simple intuition is much less helpful in complex cases such as these. But the question remains, should we consider the falling of the pen to be real, or the law of gravity that explains (or causes) this process? Should we consider the economy and the digital monetary values being moved around truly more real than the goods being traded?

While I am not able to fully address any of these questions here, I would settle for the claim that the ideal is at least not *more real* than what we are given in experience and thus has no stronger claim to the term 'real'. On the contrary, looking at ordinary language, the ideal seems to have less of a claim to the designation 'real' in many cases. As Gratton puts it in his book *Speculative Realism*: 'Realism, for most people, simply means a belief that there is a world independent of our minds or cultural beliefs' (Gratton 15). But let me be clear, this connection of the real with what can be experienced through the senses does not imply that the ideal does not exist, that it could be ignored, or that I am claiming that the ideal cannot ever be (causally) effective. I simply exclude the ideal aspects from my investigation – remaining agnostic as to their status – in order to get a handle on those aspects of what there is that my question focuses on, namely *the everyday world that we live in* as it is given in *our actual, direct experience*. Therefore, ideal objects are simply not within the scope of my investigation.

However, if pressed on this point, I would argue that here, too, we fall into the trap of the dichotomy of extremes – we focus on the extremes of the ideal and empirical/real instead of considering the various mixtures and combinations that we actually encounter, a mistake I made myself in the preceding paragraph. In this case too I would argue that, when it comes to the world we live in, both the purely experiential real and the purely speculative ideal are limit cases binding the extreme ends of the continuum of what there actually is. Our engagement with the world only discloses mixtures that become purer and purer the further one's investigation moves towards the extremes of the continuum. Since I have made clear from the beginning that I am attempting to understand the world we live in, beginning as close to engaged experience, i.e. the experiential, empirical and physical as possible, my beginning with sensible qualitative givenness is an adequate starting point.

What is new about this use of experience as a starting point?[2]

But how is this emphasis on experience new? Is it not the case that scientists and empiricists have defended such an emphasis on empirical data as a 'tribunal for our thinking' for years? Why hasn't empiricism with its focus on experience already shown reality to be fundamentally dynamic, if there really is such a correlation between direct experience and a dynamic reality, as I claim? The simplest answer that I can give to this objection is that empiricists generally do not focus on experience in a way that would enable them to see dynamic reality in its actuality. And the average scientist using the empirical method is more interested in specific problems and solutions, in discovering causal connections for example, or effective chemical structures, than in ways of understanding or describing the objects of experience adequately. This, of course, implies that there is a dichotomy, a bifurcation in the way we experience what there is (i.e. appearances) and the way we scientifically and rationally account for what there is (i.e. the inferred causes of the appearances).

This separation, between the world we experience and the world science describes, leads to scepticism and the sociopolitical problems we are currently observing: 'The bifurcation of nature is the road to scepticism because once nature is partitioned into these two systems, it is difficult, if not impossible, to provide

---

2. These paragraphs are partially based on Röck, 'Experiencing'.

a coherent explanation for how our ideas correspond to an unknowable external reality' (McHenry, *Event* 19). Whitehead notices the undue and almost invisible effect the focus on these scientific abstractions has on what we consider real and relevant and, in his philosophy, devises a conceptual scheme that is as free as possible from such abstractions and evaluations.

> What I am essentially protesting against is the bifurcation of nature into two systems of reality, which, in so far as they are real, are real in different senses. One reality would be the entities such as electrons that are the study of speculative physics. This would be the reality that is there for knowledge; although on this theory it is never known. For what is known is the other sort of reality, which is the byplay of the mind. (Whitehead, *Concept* 30)

The point here is to argue that our conceptual abstractions suggest such a distinction between a reality that is 'there for knowledge' and a reality that is the 'byplay of the mind'. But '[a]ll we know of nature is in the same boat, to sink or swim together. The constructions of science are merely expositions of the characters of things perceived' (Whitehead, *Concept* 148).

In what follows, I argue that one of the reasons for the disconnect between the way we experience reality and any conceptual or propositional (including scientific) accounts of reality is the fact that there is a fundamental structural difference between the complex, interconnected and messy multiplicity of *concrete reality*, i.e. the dynamic world we *actually live* in, and the ideally ordered world *as we conceptualise it* in thought. So, my claim is that concepts and the resulting propositions simply refer to an idealised (or abstracted version of) reality that cannot in principle provide quite the same complexity and detail as we are given in experience. It is this discrepancy in the level of complexity that distinguishes the world of our experience and the world as it is disclosed through concepts, language and knowledge.

What there is is so detailed, complex and dynamically related that it can never be captured fully through propositional language. Predicates, concepts and judgements (with the potential exception of proper names) are simply much less specific or detailed than our experiences, and with good reason. Linguistic tools are general, they need to apply to and be useful for a variety of situations, and therefore by their very nature they are unable to grasp or express concrete individual differences adequately. As Nietzsche puts it:

> Let us contemplate in particular the formation of concepts: every word becomes a concept, not just when it is meant to serve as a kind of reminder of the single, absolutely individualized original experience to which it owes its emergence, but when it has to fit countless more or less similar – that is, strictly speaking, never equal, hence blatantly unequal – cases. Every concept arises by means of the equating of the unequal. (Nietzsche 27)

The great power of language is rooted precisely in this ability to transmit relevant information clearly by disregarding the details and aspects that are not relevant for present purposes of communication. This is the advantage of abstract and general concepts and is what makes them so incredibly powerful. This is the reason why we use language, why judgements and propositions allow for logical deductions, and why intellectual manipulation can lead to further insights into general structures. Without these tools we would be stuck with the concrete singular. Without the power to abstract and generalise, we would remain bound to the immediate and the present. However, it is precisely this power that can lead us astray when it comes to accounting for reality, in its temporal, related and messy actuality, since what there is and what is thus given is always more singular, complex and malleable than our concepts suggest. '[W]e should be aware that [. . .] the world is given as positivity, as wealth, as an offer of objects that are much finer grained than the concepts with which we try to demarcate them' (Ferraris, *Positive Realism* viii).

If we want to understand the concrete reality we live in, not in abstraction, but in its concreteness, we thus have no choice but to begin with experience. But let me be clear. I am not trying to imply that we should remain with lived experience. Actual experience is our starting point; it provides the data we begin with and it provides a measuring rod against which we can assess the results of our speculations. But lived experience is not and cannot be the limit of our intellectual engagement, without seriously damaging our ability to develop new ways of thought, new technologies and new ways to flourish. I am also not trying to suggest that this starting point is adequate for any and every investigation and should thus be adopted by every philosopher. Again, the adequacy and the relevance of this approach depends on the object studied and the questions that are to be answered.

It is also important to note that language cannot be reduced to propositions in the sense introduced above. It is a mistake to reduce language to a medium that allows for judgements about truth and falsehood about the contents mediated. Language is more than a set of sentences or propositions that can be investigated as to their truth-value:

> Unfortunately theories, under their name of 'propositions,' have been handed over to logicians, who have countenanced the doctrine that their one function is to be judged as to their truth or falsehood [. . .] The existence of imaginative literature should have warned logicians that their narrow doctrine is absurd. It is difficult to believe that all logicians as they read Hamlet's speech, 'To be, or not to be: . . .' commence by judging whether the initial proposition be true or false, and keep up the task of judgment throughout the whole thirty-five lines. Surely, at some point in the reading, judgment is eclipsed by aesthetic delight. (Whitehead, *Process* 184–5)

Phenomenological descriptions, for example, allow for a way through this dichotomy between what there is and our conceptual accounts, since here language is not reduced to a vehicle for the transmission of judgeable data. *A description is neither true nor false, it is adequate or inadequate.* Furthermore, many phenomenologists actively shape or coin words and reshape the use of language to fit the experience, and phenomenological descriptions remain continuously open to revisions and adaptations.

There is no ultimate description, only more or less adequate as well as more or less detailed descriptions. Therefore, descriptions are sensitive to details, complexity and changes.

Finally, a phenomenological description is much more sensitive to the investigative perspective taken than a propositional account or a definition. Descriptions are thus explicitly research-context sensitive as well as sensitive to changes in the phenomena. Descriptions attempt to retain as much of the original phenomenon as possible, but with (at least) adequate complexity, while concepts, judgements and propositions are formed with a different aim, namely, to convey an ultimate – an ultimate essence, structure, nature or, and most of all, an ultimate answer – irrespective of the investigative perspective, the concrete changes and developments going on and irrespective of all the currently unfolding creative processes. Thus, phenomenological descriptions provide a more adequate tool to account for what there is than traditional (i.e. conceptual and propositional) approaches.

Towards Dynamic Realism: Engaged Experience[3]

Having thus clarified why it is adequate, in this case, to begin with actual experience and with open-ended descriptions instead of clear propositions or concepts in order to reveal the world as fundamentally dynamic, it is now time to clarify and define the method or approach that allows me to combine process thought, phenomenology and a focus on experience, namely 'engaged experience'. While phenomenology usually interprets actual experience as lived experience, we need to go a bit further to accommodate also the processual and ontological perspectives. I use the term 'engaged experience' to refer to this specific form of actual experience that bridges the epistemology–ontology divide.

In order to introduce engaged experience, I will first highlight in what respects traditional empirical and scientific ways

---

3. These paragraphs are partially based on Röck, 'Experiencing'.

of thinking and understanding experience (such as scientific empiricism) fall short of engaged experience. I will thus first provide a sort of negative definition of what engaged experience is not, before moving on to discuss how engaged experience can be understood positively.[4]

A processual approach to what engaged experience is not

Many contemporary philosophers seem to agree that the scientific method is the best, for some even the only, method to account for the structure of our experiences and to learn about the natural world. The two most influential thinkers of dynamic reality, Bergson and Whitehead, however, while having great respect for the scientific method, still contend that there is a role that philosophy can play in discovering and understanding experience as well as nature. They agree that there is something to reality that the scientific method cannot adequately account for and that we can access it through *engaged experience*.

---

4. Pragmatism too begins its investigation with a radicalised understanding of experience. There is a curious historical fact that situates William James's radical empiricism within a broadly phenomenological tradition. One year after Husserl's first use of the term 'phenomenology' in his *Logical Investigations*, Charles Sanders Peirce used the term to characterise the philosophy he was developing. In a letter to James about his essay 'Does Consciousness Exist?', Peirce compares his phenomenology to James's radical empiricism, and his descriptions also characterise Husserl's phenomenology: 'As I understand you, then, the proposition you are arguing is a proposition in what I called phenomenology, that is just the analysis of what kind of constituents there are in our thoughts and lives [. . .] Phenomenology has no right to appeal to logic, except to a deductive logic. On the contrary, logic must be founded on phenomenology. Psychology, you may say, observes the same facts as phenomenology does. No. It does not observe the same facts. It looks upon the same world [. . .] but what it observes in that world is different' (Peirce, *Collected Papers* 204). While there is not enough room in this book to take a close look at the understanding of experience in the pragmatist tradition and how it relates to phenomenological and processual ways of understanding experience, pragmatism provides a further way of reading experience as engaged.

So why precisely does science fall short when it comes to accessing and understanding what there is? One reason for this shortfall, which both Bergson and Whitehead agree on, is the necessary amount of abstraction involved in empirical and scientific investigations. While the immense usefulness of the sciences depends on a certain degree of abstraction, the overuse of abstractions in attaining knowledge through this method can create difficulties. Reality is split into a nature for us, which we can experience, and an objective nature that only scientists can truly access. This doubling of reality into a world of perception and a 'real world' of science beyond perception implies that 'the reality of the external world is never known but only conjectured, while the reality of appearances is known but remains purely mental or dreamlike' (McHenry, *Event* 19).

The disregard of subjectivity, experience or feelings in scientific investigations, and the correlated bifurcation of nature, is a result of the scientific method, which is not problematic for scientific progress itself, because scientists aim to

> enlarge our influence over things. Science may be speculative in its form, disinterested in its immediate ends: in other words we may give it as long a credit as it wants. But, however long the day of reckoning may be put off, some time or other the payment must be made. It is always then, in short, practical utility that science has in view. Even when it launches into theory, it is bound to adapt its behaviour to the general form of practice. (Bergson, *Creative Evolution* 358)

Such practical or informative results are much more easily obtained if the seemingly irrelevant pieces of information are disregarded; if we do not account for all that is experienced and instead focus on what appears relevant for the specific question at hand. This focus on creating useful or at least potentially useful knowledge should dissolve any doubt as to why these practical scientific strategies do not disclose reality as it really is – this is simply not the aim of such investigations. The nature of reality as such is just not an issue investigated by most scientists, nor is this question at the heart of most experiments.

More often than not, it is the philosophers who engage with specific scientific results, over-generalise them and apply them to reality in general in order to construct a new grand theory. If philosophers thus end up considering scientific concepts to be *more real* or a better guide to what there is than our experiences and feelings, then they commit the *fallacy of misplaced concreteness*, by considering atoms, gravity or black holes *more real* or at least *more fundamental* than the data provided by the world as it appears in our experience. In contrast, Whitehead argues that the concrete world we experience is *at least as real* as the world described by mathematics and science. Gravity, atoms and electromagnetism are, for instance, hugely useful and successful concepts or models, but they are not more real (or more fundamental, or even more objective) than the warmth of the sun that I can feel on my skin or the taste of an apple. It is always our body that first engages, that first feels or experiences the effects in the perceptual mode of causal efficacy that we then attribute to a scientific concept. Even the most abstract scientific concept is based on and abstracted from the engaged experiences we have. If we had no experience of the effects of 'gravity' at all, there simply would be no need for such a concept. In concrete engaged experience there is no absolute difference between the effects of gravity on our body and other experiences or feelings; these experiences vary only in degree, but not in kind. So, Whitehead contends, it makes no sense to accord gravity in its abstracted form a central status within physics while at the same time disregarding all other engaged experiences (or 'feelings', in Whitehead's terminology). As Whitehead puts it, the 'sharp division between mentality and nature has no ground in our fundamental observation. We find ourselves living within nature' (Whitehead, *Modes* 156)

Moving towards engaged experience

One fundamental problem in accounting for experience is rooted in the fact that we tend not to separate our reactions to and judgements about experience from the experience proper. This leads to a distorted understanding of experience. A good example of a conceptual distortion of experience is the claim that we can distinguish between primary and secondary properties, that some of the properties that we perceive are caused by the object alone, while others are the result of a perceptual interaction between the mind and the object. In considering experience without presuppositions, this distinction between what is given (primary property) and what needs our judgement or interpretation of experience (secondary property) cannot be argued by pointing to experience alone. The distinction between primary and secondary properties itself is not given in experience. It is a consequence of the bifurcation of nature, i.e. the distinction between the appearances or phenomena that we can experience and what we consider the (objective) cause of this experience.

All that we can actually experience are properties, and there is no immediate way of clearly distinguishing primary properties from secondary ones. In order to be able to make such a distinction, we need to bifurcate nature and introduce some further criterion that characterises objective existence, but that is not given to experience like the other qualities. This criterion tends to be the quality of being mathematically determinable with certainty. This is an ideal criterion, since it is not given directly, but can be made manifest through the acts of measuring and calculating.[5] So, the main way to distinguish primary from secondary qualities is the fact that primary qualities are

---

5. If we move to a more abstract level, from objects to matter, for example, the same structure holds. Matter is conceived as simply located, as taking up a defined extension of geometrical space, and is thus describable and measurable through geometrical modes of thought. However, modern physics, as Whitehead and others point out, seems to imply that the fundamental elements are not necessarily tied to one simple location. For a detailed discussion of this analogous line of thought, see Debaise, *Nature* 15, and consider Whitehead's discussion and rejection of simple location in *Process and Reality*.

objectively determinable, which I take to mean that they are measurable. Thus, what renders primary qualities primary is the fact that, as soon as a standard of measurement has been agreed upon, any and every correct measuring will get the same result. In contrast, secondary qualities are conceived as qualities that cannot be measured objectively, which means that philosophers were not able to quantify and standardise them in such a way as to allow recurring measurements to lead to the exact same result. However, modern science has undercut this seemingly clear distinction. If we wanted to measure length by being exact on a quantum level its status as a primary quality might become a little more problematic, while measuring wavelengths that determine colour or heat has become a fairly straightforward procedure.

I do not actually wish to argue for or against the primary status of the property of being coloured. I am simply trying to argue that the distinction between primary and secondary qualities is not rooted in experience, but in a certain way of understanding and measuring experience. This distinction is helpful for some investigations, and thus I see no reason to do away with it, but we should keep in mind that this understanding of experience is not really an empirical distinction, but a highly conceptual one. Most philosophical ways of understanding empirical experience suffer from a similar level of conceptualisation. Phenomenology is the attempt to minimise these levels of conceptualisation. Husserl, for example, proposes a similar argument with regard to the sense data theory of experience. He explains that if we investigate experience closely enough, we do not perceive sets of sense data. On the contrary, we always experience something. Only in further investigation can we analyse what is given in perception and distinguish various sense data, qualia or primary and secondary qualities from other components of the experience. So, to begin one's investigation of experience and its contents with qualia or sense data means to have already lost actual experience.

Husserl's account of what is actually given in experience consequently differs widely from what we usually consider experience to be. The object of experience, for example, is never given in isolation. It always appears in a concrete context, it has a background (whether I focus on it or not) and appears to the perceiver from a certain perspective against this background. This relation of foreground and background is furthermore correlated to my corporeal movements. If I see an apple, for example, I can walk towards it. If I do so, I expect it to become larger in my visual field. Any change in the placement of my head, the focus of my eyes or the position of my body changes the perception of the given object, if the object is given in actual sense experience. And there are quite specific ways in which the changes in my movements correlate to the appearance of the object. Husserl calls these movements and orientations of one's body that correlate to changes in what is given '*Kinaesthesen*'.[6]

While it is possible for me to make a wrong judgement about the nature of the apple and mistake a very realistic image for a real apple, this mistake will become clear as soon as I try to engage further with the apple; if, for example, I try to grasp or eat it. It is worth noting at this point that is precisely the expectation that I can eat the apple that motivates me to move towards it and attempt to bite into it. Husserl refers to this primitive form of expectation that colours all our sensory experience as 'protention'. Only thanks to this expectation can we be surprised by the fact that it is not an apple that I am experiencing but an image. We can only be surprised by experiences that *do not conform* to these expectations. So, only if there is a connection between past expectation and current experience, only if my past expectation is somehow present in the current failure to grasp the apple, will I be surprised. Husserl calls this continuation of the past into the present 'retention'.

---

6. In *Matter and Memory* (published 1896) Bergson discusses similar ideas in introducing his ontology of 'images' as a way to sidestep the opposition between 'representation' and 'thing in itself' in traditional ontologies. In this conception, the orientation of the body and its role in the constitution of perception is just as central as it is in Husserl's thought.

A further interesting aspect of sense experience is the fact that we can move around an object, thus causing changes in our perception, and still have the object given as one single object. When I move around the table for example, I experience a shift in the forms and shapes, but I only experience one table that has different sides, which I cannot actually see all at once. These different sides are co-present in my experience of the table, but not directly given, as long as I do not move around the table. Husserl calls this aspect of spatiotemporal phenomena adumbrations (*Abschattungen*). Furthermore, looking closely enough, we see that objects do not have uniform colours even when looked at from one side. The table has some brighter, some duller spots, there is a perceptual difference in even the smallest extension of colour; furthermore, these colours shift and change with our movements and with the passing of time. Ultimately, there is no single stable colour that constitutes the colour of the table, but a variation of colours that add up to what we call 'the colour' of the table.[7]

So, for Husserl, even the most mundane experience is not only a complex interaction between inner and outer, between body, movement and appearance, but also a complex interaction between foreground and background, inner and outer horizons,

---

7. Bertrand Russell claimed that our common-sense account of experience, which tends to imply a constancy of colour, is a mere convention. To say that the table has 'a colour' is to tacitly imply that for 'a normal spectator from an ordinary point of view under usual conditions of light' a colour appears, and that this is the 'real' colour of the table (Russell, *Problems* 2). But do we have to succumb to such conventionalism, especially when it comes to understanding concrete reality in its complexity? Or are there ways to account for the fact that properties are both constant and varied and still maintain a transcendental realism, as phenomenology does? Husserl's answer is that it is not actually the colour or the shape of the table that changes when we move. What changes instead is merely the way the table is adumbrated: 'One and the same shape (given "in person" as the same) appears continuously but always "in a different manner", always in different adumbrations of shape' (Husserl, *Ideas I* §87).

as well as past, present and future.[8] Actual experience is thus much more than merely noticing, registering and representing of data, and thus a lot more complex than most empirical accounts suggest. If we furthermore acknowledge that experience exists in the world, insofar as we as experiencing subjects are part of this objective world, then experience is more than a merely epistemological problem. It is also an ontological problem. This dual structure not only holds for experience, but for consciousness in general; it is an essential feature of the life of the mind. Thus, it is adequate to talk about two aspects in accounting for consciousness (and, *mutatis mutandis*, for experience):

> (1) *Empirically* it is contained in the world; (2) *Cognitively* it contains the world. Although these relations are coeval, their joint understanding faces the difficulty that whereas the empirical relation is accessible to natural inquiry, the cognitive relation is not. Empirical knowledge can only presuppose it; reflection alone can clarify it. (Chapman 79)

This understanding of experience as an objective and ontological part of the world also undercuts the traditional epistemological distinctions between purely subjective experience and objective data, and renders experience an interactive and subjective-objective form of engagement.

So far, I have shown how interconnected, correlated and integrated experience actually is, and how these complex and interactive structures are often overlooked in traditional accounts of experience. In a final step, I now try to give a positive account of engaged experience, and of how engaged experience can take advantage of this dual structure to uncover what there is as it is.

---

8. In this case too, Bergson discusses similar issues. However, he does so, not regarding perception, but with regard to ontological and metaphysical questions, namely temporality, change and presence. Bergson argues that the past is retained and is indivisible from the present; he is, however, more interested in the 'automatic' (Bergson, *Creative Mind* 153) and absolute preservation of the past in every present, and the resulting 'undivided' and durational 'present' (Bergson, *Creative Mind* 152).

Engaged experience

As the term suggests, 'engaged experience' amounts to an active and engaged understanding of experience. It is thus situated between the activity of being engaged and the passivity of experiencing. Engaged experience is actively engaged in two ways. First, it is engaged in actively uncovering as clearly as possible common preconceptions that shape our common-sense understanding and use of sense experience. This engagement is situated on the level of epistemology and is focused on preventing misinterpretations of what experience is and of what experiences can uncover. Its aim is to free actual experience from the conceptual frameworks that make it so tricky to see what is given instead of seeing what we think we see (e.g. sense data or primary and secondary qualities). The less active conceptual influence we layer on top of what is actually given, the more what there is can shine through. This aspect of active liberation is a matter of degree. And while we might never be fully rid of conceptual frameworks and preconceptions, it is worth trying to be as free of these conceptual hindrances as possible in order to minimise conceptual distortions.

This first aspect of engagement in engaged experience puts us in the seemingly contradictory position of having to work at developing an adequate practice of experience before we can experience adequately. Experience is not naturally accessible to us in its most adequate form, nor do we have immediate access to its most adequate definition. There is, however, a fundamental problem inherent to this approach, namely the fact that we always already are experiencing beings. There is no outside of experience from which we could examine, probe and investigate experience 'objectively'. So, engaged experience can only happen haphazardly, while we experience, in the course of experiencing, and it cannot be considered a preparatory step to be taken before experience begins – there is no *before experience for the essentially experiencing beings that we are*. We need to learn to see while we are engaged in seeing; we can only uncover engaged experience while we are experiencing.

So, on the one hand, engaged experience is engaged in an attempt to shed preconceptions, and in this sense it has a lot in common with the project of phenomenology. Engaged experience is, however, also engaged in a second, ontological sense. It describes an experience that is directly engaged with what is experienced. Engaged experience is thus conceived as a form of direct and immediate and interactive access to what there is – without leading to immediate knowledge about what there is. In Bergson, this aspect of experience is expressed through the metaphors of entering into the object through sympathy. This aspect of engaged experience is roughly equivalent to what Whitehead describes as 'causal efficacy'. However, this direct grasping or immediate feeling becomes noticeable only because of what I have described as the first sense of being engaged as part of engaged experience, precisely because we are not as distracted by preconceptions and thus are more receptive to actual experience. Secondly, such direct access is possible because on an ontological level we as experiencing beings are part of this world, just as our experience is part of this world.

In sum, two things can be said about engaged experience. First, it engages in minimising subjective distortions and conceptual structuring of what is experienced and tries to allow for the world to actively structure experience. And secondly, this direct structuring of the subject/mind/perception by the world is possible because we as experiencing beings are always already intimately related to the world and integrated into the world on an ontological level. At this point, I would like to provide my usual caveat and emphasise that engaged experience does not stand in conflict or competition with more traditional ways of understanding experience as registration and representation. It is simply a further way to understand and engage with experience. I would like to emphasise further that it is not the case that every moment of experience should always only be investigated as a form of engaged experience. On the contrary, a focus on engaged experience and what is given in engaged experience is not necessarily helpful in answering most scientific questions or in answering most of the practical questions we are confronted with every day.

So far, I have laid out my project by establishing the idea of more or less adequate correlations between thinking and being, between epistemological approaches and the kind of reality that they can uncover. I have also taken the time to root these claims in the traditions that I make most use of, phenomenology and process thought, using a more historical and scholarly approach. I have finally introduced the idea of engaged experience as an epistemic/ontological approach that is able to uncover a dynamic reality. Now it is time to apply all of these results to the question of what there is, to properly begin the search for the hallmark properties of what is real from within the correlation between phenomenology and process thought, i.e. engaged experience.

10

Uncovering the Real as Physical: Naturalism and Materialism

Let me begin the search for the hallmark properties of the real by looking at a common-sense contemporary interpretation of what it means for something to be 'real': the real is what the positive sciences uncover and describe. In order to probe this intuition, I will take a look at naturalism, scientific realism and reductionism. Whether the claims of science are considered true propositions about what there is, or whether they are merely conceptual constructs that in some way relate to reality, to many the practical and technological advances made possible by science indicate that the scientific method can provide some privileged access to the real. These kinds of positions are generally considered to be 'naturalistic' (or 'physicalistic').[1]

Here too we can distinguish an ontological as well as an epistemological dimension. The term 'naturalism' indicates the ontological claim that only natural laws and forces are considered real; everything that is exists as part of the causal nexus governing spatiotemporal reality. This leads to the epistemological conclusion that all phenomena can and should be explained in terms of natural laws and physical causes. Scientific realism combines this position with the additional claim that these scientific

---

1. For the purposes of this book I do not clearly distinguish between 'naturalism', 'materialism' and 'physicalism', even if there are contentious ongoing debates about whether this is adequate or not. However, since the various positions overlap substantially with regard to the issues at stake here, the distinctions are not relevant for present purposes.

explanations provide the best way to grasp to what there is: 'It is the thesis that most of the unobservable entities posited by our best scientific theories actually exist, and exist independent of our minds, conceptual schemes, and the like' (Greenough and Lynch 5). Thus, a *scientific realist* will claim that scientific propositions, theories and models are our best bet, if we want to discover what actually is real. Considering that scientists have discovered so many successful, testable, provable and practically useful insights, and generated useful descriptions of what there is, descriptions that *work* (at least on the levels of magnitude commonly accessible to humans or used in feats of engineering and for technological advances), it is no surprise that we first look to science for an adequate account of what there is.

This interpretation of the real as what scientists work with, as what can be discovered through scientific methods, could thus provide a very stable epistemic foundation to uncover the real. However, in pursuing this path, we face the problem that scientists themselves are not quite convinced that what they describe is the actual reality, nor do most scientists seem convinced that they have found a definitive answer to the question of what is. Usually, scientists prefer to work in terms of likely hypotheses and testable theories, making no claims as to the truth of these theories, or the reality of the entities and laws that these theories imply. Generally speaking, science does not deal in truths but in degrees of persuasiveness and conviction. Therefore, it seems somewhat presumptuous (and rather unscientific) to claim that science can and should tell us once and for all (with certainty) what is real. And philosophy does not seem adequate to convince scientists of the certainty or truth of their hypothetical claims. It does seem quite wrongheaded to advise physicists to unquestioningly accept and presuppose the laws of logic or to accept a priori reasoning, as implied by scientific realism, even if there is no empirical evidence for it (Markosian). I agree with Ladyman and Ross when they argue that '[p]hysicists do not believe there are such things as good a priori grounds for holding beliefs about the constitution of the physical world, and we suggest that only a foolhardy philosopher should be willing to quarrel with them on the basis of his or her hunches' (Ladyman and Ross 18).

Instead of being able to leave this question to science, philosophy has to follow its own path in testing and reflecting on the nature of natural laws and the status of scientific models. So, in what sense are these kinds of laws, structures or things, presupposed and sometimes even successfully predicted by science, 'real'? They are not directly given in experience, so how can they provide us with a better understanding of the real world we live in? In German Idealism there is a way to understand 'real' that can aid at this point. The German terms for 'real' and 'reality', namely *wirklich* and *Wirklichkeit*, emphasise a central effective and dynamic aspect in their rendering of what is real. Ultimately, what is real is simply what has an effect (*Wirkung*) – efficacy determines what is real, it is the hallmark property of the real. This understanding of the real as that which can have an effect has a long philosophical history. Plato, the first idealist, already suggested this understanding of the real in the *Sophist*. He maintains that being is the δύναμις (the power/ability) to affect and to be affected (*Sophist* 247e). Whatever can exert an influence and thus have an effect or suffer an effect is to be considered to be and to be real.

If we adopt this understanding of 'real' as that which has an effect, without further qualification, in order to understand how entities such as atoms or natural laws are real, then many things beyond natural laws or exotic particles fall under this same understanding of the real. By this definition a dream or an idea is just as real, i.e. effective, as a stone. Maybe even more real, since ideas, ideals and images are able to mobilise entire generations (consider the ideals of 'Liberté, Égalité, Fraternité' that changed the world) and in all likelihood have bigger and arguably more lasting effects on society than a stone or a particle might have on anything it comes into causal contact with. Thus, if to be real is to bring forth or suffer action or change, if it is to be effective, then ideals, ideas and concepts should be considered actually real, while stones or particles, being quite effectually inert, turn out to be inadequate candidates for a paradigmatic understanding of what is real. While it is not surprising that this is a position that most idealists would hold, not too many scientists or scientific realists would agree with this account of what is real. Therefore, in order to render this concept of reality as efficacy scientifically valid and valuable, a second criterion needs to be introduced, one that will help us to exclude ideals and dreams, but that will still allow us to include all manner of scientific objects, from particles and stones up to forces and constructs such as dark matter.

Measurability could provide a very useful additional criterion here. So, the hallmark properties of the real would be 1) to be able to exert an influence or suffer an effect and 2) to be amenable to mathematical treatment, i.e. to be measurable and quantifiable. So, something's reality would then be bound to and determined by *efficacy* as well as by *being measurable against a scale*. And I do think it is fair to claim that the scientific worldview presupposes *measurable effectiveness* as the hallmark property of the real. However, in making this move from the real as effective to the real as effective and quantifiable, a quite subjective epistemological qualification slipped into our discussion, since *only what humans can measure and thus quantify is actually quantifiable*. Nature does not measure itself; it is the human mind that measures against a scale. For present purposes it is now quite inconsequential whether the possibility to be quantified is an ontological property, a power, or merely the result of an epistemic process. Even if the possibility to be quantified is an ontological property, disposition or power, that does not change the fact that this property, disposition or power is still only realised or accessible via actually measuring the object in possession of this quality, or by realising or actualising this power through measuring it. We can determine whether something is actually ('really') quantifiable only via the epistemic process of measuring – which is a subjective process.

Whether this introduction of a subject-relative definition in a scientific, objective account of the hallmark properties of what is real is argumentatively sound and not simply a category mistake is at least debatable. Be that as it may, the simple fact that only the effective quantifiable aspects of reality are the proper objects of investigation for modern experimental science does not provide any argumentative basis for the hypothesis that these properties most fundamentally or even adequately characterise what there is. This would only be the case if we wanted to define 'real' exclusively as that which can be described by scientific means – which a priori excludes fields of study such as aesthetics and morality, as well as issues such as intentionality and phenomenologically given quality. And the effectiveness of scientific discoveries alone does not provide a sufficient ground to limit reality to what can be quantified.

Science ultimately draws from two sources, namely empirical experience as well as conceptual presuppositions (a vision of reality that grounds the empirical investigations), i.e. an interpretation of what there is. Science

> has been in large part the history of a marriage between two sources of inspiration. One source is our probing of the manifest world, through observation and experiment, conditioned by our success at inventing and deploying equipment that enables us to extend or exceed our powers of perception. The other source is a vision of reality at the center of which there often stands an ontological program: a view of the kinds of things that there ultimately are and of the ways in which they connect. Such were the ontological programs associated with the science of Aristotle, of Newton, and of Einstein. (Unger and Smolin xiii)

One challenge for scientific realism is thus to 'distinguish what we in fact know – the hard empirical residue of scientific discovery – from the lens of assumptions through which we are accustomed to see the larger significance of these factual findings' (Unger and Smolin xiii). Whether such a clear-cut distinction is in fact possible is doubtful. Most forms of realism of the twentieth and twenty-first centuries that were grounded in science and its methodology relied heavily on the presupposition of a lawfully ordered material and physical universe, on what Unger and Smolin call the Newtonian paradigm:

> Under the Newtonian paradigm, we construct a configuration space within which the movements and changes of a certain range of phenomena can be explained by unchanging laws. The range of experience defined by the configuration space and explained by the laws can in principle be reproduced, either by being found in another part of the universe or by being deliberately copied by the scientist. The recurrence of the same movements and the same changes under the same conditions, or the same provocations, confirms the validity of the laws. (Unger and Smolin 19)

And while this procedure based on reproducibility has led to unrivalled insights into aspects of what there is, it is an inadequate approach to cosmology (i.e. the metaphysics of the natural world) and ontology. This methodology, by its very nature, is inadequate to understand the universe including its becoming (the history of our universe), i.e. reality as a whole, since there is only one single reality available to us as observable. Any claim about the structure or performance of the whole is necessarily unrepeatable and thus not amenable to the scientific method strictly speaking. In the case of cosmology, it 'is no longer thinkable, even in principle, to prepare or even to discover copies for what we are to explain, now the entire universe, so that we can test the constant validity of the laws' (Unger and Smolin 21). Not even the idea of a multiverse or parallel universes can offer a way out, as these constructs implied by mathematical calculations and speculations are unobservable.[2]

---

2. There are many further problems with using any multiverse theory to avoid these issues. Consider the following: 'Deaf to Newton's warning not to feign hypotheses, we may appeal to the idea of multiple, parallel universes in an effort to rescue the cosmological uses of the Newtonian paradigm. If, however, these other universes are, as they must be, causally unconnected with our own, and no light-borne information can travel from them to us, this conjecture will amount to no more than a vain metaphysical fantasy, disguised as science' (Unger and Smolin 21).

The Epistemology of Scientific Materialism or Physicalism

Let me look at a variation of understanding the real as what is material or physical, namely scientific materialism or physicalism. Both positions are considered to be reductive and imply that what is real can be explained by reference to matter and material interactions alone. This means that even phenomena such as consciousness and the like are considered to be reducible to a material or physical basis. While scientific materialists generally hold that all phenomena are to be explained by reference to physical matter and its law-governed interactions alone, physicalists restrict what they consider to be meaningful statements to claims about physical elements, bodies or processes that are in principle verifiable. Thus, a materialist will generally hold that any phenomenon can be explained by reducing it to its constitutive matter and its law-governed interactions with other bits of matter, while a physicalist will consider things such as space-time, forces, dark matter and so on to be irreducibly fundamental in any account of what there is. But this distinction is tenuous, and there are many thinkers who consider 'materialism' and 'physicalism' to be synonymous.

However, these sorts of positions hinge on how 'matter' or its modern equivalent, 'physical elements, bodies or processes', are understood. Both materialists as well as physicalists tend to conceive of matter or physical existence as tangible or measurable stuff that makes up reality; whether this stuff is string-like, particle-like, or takes any other form does not make a substantial difference for my argument. The resulting understanding of material nature is usually that of a lawfully organised sum of pieces of matter (or strings and so on), that do *not* have any *internal principle of movement*.[3] By this I mean that these pieces of natural matter remain inert, over any length of time, if no external forces

---

3. This phrase will be discussed in more detail in the following chapters. But just to quickly outline what is meant, the main difference between such physicalist/naturalist and processual approaches is that from a processual

have an effect on them and cause them to move or transform. If nature is thus understood, it becomes inherently stable and static, and its material pieces are only connected through spatial as well as causal relations.

Even though reductive materialism or physicalism have been very influential points of view, it is not at all clear that the terms 'matter' or 'physical existence' actually have a unified meaning or that we are in possession of a unified understanding of them. Within the analytic tradition, matter is generally understood either as composed of 'partless particles' (i.e. atoms) or as 'gunk', where 'every part has a proper part' (i.e. infinitely divisible matter). Ladyman, Ross and Spurrett argue that these options were debated first by Democritus and Anaxagoras, discussed again by Boyle, Locke and Gassendi on the side of the atomists, and Descartes and Leibniz on the side of the gunkists:

> It is preposterous that in spite of the developments in the scientific understanding of matter that have occurred since then, contemporary metaphysicians blithely continue to suppose that the dichotomy between atoms and gunk remains relevant, and that it can be addressed a priori. Precisely what physics has taught us is that matter in the sense of extended stuff is an emergent phenomenon that has no counterpart in fundamental ontology. (Ladyman and Ross 20)

There are, however, ways to understand matter that are not based on the idea of smallest spatial parts or infinitely divisible matter, that do remain more in line with contemporary scientific results by remaining faithful to the actual dynamicity and complexity of the kinds of real compositions that are described by science. For example, on closer inspection, seemingly static material composita such as H_2O are actually 'constantly forming, dissipating, and reforming over short time periods in such a way as to give rise to the familiar properties of the macroscopic kind

---

perspective every process (this includes material entities such as stones) has some form of internality or perspective that contributes to its development.

water' (Ladyman and Ross 21). But this issue does not only apply to material composita, it applies to matter in general. 'The Newtonian description of matter abstracts matter from time. It conceives matter "at an instant". So does Descartes' description' (Whitehead, *Modes* 88–9). Instead of considering this view of matter 'at an instant' merely a useful conceptual abstraction, many philosophers of science take it as an accurate description. However, for Whitehead,

> it is nonsense to conceive of nature as a static fact, even for an instant devoid of duration. There is no nature apart from transition, and there is no transition apart from temporal durations. This is the reason why the notion of an instant of time, conceived as a primary simple fact, is nonsense. (Whitehead, *Modes* 152)

We are committing the *fallacy of misplaced concreteness* if we think matter 'at an instant', as essentially eternal or atemporal. This specific instant of the fallacy of misplaced concreteness, Whitehead terms the *fallacy of simple location*. This fallacy is rooted in the doctrine of external relations that characterises the Newtonian and Cartesian descriptions of matter, which presupposes that material entities are fundamentally non-relational, i.e. simply located in both space and time. Any material entity is thus thought to be located 'in a definite finite region of space, and throughout a definite finite duration of time, apart from any essential reference of the relations of the bit of matter to other regions of space and to other durations in time' (Whitehead, *Science* 58).

If, however, matter or material composita are not considered to be simply located nor static, then this leaves room for a more complex, interrelated and dynamic understanding of matter that can accommodate the kinds of scientific insights implied by relativity and that can also accommodate the kinds of results described by quantum physics. The price for this shift in our understanding of matter is that it is not compatible with traditional forms of materialism and the resulting Newtonian, mechanistic understanding of reality. It leads to an understanding of matter that runs counter to established ways of thinking and counter to our social and culturally informed intuitions.

Bergson's understanding of matter is an example of such a dynamic understanding.[4] Bergson develops an understanding of emerging, evolving, creative materiality that unifies the elements of quantity (extension) and quality (structure, order): he conceives of matter as geometrical and quantitative while still associating it with the quality of duration. In order to indicate this unusual way of conceiving matter, he introduces the term 'image'. So, according to Bergson, matter is an *image,* something that is located between *representation* and *thing-in-itself.*

Bergson begins his investigation by closely examining actual experiences and basing his investigations on the results of these observations. According to Bergson, in everyday life, matter is given to our senses as completely independent from our thought processes or our experiences. We experience matter as independent and objective; in Husserl's terminology, it is given as transcendent. This observation leads Bergson to the conviction that we cannot begin our investigation on an epistemological level; we cannot simply begin with the unexamined claim that the matter that we are given in experience is a mere representation. This is the case precisely because matter is not given as a representation or as an image, but as transcendent, as existing independently. Furthermore, we also have the impression that the *material object itself* is given to us. This leads Bergson to the conviction that what there is cannot be absolutely different from what we are given in perception. Therefore, any investigation into the nature of materiality cannot begin with the claim that matter is purely objective, since it is also given to us in experience; nor can we base our investigations on the claim that it is purely subjective, since it appears as independent. Taking experience seriously thus leads Bergson to claim that material objects should not be taken to be completely transcendent things-in-themselves,

---

4. For arguments to this effect, see Dolbeault. For different ways to conceptualise matter as dynamic that are rooted in Schelling's philosophy, see Grant.

which need – in a second step – to be related to experience in some way. On the contrary, they are directly accessible, even if they can never be fully known (Bergson, *Matter* 10). An investigation into the nature of matter should therefore begin from a starting point that combines idealism and objectivism. In order to do so, we need to open our thinking to the idea that existence and appearance are associated, or correlated as Husserl would say, without the one being reducible to the other.

Having thus established Bergson's epistemological approach, let me take a closer look at the resulting ontological or metaphysical understanding of matter as 'image'. 'Matter', as Bergson conceives it, consists of heterogeneous qualities. It is characterised both by the kinds of mathematically describable quantitative qualities that are traditionally associated with matter by thinkers such as Descartes, but also by what are often referred to as *secondary qualities*. Thus, Bergson simply rejects the distinction between primary and secondary qualities, and in doing so agrees with Berkeley's claim that secondary qualities of matter are just as real as the primary ones (Bergson, *Matter* 9–11). There is qualitative variation to matter and thus matter can only be considered to have a certain degree of mathematisable extension – matter simply is not essentially divisible (Bergson, *Matter* 220, 247) or essentially mathematisable, because it is also qualitatively determined.

There is no such thing as fully 'inorganic', i.e. completely 'unorganised' and inert matter. According to Bergson, matter is just as much internally regulated, i.e. organised, as life is, even though the organisation of life allows for an almost infinitely larger degree of freedom and creativity. Therefore, there is still some, admittedly usually incredibly slow and incredibly minute, but nonetheless active internal organisation in matter. The slow process involved in the shifting of tectonic plates, the generation of minerals and so on can provide large-scale examples of the kinds of activities Bergson had in mind. From the point of view of particle physics, matter is made out of a highly organised structure of particles, and even if the movements of these particles were describable with mechanical precision (which they are not – we can only come to terms with these movements through statistical means), this organisation is itself subject to change. According to our best science, these structures characterising matter as we know it have ultimately evolved from the creative explosion that was the Big Bang; they thus have a history and a becoming.

With Bergson one can thus argue that while matter can successfully be thought as relatively inert and stable, and it is often very convenient to think of it in just this way, this is not the whole story. In investigating matter, we should engage with the actual complexity of what there is instead of beginning with the idealised preconception that matter is that which can be fully reduced to a clearly quantifiable extension, or that it forms fully isolable systems (Bergson, *Creative Evolution* 13). This position has an interesting consequence: If matter is not merely extended, or characterised by primary qualities, but is also inherently qualitative – if it is not merely passive but also (to a small degree) active – how can it be absolutely distinguished from mind and experience? The answer to this question is simply that there is no absolute distinction between mind and matter. There are differences in degree, but not in kind: the mind has an extensive dimension like matter, and physical matter endures just like the mind. Therefore, there is no reason 'why a duration, and so a form of existence like our own, should not be attributed to the systems that science isolates, provided such systems are reintegrated into the Whole' (Bergson, *Creative Evolution* 14).

The Copenhagen interpretation of quantum physics, which to my knowledge is still considered a standard interpretation, provides us with a similarly ambivalent or dual understanding of the nature of matter, namely as being wave-like as well as particle-like, depending on the circumstances.[5] If the Copenhagen interpretation is not merely taken as a set of computational rules

---

5. The decoherence histories (or consistent histories) approach does amend this interpretation in order to allow for predictability, but to my knowledge it does not affect the relevant issues discussed here.

describing phenomena completely unconnected to reality, but as an aid in understanding the world we live in, then it presents us with a similarly fundamental role for subjectivity. It is that which determines these circumstances through the presence or absence of an observer.[6] Thus, according to the standard interpretation of quantum phenomena, matter behaves only in the familiar discrete way under certain circumstances – when it is observed, when a subject is present. Under these circumstances matter turns out to be discrete and thus cleanly divisible. In other circumstances, however, it behaves in a continuous way, being characterised by qualities such as frequency and amplitude. This qualitatively determined wave-like behaviour renders any division a discretionary act, performed by a conscious observer. Both types of behaviour are fundamental to the understanding of matter in quantum physics, and thus only by investigating both aspects can we truly understand the full range of qualities exhibited by matter – from simple extension to durational wavelength and frequency. Furthermore, the idea that matter 'behaves' differently in different circumstances, that it 'exhibits different properties' in different situations, suggests a view of matter that is not purely Newtonian, i.e. static and passive.

Ultimately, if neither the standard interpretation of quantum physics nor our actual experience can substantiate the claim that matter is purely passive (i.e. has no internal principle of motion), nor that it is reducible to its mathematical properties and nothing more, then this claim can only have its origin in some conceptual configuration, some conclusion born in the minds of philosophers (or scientists):

> We enjoy our mathematical powers for natural reasons. We develop them at first inspired by nature, eviscerated of time and particularity, and then at a distance from the original sources of

---

6. This, of course, implies a rejection of the instrumentalism implied by the Copenhagen interpretation, which in any case is based on an artificial isolation of the quantum system and its separation from the world of which it is supposedly the foundation.

our inspiration. Mathematics, however, is smaller, not greater, than nature. It achieves its force through a simplification that we can easily persuade ourselves to mistake for a revelation and a liberation. (Unger and Smolin 18)

Even though contemporary sciences, from physics to biology, tend to paint quite a complex, temporal and dynamic picture of nature, the traditional reductive (and at heart Newtonian) preconceptions of a static, perfectly law-governed material nature still shape our philosophical intuitions and our pre-scientific understanding of what there is. These preconceptions render it even more difficult to see what is given as it is given. To a large extent contemporary science has moved on from the Newtonian worldview, substituting matter for energy, for example, linear space and time with space-time, determinism for singularities in social and dynamic systems and so on; but the way nature is thought is still fundamentally influenced by the way Newton described the world. This means that the issues discussed in these paragraphs are not issues that can be solved by physicists. More science is not going to provide better solutions to these problems. This is a cultural and conceptual issue, and thus one that can only be tackled by philosophy.

Dynamic and Relational Forms of Scientific Realism

In what follows, I will present two forms of scientific realism that do not follow the traditional Newtonian understanding of reality and that overlap with dynamic realism in substantial ways. I will look at ontic structural realism mainly as it has been proposed by Ladyman and Ross, as well as at Sellars's transcendental scientific realism.

The reasons I chose to focus on (ontic) structural realism are that first, structural realism is generally considered to be one of the most defensible forms of scientific realism. The main reasoning is that the unrivalled success of the sciences would be inexplicable if scientific theories did not describe what there is at least approximately, which is structural realism in a nutshell. Secondly, I chose to focus on ontic structural realism specifically because, in contrast to structural realism, it is more optimistic about the possibility of developing an ontology, i.e. we do not need to remain agnostic about the properties characterising the ontic level. This position thus combines the epistemic advantages of scientific structuralism with an ontological description of reality that reflects the no-thing relational structure implied by dynamic realism, since ontic structural realism is an account of reality as internally related and, based on the results of modern physics, it can help support the claim that dynamic realism is compatible with contemporary science, at least with regard to its claim that reality is fundamentally relational.

I will then introduce Sellars's transcendental scientific realism, since his 'scientific realism [. . .] turns out not to be founded in naturalistic or scientistic prejudice, but to be the necessary result of an analysis of the phenomenology of perception on the one hand, together with Sellars' adaptation of the transcendental methodology' (Haag 149). This is a strategy that undercuts the subject–object distinction and closely resembles the strategies employed in the accounts of what there is presented in Parts II and III. Furthermore, Sellars also focuses on the dynamic and processual elements discovered by the sciences, and thus can help to make the argument that the dynamic aspect of dynamic realism is also compatible with contemporary science.

The ultimate aim in discussing these positions at this point is to show that neither the central tenet of dynamic realism, its internal relationality, nor its presupposition of genuine change or processualism stand in conflict with contemporary science. On the contrary, dynamic realism is more compatible with contemporary science than many other metaphysical accounts of reality that take their cues from a Newtonian, mechanistic and deterministic view of reality. Modern science, especially in the fields of quantum physics and astrophysics as well as in contemporary biology, support the idea that what there is is fundamentally relational as well as genuinely dynamic.

Reality as internally related: ontic structural realism

These realists take as their guideline the relational descriptions generated by physics and thus consider reality to be fundamentally relational and not a set of things, entities or atoms. But this does not mean that everyday things do not exist; they are simply not fundamental:

> According to the account we will give, science tells us many surprising things, but it does not impugn the everyday status of objects like tables and baseballs. There are, we will argue, aspects of the world with sufficient cohesion at our scale that a group of cognitive systems with practically motivated interest in tracking them [i.e. human beings with practical aims] would sort them into types for book-keeping purposes. (Ladyman and Ross 5)

Tables and baseballs are thus not truly emergent phenomena, they are groupings, sets of structures that we find useful to group. Thus, ontic structural realists agree with Bergson's claim that we often think reality as a set of individual elements or things because of a veil of prejudice, rooted in language, habit and our tendency to engage with the surrounding environment according to specific aims. To ontic structural realists, objects are simply 'pragmatic devices used by agents to orient themselves [. . .] and to construct approximate representations of the world' (Ladyman and Ross 130), just as objects are pragmatic devices to refer to sets of closely related and stable processes for process thinkers.

But things are not simply wholes composed of fundamental structures. Part of the ontic realist project is the displacement of the part/whole distinction, i.e. of the mode of explaining what there is through higher and lower levels, with a new way of distinguishing fundamental science from the special sciences taking its place. It is not the case that fundamental physics describes the parts or elements that compose the wholes that the other sciences investigate. Instead, fundamental physics describes structures that apply to every aspect of the universe, while the special sciences describe structures that only hold for certain regions of the universe. What is fundamental can be understood in two ways, either as that which is everywhere, or as what is basic. Both process thinkers as well as ontic structural realists agree that 'we don't take ourselves to be asking about a putative physical "bottom" of reality. Instead [. . .] by "fundamental" physics we will refer to that part of physics about which measurements taken anywhere in the universe carry information' (Ladyman and Roass 55). The difference between this position and dynamic realism is that for dynamic realism, philosophy is to develop doctrines in terms of which all experience can be explained, while ontic structural realists such as Ladyman and Ross hold that metaphysics is to develop doctrines in terms of which every measurement of fundamental physics can be accounted for.

Ontic structural realists hold that what there is is fundamentally relational, which leads them to argue either for the elimination of things in favour of structures altogether (radical structuralism or eliminativism), or to claim that if there are individuals, they have no intrinsic properties, but only relational properties. Since the first claim is more radical and closer to the position of process thought, I will engage with this version of ontic structural realism. To hold that there are no things, but only (related) structures, means that there are no independent things, no substances, atoms, elements or entities that could be considered to be bearers of relationships; instead, what there is, just as Whitehead and Bergson argued, is structural ontological interdependence that either bears or exhibits properties:

> Ontic Structural Realism (OSR) is the view that the world has an objective modal structure that is ontologically fundamental, in the sense of not supervening on the intrinsic properties of a set of individuals. According to OSR, even the identity and individuality of objects depends on the relational structure of the world. Hence, a first approximation to our metaphysics is: 'There are no things. Structure is all there is.' (Ladyman and Ross 131)

So, what exactly is this modal structure? It is the nomological structure shaping everything there is; it is thus fundamental in the sense introduced above. This nomological or modal structure should not, however, be identified with the 'causal structure', since there are properties discovered in fundamental physics (for example, entanglement) that undercut the enlightenment idea of determination through efficient cause and effect.

So how would such structures now relate to processes? If there are only structures, how could there be processes? To me, the answer seems simple. If one takes the internal relatedness of processes seriously and abstracts duration from them, what would be left is an ontic structural reality as described by Ross and Ladyman. Or to put it differently, if these fundamental ontic structures were conceived as temporal, dynamic or evolutionary in nature, the result would be a process ontology. So, the main general conceptual difference between process ontologies and ontic structural realism is, once again, the role that time, temporality and genuine change are afforded in the respective accounts of reality.

Reality as dynamic: Sellars's transcendental scientific realism

Before I move on, I would like to discuss one final form of realism that is based on a thorough reflection on science and its results. This is a form of scientific realism that is shaped by the dynamism of what there is, namely transcendental scientific realism, as it was developed by Wilfrid Sellars. His position is often considered a bridge between traditional metaphysical stances and a future process metaphysics that has a firmer footing in a traditional use and engagement with science, and a smaller footing in speculation than Whitehead's, Bergson's or Deleuze's positions. I will still be considering Sellars as a process thinker, not only because he was explicitly committed to a future process metaphysics, but also because his process monism, even if it was never systematically developed,[7] seems to share the same

---

7. There are readers of Sellars who would deny such a processual interpretation, or at least find it highly questionable. In my eyes Johanna Seibt, throughout

fundamental structures that I identified in other process thinkers, namely 1) a rejection of (mere) metaphysical speculation that is not bound by engaged (and examined) experience (or scientific developments in the case of Sellars), 2) a rejection of empirical knowledge based on immediate (not clarified) experience, and 3) – depending on how one reads Sellars – an attempt to connect mind and world, by placing causes and norms on the extreme ends of a continuum that encompasses both mind and world (Seibt). Sellars would thus agree with process philosophers as well as phenomenologists in arguing that reductive interpretations of what there is are overly simplistic. However, while Whitehead, for example, dismisses reductive materialistic or naturalistic ways of understanding nature as lifeless, because besides excluding all sorts of relevant phenomena they also generate a form of alienation, Sellars upholds the value of naturalism.

To Whitehead, reductive and naturalistic approaches are inadequate to describe the dynamic creativity that characterises nature. Similar claims can be made from the perspective of phenomenology. Any reductive and materialist understanding of nature severs the living subject from its world, thus undercutting the phenomenological premise that the subject is always already related to its world. These positions are echoed in Sellars's famous view that contemporary philosophy is in the unenviable position of having to navigate two equally complex but radically different ways of conceiving humanity-in-the-world, namely the manifest and the scientific image. The contemporary philosopher

> is confronted not by one complex many dimensional picture, the unity of which, such as it is, he must come to appreciate; but by *two* pictures of essentially the same order of complexity, each of which purports to be a complete picture of man-in-the-world, and which, after separate scrutiny, he must fuse into one vision. (Sellars, *Science* 4)

---

her work, has shown clearly how such an interpretation is not only possible, but also highly fruitful in understanding and developing Sellars's thought.

The issue here is not the fact that science provides us with a more detailed or finer-grained account of what there is than the manifest image does; the issue is that science involves the generation of a distinct categorical structure. According to Sellars, modern science breaks with the (categorical) structure of the manifest image; thus he diagnoses a form of bifurcation of nature. Furthermore, this distinct categorical structure does not simply order data collected into a new whole, creating a new image of humanity-in-the-world, but it also influences the categorical structure of the manifest image, sometimes to such an extent that the (categorical) structure pertaining to the manifest image is lost – not fused or integrated, but lost.

This is precisely the issue that many phenomenologists and process thinkers are attempting to tackle in their writings. However, these thinkers go further in their critical assessment. While Sellars argues that philosophers have always engaged in spelling out the categorical structure of the manifest image, phenomenologists and process philosophers would argue that for most of the history of philosophy, the qualitative structures presenting themselves in the manifest image tended to be hidden by the categorical structures forced on experience through reason and rationality, and are simply disguised further by the categorical structures that result from modern science. But they agree on the ultimate aim, namely the integration of these levels.

> We should, as the classical pragmatists did, actively seek a dialogue between natural-scientific and humanistic orientations, arguing that in an important sense all sciences are human sciences, committed to viewing the world from a human perspective. Instead of polarization, dualism, or dichotomies, I would argue for a continuous nonscientistic rethinking of the unity of science—clearly not in the logical positivists' (scientistic) sense but in a sense continuously learning from both sides of the supposed dichotomy. (Pihlström, 'New Directions' 207)

What distinguishes Sellars from other process thinkers discussed in this book is his full-throated defence of naturalism and his reluctance to engage in speculation. According to Sellars, ontology is to be the '"midwife" of a description of reality as conceived in science' ('Structure' §65). Thus, it is the business of ontology 'to project categories relative to a given state of scientific development, governed by the regulative notion of a complete description of reality by the ideal ('Peircean') scientific theory, then the state of scientific development determines which ontological work can be meaningfully undertaken at which time' (Seibt 191). Which is to say that while most process thinkers and most phenomenologists looked towards examined engaged experience to limit their speculations, Sellars looks towards the natural sciences. This means that, for Sellars, ontology has to continuously grow and adapt to the emergence of new scientific discoveries. And this is the interesting overlap – both sides agree that there is no stable, unchanging or ultimate basis for the development of an ultimate or static ontology. The ontological system is to be continuously adapted.

Sellars argues that as a result of this open-ended nature, it would be wrong to presuppose that there is an ultimate vision of the place of humanity-in-the-world. This is the case for two reasons; first, we are continually broadening our horizons and learning new things that force us to revise our general view of the world. Secondly, there are no reasons to consider the way humans are in-the-world to be itself final or stable (de Vries 8). The way we engage and clarify experience always changes, and so does the scientific account of what there is ('Structure' §65). For Sellars, there is a relevant history of scientific descriptions of reality and of the way humans relate to the world, just as there is a history of *Being* for Heidegger, leading to a fundamentally historically situated view of ontological descriptions.

The scientific method relies on mediating approaches, using reduction, abstraction, measuring and quantification to learn more about its objects. While these methods have immense advantages and have led to an incredible amount of knowledge, by their very nature they cannot fully account for what there actually is, in its concrete complexity. These methods have been developed to reduce this complexity, to clarify and simplify – to render what there is understandable. Abstraction by definition abstracts from what is, by excluding aspects that are deemed irrelevant for the investigation at hand, while reduction is the process of reducing the actual complexity to what is considered essential. This tendency towards abstraction, reduction and simplification in science is neither surprising nor problematic, since generally speaking, scientists are not interested in the concrete singular or in accounting for every detail of the world we live in.

Husserl's most relevant insight with regard to the relation between lived reality and the sciences is the fact that the everyday world is fundamental even for the most abstract of sciences. He argues that any scientific engagement or discovery is only possible on the basis of our experience of the everyday world, and is thus only possible on the basis of a theoretical engagement with this everyday world: 'given prior is the world as the everyday world, and within this arise man's theoretical interest and the sciences related to the world [. . .]' (Husserl, *Ideas II* §53). The world as we experience it every day is both the location of and the ground for as well as the object of scientific research. This of course means that in order to gain philosophical insight or knowledge about what there is – as it is, in all its concrete complexity – we cannot simply begin with or let the investigation only be guided by the abstract results of science, since science begins with an abstracted and reduced version of what there is. Furthermore, as I argued before, *what there is* is not an object among other objects. The cosmos is a singular object, it is unique and all-encompassing. Thus, the traditional scientific methods of comparison, repetition and experimentation do not work when it comes to understanding what there is. There is no 'non-reality' that we could contrast with what there is, nor can we re-run the Big Bang, the evolution of sentient beings, or the Second World War. For investigations that focus on ultimately unrepeatable and incomparable singularities, the scientific method is simply not the most adequate method of investigation available. This argument can be taken further; if we were fussily exact and extremely precise in our investigation of what there is in all its detail, then there is not one object, event, thought or entity that is ever truly repeatable. Everything is radically singular, if we do not abstract from any of its qualities, including its relations, its temporal location and so on.

To gain insight into what there is in its singularity as well as its full dynamic complexity, we can either begin our investigation with experience to then compare the results with scientific accounts, or, ideally, both approaches could be used side by side, limiting and informing each other, to achieve a more adequate understanding. While it is absolutely legitimate – and I would even say necessary – to compare and evaluate philosophical or phenomenological descriptions against the results of scientific research, in our current intellectual climate, where the relevance of science is overemphasised, it seems more adequate for our investigation to focus mainly on the world as it is given.

11

Moving from the World of Science to the Life-World

> The concepts we deploy, the abstractions we construct, our very modes of thought are no longer able to deepen or develop our experience of nature; they only obscure its meaning. (Debaise, *Nature* 1)

Since I am trying to uncover this world as it is actually given, without preconceptions, I will now be taking an agnostic stance as to what things are; thus, following the phenomenological method, I will be asking *how* this everyday world is given, *how* it is accessible to us, not what it is. The aim of this procedure is to discover *what we can learn about what there is from our descriptions of how this world is given*.

Husserl proposes two different ways in which we can think how this world is given. In his early writings he characterises the world to be given as the horizon of all horizons, which in his later work transforms into an account of the world as life-world. Both characterisations attempt to describe how the concrete world of our experience is present for experience. In what follows, I will discuss whether either description (or both) can provide us with the hallmark properties that characterise the unique, concrete real as it is given in experience.

Husserl first understands what there is, the world, as the horizon of horizons (Husserl, *Ideas I* §1) and thus as the outer limit for all potential givenness (intention) and meaning. The term 'horizon' for Husserl denotes aspects that are not directly experienced, but that constitute the outer limit of our experience, while still pointing towards further possible experiences. Just as the experience of the horizon in a literal sense depends on one's physical position and direction, so does the experience of the world as horizon depend on the locatedness of the experiencing subject. The horizon of meaning, for example, is the background meanings that constitute and influence our present experiences, but that aren't actually present. In appreciating the colour of the pillow that I bought from Primark, I can follow the horizon of colour theory, the horizon of remembering other pillows that I had in the past, or the economic horizon constituted by the fact that me buying this item makes me a contributor to an exploitative economic system. All of these horizons are opened up and thus made possible as lines of thought by my initial engagement with the pillow. Whether I follow any of these horizons or none is another matter. Next to such outer horizons, there are inner horizons characterising phenomena; there is always more detail about a phenomenon to be discovered, since concrete givenness is ultimately inexhaustible in its complexity.

When Husserl thus says that the world is the horizon of all horizons, what he is claiming is that what there is is the ultimate horizon for human engagement in general. This, however, is not a fixed or final horizon, but one that shifts, evolves and moves with the movements, shifts and evolutions of the inner and outer horizons of experience. The world as the horizon of horizons (and similar things can be argued in the case of the life-world, which I will discuss later) is never fully understandable as an object, nor is it ultimately graspable in its entirety. Neither world can ever be an *object* of knowledge, since the world as horizon extends both spatially as well as temporally: it stretches out into infinite space but is also given as 'endlessly becoming and having endlessly become in time' (Husserl, *Ideas I* §27). However abstract, theoretical, transcendent or mystical one's thoughts and theories are, they are given to the thinker as a living being living in, through and with this world, within this ultimate horizon. It is this fact of being situated, this being located, that opens up this horizon of givenness. However far we go in our thoughts, experience, lives, the horizon stretches and moves with us so that it always remains the outer edge of what can be given. Just as any answer opens up new questions, any move towards the horizon discloses that, actually, the horizon is even further out. Thus, the world cannot be conceived as the sum of all things or facts.

The *Alltagswelt* (everyday world) as it is experienced in the natural attitude is the basis from within which any horizon can be travelled towards. It is always this same everyday world that provides the ground or fundament for all the conceptual or experiential horizon-worlds that we build in order to interpret and understand this world we live in, be it the world of knowledge, the world of religion, or the world of science. We act, feel, know, work, research *and* live in the world, and we do so in a world that appears consistent and continuous. The continuous experience with the world and its 'style' of existence is the basis for our continuous acting and feeling and researching in the first place. So, there is a unified style to what is experientiable.

What is given as the everyday world is in a sense fundamental, but there are a multitude of horizons, some with similar styles, some with different styles of givenness. In our experience, what there is as given in and with the everyday world has a style of givenness that is different from the style of givenness that numbers, memories, ideals or phantasies, for example, have. What is given as the everyday world opens up a specific horizon endowed by characteristics that, given a sufficient amount of investigation, distinguish it from other horizons or regions of being, be they ideal or conceptual, scientific or phantasmatic. And even if we sometimes make mistakes, if we mistake a dream or a hallucination for a sense experience, or a calculation error for a scientific discovery, sooner or later we realise that what we experience does not fit the style of the horizonal givenness in question and that we simply misinterpreted the experience, its sense, meaning or relevance.[1] It is this phenomenologically accessible style of the

---

1. This is only the case, of course, if we have not redefined or reinterpreted the style of the world to fit our dreams and hallucinations. Which would mean

real, of the world as the horizon of horizons, which distinguishes it from other ways of being given, that I am trying to uncover in my attempt to look for the hallmark properties of what is real.

This understanding the world as the horizon of all horizons is, however, quite one-sided, since it is a purely formal characterisation and does not easily accommodate the qualitative complexity and relational, dynamic intricacy of what there is. Acknowledging this shortfall, Husserl kept refining and developing his phenomenological approach in various ways, to account for more qualitative and evolutionary aspects.[2] Just to provide one example, at the stage of *Ideas II* Husserl starts to distinguish different regions within this world-horizon, and thus begins to give shape to various world-horizons. He distinguishes the homeworld (*Heimwelt*), the environing world (*Umwelt*), the world of things (*Dingwelt*) and the world of spirit (*geistige Welt*), which refers to the world of persons in intersubjective community (Husserl, *Ideas II* §3). But all these worlds are still situated in or related to the world as the horizon of horizons.

In *The Crisis of European Sciences*, however, Husserl introduces the idea of the life-world (*Lebenswelt*), which is a much more qualitatively developed and fleshed-out understanding of the world-as-horizon. The phenomenon described remains the same, namely the concrete world of our sense experience, and it is still the ultimate open horizon for meaning and appearance. But there is a genetic, physical and embodied focus to the investigations of the life-world;[3] it is the temporal world that we actually encounter,

---

that we have left the level of actual experience by preferring our interpretation of what there is to our actual experience of what there is.

2. While I am only presenting the earliest and the latest stage in Husserl's attempt to come to terms with the world as it is given in the natural attitude, in an oversimplified manner, there are many renderings and complications infringing on this issue.

3. The development from the world as horizon of horizons to the life-world is much more continuous than many would have. In his lectures on the basic problems of phenomenology (*Grundprobleme der Philosophie* 1910/11), Husserl addresses the 'natural concept of the world' (*natürlicher Weltbegriff*) and how our bodily situatedness relates to our orientation in the world

not only conceptually, but also on a physical or bodily level. It is the temporal world of our everyday embodied existence as well as the world as the horizon of horizons, i.e. the world as the limits of appearance. This life-world is what there is *before our conceptual or intellectual engagement*. It is described as 'pre-scientific', 'pre-given', 'always already there' (*immer schon da*) and 'familiar' (Husserl, *Crisis* §36). But this pre-scientific givenness does not remain in a purely theoretical atemporal or eternal limbo; the life-world is a product of meaning, of sedimentation, of becoming – it has a history. As Husserl explains, the life-world is not completely separate from the world of science, the world of thought and culture. These forms of interpreting and engaging with the life-world 'flow into' (*strömen ein*) (Husserl, *Crisis* §§59–60) the life-world and help shape and form it. This *flowing in* enriches the life-world by creating layers upon layers of sedimentation, of meaning, interaction and engagement. So, the life-world, even as a pre-scientific world, is always the contemporary life-world, a result of sedimentations influenced by culture and sciences, and not some eternal, pure or originary world of innocence that we could return to. Husserl's descriptions disclose this life-world as something that is neither objective, in the sense of mind-independent, nor purely subjective, in the sense of mind-dependent. The life-world is a confluence, a co-constitutive meeting of world and humans, of science and culture, by which I mean there would be no social, cultural and biological life-world without humans,[4] but also no humans without the objective biological, chemical and physical structures and affordances provided by this world.

(Husserl, *Phänomenologie* 124). He furthermore argues that the general thesis (*Generalthesis*), i.e. the thesis at the basis of the natural attitude, is not an empirical thesis, but is absolute and a priori (Husserl, *Phänomenologie* 136).

4. And while I engage with this question in the next section in much more detail, I just want to clarify at this point that this does not imply that there would be no world without human beings. The world did not suddenly spring into being with the emergence of human consciousness (whether it did so in correlation with divine consciousness is another matter, but that is not a question I address).

Let me summarise the results of our investigation into the life-world and the world as horizon with regard to uncovering the hallmark properties of what there is. Every possible experience is an experience given in and of this world; it is the horizon of all givenness and thus of all meaning, scientific discovery, transcendent thought as well as spiritual enlightenment. There is nothing beyond this world, as this world is always the outer limit of what can be given, what can be present for us as conscious and bodily human beings. In addition to the radical immanence that is presupposed by the world as the horizon of all horizons, the descriptions of the life-world also disclose a temporal as well as relational dimension to what there is. The life-world is historical, interconnected and thus layered with and connected to cultural and scientific developments. It is not a pure realm of mind-independent life before the advent of science, culture and reflection.[5] In a manner of speaking this world, itself has a history, a becoming – a life.

One way to take these descriptions seriously is to ask what distinguishes the disclosure through the lens of the life-world from other forms of uncovering the world, for example, the empirical and scientific interpretations of the world that were discussed in the preceding chapter. First, they are distinct in so far as the life-world is, arguably, the basis for any science. Every

---

5. The historical roots of the life-world itself lie in the idea of a natural concept of world (*natürlicher Weltbegriff*), the idea of a pre-scientific world of immediate experience, as developed by empirico-criticists such as Richard Avenarius or Ernst Mach. Both thinkers claim that any judgements about something beyond the horizon of experience is pure metaphysics and should not be considered to be part of any genuine philosophical reflection. This kind of empiricist position is often characterised as a 'subjectivist positivism', as its proponents consider experiences to be the result of a physiological and psychological constitution, and a strict distinction between these aspects, psychological and physiological, is considered impossible. Only experiences, whether sense perception, measurements or findings, could be the proper object of scientific investigations, and immediate experiences especially were thought to disclose the integrated natural world (*natürliche Welt*) prior to scientific theory and conceptualisation.

scientist lives, breathes and eats in the life-world and ultimately investigates limited, abstracted, reduced or idealised aspects of it. But secondly, and this aspect is just as fundamental, the life-world is intimately and explicitly connected with actually lived life, while any objective scientific engagement with this world tends to aim at an uninvolved approach, effectively attempting to minimise the subjective or lived involvement. Any investigation that begins with the life-world, as I understand it, begins with an intermediate position that does not reduce the concrete temporal complexity of the world that we live in either to its subjective or its objective aspects, but attempts to account for the actual interconnectedness that is given in experience.

Last but not least, on a purely linguistic level, Husserl uses the term 'life' to indicate the *differentia specifica* that distinguishes the life-world from any other characterisation of the world. Therefore, I will continue by considering whether 'life' could be the distinguishing hallmark feature of what there is.

Phenomenological Issues Connected to Life and Moving to Ontology

If we thus take life to be the distinguishing feature characterising the life-world, then how should we understand life in concrete or phenomenologically descriptive terms? A problematic issue, since from a phenomenological point of view, 'life' is a very difficult phenomenon to come to terms with. There is no such thing as the phenomenon of life or a specific experience that we could determine as an experience of life. What we can experience are living beings, dying beings, dead beings or non-living entities, but not life itself. Life is, furthermore, a unique characteristic in that it is never actually given or present at an instant but can only be detected or inferred through observation over time. We can only perceive something as alive if it moves, reacts, grows, metabolises and so on *over time*, and even if an entity performs all of these actions, sometimes we are still not sure if life is actually present. Life, like *the* world as a whole (be it in the form of the horizon of horizons or the life-world), is not the kind of phenomenon that can ever be perceived outright. Furthermore, we can only experience as long as we ourselves are alive. A conscious perceiver's being alive is a necessary condition for there to be conscious experience at all, and there is no way to take what it is like to experience life from the perspective of a living being and compare it to the experience from the perspective of a non-living entity, in order to see what difference one's being alive makes in one's perception of life. All intentional or conscious experience is at least tinged with the experiencer's being alive. To us human beings, our own being alive is always immediately present – until it is absent and, in its absence, takes with it our presence.

Finally, there is the fact that there is inordinate variation in the manifestations and presentations of life. In talking about life, we could intend anything from the life of the biosphere to the life of a cell. What is it that ties all these forms of life together? And what could it mean to claim that it is this aspect that uniquely characterises the world we are given, the world we are living in? In order to answer these questions, we have to go beyond phenomenology and look towards an ontological description of this life-world as the world which makes life possible in the first place, and that furthermore is, in a certain sense, itself alive.[6]

---

6. At this point it seems important to head off on a tangent to quickly address Michel Henry and his phenomenology of life, in order to distinguish his approach from the present discussion. Henry argues that intentional givenness or consciousness of something is not the only mode of appearance. There is another way that appearance can happen, according to Henry, namely as a pre-intentional givenness that conscious givenness rests on, i.e. 'life' or 'transcendental affectivity'. Henry's reflections follow a different route compared to what is discussed here, since his use of the term 'life' has no ontological or biological connotations and is thus used in a purely transcendental-phenomenological manner. It is simply used to refer to the self-appearing of appearing – the becoming appearance of the fact that phenomena appear – in distinction to the ek-static mode of appearing that is founded in intentionality. While intentionality is open to the appearance of something other, for Henry life is a form of self-experience that is enclosed in itself. This self-experience is the condition of possibility for

And while I would grant that beginning our investigation into the hallmark features of what there is with the idea of life as an ontological concept is somewhat arbitrary, I would also argue that, at least physically and biologically speaking, being alive is one of the most fundamental and undoubtedly real activities that an investigation into the concreteness of what there is could begin with. Is it not life that brought forth and continues to bring forth the human intellect and with it intelligibility itself? Therefore, while the thesis that life is *the* foundational condition for both appearance as such as well as the existence of intentionality cannot be borne out phenomenologically, it seems a pretty sound speculative claim – a claim that I hope will convince most readers outright. This, however, does not mean that there is no world without conscious beings, since, from a phenomenological perspective, for something to exist it is not necessary that it actually appears (as Berkeley argued). To the best of my knowledge, no serious phenomenologist claims that the world did not exist before the advent of and constitution through human experience, since '[i]n brief, consciousness gives meaning, not existence, to the world around us' (Smith 75).

An Aristotelian Look at Life between Empiricism and Speculation

Before we can assess whether life is truly the hallmark distinguishing feature of the life-world, we need to generate a basic understanding of the term in the context of theoretical and natural philosophy – the context we are operating in. One way to do so is to go back to the first philosopher who investigated this phenomenon thoroughly, namely Aristotle. Aristotle's attempt

---

any appearance at all. It is also noteworthy that this reading of life as a fundamental mode of appearing, if read ontologically, already brings us very close to Whitehead's idea of feeling and prehension, two concepts that were discussed in Part III of this book.

to understand 'life' is especially interesting for the purposes of this book, since he investigates life by situating it within a speculative, philosophical, historical as well as a scientific, i.e. biological, context. Aristotle was the first philosopher to cross the lines between metaphysics, science, experience and epistemology in his investigation of life, and I would claim that this combination of perspectives is a necessary step, since it is life itself that cuts across all of these categories or distinctions. It is the multifaceted and complex nature of life that makes such a wide-ranging investigation necessary. In this regard, 'life' is just as complex as 'reality', a term that, as I argued in Part I, cuts across the divisions between metaphysical speculation, epistemology and science. Aristotle's resulting syncretistic approach is nowhere more evident than in his *De anima*, where he investigates life through metaphysical speculation, while using descriptive, i.e. empirical, as well as subjective standards to inform and limit this speculative exploration. In this book, life is 'discussed in terms of geometrical systematicity, in terms of natural philosophy, and in terms of affect, imagination, and cognition' (Thacker 19). In this sense, the syncretistic approach that shapes *De anima* is a blueprint for the type of investigation that is attempted in this book.

The easiest way to grasp Aristotle's understanding of life is to situate it within the natural cosmos and the hierarchy of beings that he presupposes. Aristotle famously distinguishes between natural beings (*physei onta*) and beings that do not exist naturally (*technē onta*), and he argues that only natural beings/bodies have the ability to be alive in the first place. This does not mean that natural beings are automatically alive, but merely that these are the only beings that have the potential (*dynamis*) to be alive, if further conditions are met. As distinct from the *technē onta*, natural beings have, as Aristotle argues in the *Physics*, the principle of motion and stationariness in themselves (*en heautō archēn echei kineseōs kai staseōs*, *Physics* 192b13),[7] whereas, strictly

---

7. The *physei onta* listed by Aristotle are animals and their parts, plants and simple bodies (*hapla tōn somatōn*) such as earth, fire, air and water (*Physics* 192b10).

speaking, the *technē onta* do not possess such an internal principle of motion (*Physics* 192b18).[8] In *Physics* 192b19 Aristotle provides further details of the internal principle of motion possessed by the *physei onta*. He specifies that these natural beings *have an 'ingrown' tendency towards alteration* (*oudemian hormēn echei metabolēs emphyton*, *Physics* 192b19).

However, in *De anima* Aristotle takes this description further and relates it to the question of life. Here he presupposes the distinction introduced in the *Physics* between the *technē onta* and the *physei onta* (natural beings) and focuses on the *physei onta* by discussing the difference between natural beings that are alive and natural beings that are not alive. Aristotle explains that a *living being* is a natural body (*somatos physikou*, *De anima* 412a20) further characterised by the fact 1) that it is *animated* by a *psychē* (*De anima* 412a20, 415b8), 2) that it is at least in need of nourishment (*De anima* 413a22) and 3) that it has an ingrown tendency towards alteration (just as every natural being or body does). While this ingrown tendency towards alteration is a general *dynamis* to move and change in non-living bodies, in living bodies this tendency can be understood in a more specific or precise way, namely *as the ability to grow and decay* (*De anima* 412a14).

What can we learn from this account? Aristotle argues that there are natural bodies, characterised by an inherent principle of motion and stationariness. Only natural bodies possessing this principle have the potential to be living bodies. Furthermore, natural bodies can only be considered alive if a set of further criteria is fulfilled, namely animation through *psychē*, the need for nourishment to maintain life and the possession of an ingrown tendency towards alteration, which in the case of living beings is understood as growth and decay. Of course, for Aristotle, the descriptive account of what characterises life presented so far does not suffice. In order to be able to understand life adequately,

---

8. This, however, does not entail that they are unchanging. According to Aristotle, the *technē onta* can also be considered to have these principles, but only by virtue of the primary bodies they are composed of (*Physics* 192b20).

he argues, insight into a general principle is needed, a principle that can ground and thus account for all of the features observed in living bodies.

Aristotle argues that this principle of life is the *psychē*, because *it is what can account for life without being itself alive.*[9] In the terminology of Aristotle, the *psychē* turns out to be the *ousia* (essence) and thus the *entelecheia*, the actualisation or entelechy, of the natural living body (*De anima* 412a21). This principle of life, the *psychē*, has thus a unique and interesting dual nature. Insofar as the *psychē* is an *ousia*, it cannot be moving or changing, since any essence is complete and thus unchanging. Furthermore, it is the essence that guarantees the identity of the individual entity possessing it. But at the same time the *psychē* is closely associated with the life of living beings and thus the movements, changes and developments involved in being alive and characterising life. The *psychē* is the *unmoving principle of life* and is, at the same time, *the principle of movement*.

But how can it be both? One way out of this dilemma is to claim that the *psychē* is the *unmoving origin of all movement*; this characterisation is, however, already associated with the unmoved mover, i.e. the divine principle. And while there is much literature on the precise relation between the soul and the divine, it seems inappropriate simply to identify the *psychē* with divine being in quite as straightforward a manner as this argument would imply. Another, altogether more plausible way to come to terms with these difficulties is to claim that the *psychē* itself is somehow split in two. There is an essence (*ousia*) to *psychē* – this aspect can act as a principle of life and is common to all forms of life – and then there is the concretely embodied aspect of *psychē*, which changes and develops with every individual lived life. This dual interpretation would imply that one and the same principle is the cause of life and is what is actually alive, which is, after all, a thoroughly Aristotelian thought. This dual nature of the *psychē* would then make it possible to consider the (potentially divine)

---

9. For a subtle account of the relation between *psychē* and life, see Thacker 14.

cause of a living process and what is undergoing this process of life to be identical. This notion is at the heart of any processual account of reality.

So far, I have tried to characterise 'life' in an Aristotelian fashion, thus understanding it in terms of subjectivity, internality or experience and an ingrown tendency towards change, while largely disregarding the third Aristotelian characterisation, namely the need for nourishment. I have also discussed the ambivalent nature of this approach, which on the one hand provides a principle of life, but on the other hand remains somewhat descriptive. In what follows, I use these insights to investigate which hallmark properties of what there is result, if we consider it as *reality alive* or *living nature*. In doing so I follow Aristotle in looking at life as a point of departure that is situated between description and speculation, which in my case translates to a starting point between phenomenology and process philosophy.

From the Life-World to a World Alive

Having examined the concept of 'life' a bit more closely, let me now return to our original question as to how we should spell out the difference between Husserl's life-world and other worlds, in particular the world of science, and how this can help us uncover the hallmark features of what there is. So far, we had concluded that in contrast to the world of science, the life-world is characterised by 1) the presence and relevance of subjectivity as experience and 2) a historical dimension, i.e. it possesses a history, a changing, temporally extended and thus dynamic nature. These two characterisations can be connected to Aristotle's first and third criterion for life, namely, *psychē* or animation and the historical or dynamic dimension implicit in the ingrown tendency towards alteration. Being alive means having a history. There is a connection between subjectivity or experience and a historical and thus temporal and dynamic dimension, because '[w]herever anything lives, there is, open somewhere, a register in which time is being inscribed' (Bergson, *Creative Evolution* 20).

The structural analogies between Husserl's characterisation of the life-world and the Aristotelian account of life thus also characterise process ontological descriptions of reality. Process thinkers tend to describe what there is as having some form of internality (or some form of non-conscious proto-subjectivity) and they consider reality to be fundamentally temporal and dynamic, i.e. historical in the sense that the present is always to be understood as a product of the past. Therefore, in order to describe this reality, the term 'life' is often used by process thinkers to convey two main ideas, namely 1) that the subjective dimension characterising what there is cannot strictly be separated from objective existence and 2) that time, history, becoming not only forms and shapes conscious existence, but also shapes physical existence. What there is is a result of past events, it is 'the prolongation of the past into the present, or, in a word, *duration*, acting and irreversible' (Bergson, *Creative Evolution* 20).

While process thinkers tend to agree with Aristotle's assessment that natural bodies have an ingrown tendency towards alteration and that they have the potential to be alive, they tend to disagree with the Aristotelian claim that this potential is ultimately to be limited to natural bodies. Instead, dynamic ontologists hold that everything can be considered 'alive', that everything has an ingrown tendency towards alteration and that everything has an internal, experiential dimension. In thus applying the term 'life' to everything there is, process thinkers tend to disregard the Aristotelian distinction between *natural bodies* and *living bodies*, and to thus reject the claim that it is the *psychē* acting as the body's *causa formalis* (*De anima* 412a19) that renders a body a living body.[10] For process thinkers, everything

---

10. There is a further strand of thought that connects life to ideas, concepts or the intellect, that has shaped a whole tradition of metaphysical thought that reflects on the life of concepts and ideas. However, life here is not

has an ingrown tendency towards alteration and an interiority or history, while not everything has a subjective consciousness or a *psychē* as its *causa formalis*; this only holds for living bodies. From the point of view of speculative process philosophy, the usual association of internality with subjectivity or consciousness is simply not necessary.[11] In the words of Whitehead:

> In the first place we must distinguish life from mentality. Mentality involves conceptual experience [. . .] The most obvious example of conceptual experience is the entertainment of alternatives. Life lies below this grade of mentality. (Whitehead, *Modes* 166)

From a process ontological perspective, to claim that something is alive or has life is usually merely to claim that it is processual, that it is constituted by the processes of becoming, being and perishing, with the added condition *that this process is not to be attributed exclusively to external causes, but that it is also the expression of an ingrown tendency towards alteration – it has an internal cause.*

Let me discuss this last condition in a little more detail. For a genuinely dynamic understanding of reality, it is not enough simply to focus on a temporal interaction of subject and object. The processual approach implies a stronger claim, namely an (at least partial) *overlap* or even *identity* between the cause of

---

understood in a biological or biographical sense (βίος), but as animated and metaphysically determined and determinable life (ζωή). Thus, *zoe* characterises the gods in the Platonic dialogues, and Aristotle uses the term to characterise divine intelligence (*Metaphysics* XII). *Bios*, however, does not apply to the gods or the intelligence for either thinker, as the term implies mortality. Zoe ultimately describes the capability to move itself in accordance with one's aim, as an ingrown tendency towards alteration that is tinged with intentionality and teleology. This is the meaning of 'life' in Plato's claim that the ideas are alive, and Hegel's description of the 'movement of the concept' as an expression of the life of the spirit.

11. This is why this approach is not necessarily a form of anthropomorphising. There is a claim regarding a fundamental continuity or similarity in what there is, as any metaphysical concept of being will claim. But there is sufficient difference between human beings and stones built into this system to provide a substantial counter to the charge of anthropomorphism.

a process and that which is going on, the process itself. This partial overlap or identity means that we are entering the realm of self-causation. Life is a good example to elucidate this idea. In growing and unfolding, living beings become what they are. They absolutely are influenced by external factors, their environment, their experiences, their sources of nourishment and so on, but their becoming is also determined by internal predispositions and decisions, whether the result of genetic disposition, instinct, learning or reflection, or a combination of these. Interestingly, as I argued before, one of the few instances where Aristotle allows such an identity or at least partial overlap of the causing principle and what is undergoing this process is precisely the case of the *psychē* as the form of the living body and the cause of movement in living bodies.

In our contemporary intellectual climate, however, focused on clarity, distinctness and precision as it is, it is rather difficult to argue for the confluence and mingling of internal and external causation and thus a fundamental dynamic relationality. The idea of wilfully inserting complexity into our conceptual accounts is alien to our times. While there is nothing wrong with striving for clarity and simplicity as such, this approach becomes inadequate when one's object of study is as complex, as interrelated and all-encompassing as 'reality' or 'life'. Process thinkers and phenomenologists, therefore, often insist on using terms that defy current intellectual fashions, not necessarily in order to confuse, but in order to force us to reconsider our preconceptions. While terms such as 'life' or cognates such as 'organism' do suggest a subjectivist approach, which could potentially imply forms of anthropomorphism, vitalism or panpsychism, it also suggests an understanding of reality that is interconnected and dynamic. These apparently subjective terms are quite consciously introduced in order to avoid an overly simplistic, mechanistic or scientistic interpretation of what there is. Furthermore, it is not easy to find a term that is able to intuitively convey the fact that our life-world cannot be fully explained through external or material causation, but that any adequate explanation of what there is also has to take into account the active *ingrown* (and *creative*) tendency towards change, i.e. internally determined becoming. Thus, even if terms such as 'life', when used to describe what there is, might seem inappropriate or confusing to some readers, they do aid in avoiding misunderstandings and in conveying the fact that there is no absolute subject–object distinction, and that becoming, i.e. dynamism and temporality, play a fundamental role in shaping what is real. These terms emphasise the fact that there is some sort of internal relationality or perspective to what there is, thus undercutting reductive, mechanistic or other one-sided interpretations.

What about Nature as a Characterisation of What There Is?[12]

There is a close connection between the concepts of 'life' and 'nature' when it comes to the question of what there is. In what follows, I will first quickly introduce the ancient Greek understanding of *physis* (nature) and provide an account of Aristotle's use of the term, before I discuss the possibility of using the term 'nature' instead of 'life'.

We possess a long tradition of conceiving of the world as a natural, becoming and living cosmos. When, for example, the earliest ancient Greek poets, scientists and thinkers looked at the world, they saw one living natural organism: 'The insight that the world is a system, is organic, therefore both orderly and alive, is the Greek view as far back as we have records' (Cairns xvii).[13] This natural world was understood as fundamentally characterised by materiality, growth and life. 'This conception was to the Greeks

---

12. This part is based on Röck, 'Concept'.
13. There are many contributions on the roots of the concept of *physis* in Greek theology. One excellent if older example is Heidel, who claims that the λόγος περὶ φύσεως succeeds the μῦθος περὶ θεῶν in a natural transition (Heidel 89).

so obvious that the fact of natural growth lay at the foundation of their thought. Growth implies life, and life implies motion. This is true of Greek thought always' (Heidel 98). Considering this close connection, which is also evident in Aristotle's accounts I have presented so far, it seems to be worth looking at whether focusing on 'nature' instead of 'life' would not solve some of the conceptual and linguistic problems mentioned in the previous paragraphs. In looking at the concept of 'nature' I am thus attempting to assess whether nature allows for a similar characterisation of what there is as dynamic and internally determined, while at the same time not suffering from some of the issues connected to life, i.e. its connection with *psychē* (i.e. subjectivity, vitalism, panpsychism or anthropomorphism), as well as the potential concerns that could result from the fact that Aristotle's second criterion for life, namely to be in need of nourishment, has simply been disregarded in the discussion so far.

Looking at Aristotle's use of *physis* (nature) unearths him as a more dynamic thinker than is usually acknowledged. In introducing the Aristotelian distinction between natural beings (*physei onta*) and beings that do not exist naturally (*technē onta*), I mentioned that Aristotle characterised natural beings as having the principle of motion as well as the principle of stationariness in themselves (*en heautō archēn echei kineseōs kai staseōs*, Physics 192b13). Most Western interpreters emphasised the second principle of stationariness, subordinating motion to stability. This view has its roots in an influential claim made repeatedly in the *Metaphysics*, namely that every change or motion presupposes something (stable) that undergoes that change or motion. However, when it comes to physical nature, it is just as adequate to read Aristotle as a philosopher who considers movement and change to be fundamental, and many passages concerned with *physis* actually justify such an interpretation. The reason behind this shift seems to be a difference in the respective objects of investigation. When we want to understand ideal nature, the *ousia* as the essence of what there is from a metaphysical or categorical-linguistic perspective, the investigations in the *Metaphysics* or the *Categories* are most relevant. Both of these sets of investigations tend to emphasise stability and consider actual physical change to be either irrelevant to what truly is (*Categories*) or at least secondary, with *ousia* and/or *dynamis* being primary (*Metaphysics*). However, the kind of investigation into life or physical nature that focuses on the actually given phenomena and that can be found in parts of *De anima* and in the *Physics* leads to an understanding of what there is that is much more, or even fundamentally, dynamic.

Instead of following the traditional interpretations in considering stability as fundamental and change as merely accidental when it comes to concrete *physis* (nature), one can thus emphasise the principle of motion and consider stability as an effect of continuous motion, as the term *physis* in its early use in Greek allows us to do:

> 'Physis' was not only used to refer to the *becoming nature* of plants, but to the *becoming nature* of beings in general. So, the nature or essence of every being (φύσις τῶν ὄντων) could be considered a result of its becoming [. . .] *Physis* thus does not simply refer to inert matter or the material principle out of which the world was generated, but it also refers to becoming *nature* and thus to the becoming essence of world, which also includes man and his relation to the world. The kind of being referred to through 'physis' is not an unchanging, ideal or abstract entity that hides behind moving nature. This kind of being is an integral part of changing and becoming reality. As such 'physis' does not only refer to the becoming existence of organic nature, it conveys the *becoming nature* of every being. (Röck, 'Concept' 12, 14)

In the third chapter of the *Physics*, for example, Aristotle defines *physis* as the principle of movement and change (*physis men estin archē kineseōs kai metabolēs*, *Physics* 200a9), and in the *Metaphysics*, he claims that *physis* in its first meaning refers to those beings that have the beginning of movement in themselves (*Metaphysics* 1015a13). The quote I find most powerful in this regard is a passage of the *Physics* that I mentioned in my discussion of 'life'. In *Physics* 192b19, Aristotle claims that the *physei onta* have an ingrown tendency towards alteration (*oudemian hormēn echei metabolēs emphyton*).[14] Of course, these quotations are not intended to prove that Aristotle was actually a process thinker. No doubt, within the Aristotelian framework, the ingrown tendency towards change still needs to be actualised through a causally active form[15] or mover and to be kept in existence by the unmoved mover. Nevertheless, the fact that the grandfather of substance ontology, when investigating nature, discovers an ingrown tendency towards alteration suggests that his stance is quite a bit more nuanced than he is often given credit for.[16]

The use of the term *physis* has at least one major advantage in comparison with 'life', namely that it refers to the internal ability to move in accordance with an aim (i.e. it has an internal principle of motion), without necessarily implying a connection to *psychē*, subjectivity or animation. *Physis* simply names nature as self-guided and at least partially self-caused growing and unfolding (and thus disclosing) being-there that results in essential existence. So, nature as a living process does not presuppose animation or nourishment; instead, it is to be understood in a very broad sense as referring to that which grows and unfolds, what brings forth in a continuous dynamic movement. Looking at these possibilities

---

14. There is also a little book on becoming and destruction, *De generatione et corruptione*, that can be used to push this argument even further.
15. There are instances where the causally acting form is the form of what is moving, as is the case for the *psychē*.
16. This impression is confirmed when we look at the structure of the *Physics* itself. While the first main part (Books 1–4) is concerned with nature, the second main part (Books 5–8) can be considered an investigation into motion and thus change. Now of course, the whole issue is much more complex than the quick outlines in this book might suggest. One might want to discuss the issue of active and passive changes, the question of whether *physis* can be understood as becoming and changing nature (as I have done) or whether it has to be understood as the nature of something (essence) – even though we are not certain of what exactly the difference is and if there even is a substantial difference – and so on. However, even if the expositions provided are an oversimplification, what cannot be disputed is the fact that movement and change, while they are quite marginal in the *Metaphysics* and the *Categories*, are fundamental aspects of the investigation in the *Physics* and other works focused on nature and natural beings.

afforded by the ancient Greek concept of nature in general and the Aristotelian treatment of *physis* specifically, it might seem more adequate to dispense with the additional complexity introduced by focusing the search for the hallmark properties of what there is on life. It seems only fitting to attempt to simplify this investigation by taking a closer look at the concept of nature as a potential candidate for clarifying or modifying the hallmark features of what is real that we have discovered so far, namely an *active* and *ingrown tendency towards change*.

Even if this strategy promises to simplify some of the issues mentioned earlier, it does so by introducing a whole host of new problems, the first of which is the question of what nature is. Should nature be understood along the lines of the reductive, materialist and naturalist positions introduced at the beginning of Part IV, or should it be read in connection with life and the idea of ingrown tendencies as is suggested by Aristotle's arguments? These two aspects of understanding nature as mechanically organised or as organically structured have shaped many discussions around nature, including phenomenological investigations. Many phenomenologists, and especially the early Husserl, have a somewhat ambiguous relationship to the question of nature and the question whether one should distinguish between *physical* (i.e. material) *nature* and *nature alive*. In *Ideas II* Husserl still argues that the traditional distinction separating mere (physical) nature from living nature is adequate and helpful in coming to terms with nature. He even introduces a non-extensional property, whose presence or absence grounds this distinction between the merely passive *material nature* and *living animal nature* (Husserl, *Ideas II* §12; *Cartesian Meditations*). This strict opposition between scientifically discoverable nature and lived nature is, however, weakened in later writings. In *The Crisis of European Sciences* for example, Husserl explicitly criticises the scientific tendency to turn nature into a simple object by distinguishing it cleanly and clearly from the life-world and from experience in general.

This is precisely the issue concerning nature as event that Whitehead investigates in his philosophy. Here, too, nature is conceived as what there is beyond the ubiquitous bifurcation into objective scientific, mathematical or geometric accounts and subjective experience. Its first conceptualisation in *The Concept of Nature* bears many similarities to phenomenological accounts, including the exclusion of a metaphysical stance, before ripening into the more speculative position that is presented in *Process and Reality*. Nonetheless, the attempt to overcome the bifurcation shapes Whitehead's view of nature throughout and is evident in his characterisation of nature: 'Nature is that which we observe in perception through the senses' (Whitehead, *Concept* 3). But Whitehead also states that 'The immediate fact for awareness is the whole occurrence of nature. It is nature as an event present for sense-awareness, and essentially passing' (Whitehead, *Concept* 14). This rather phenomenological dualism can be summed up as follows:

> Nature is perceived as dependent on perception, as we experience it only according to a perspective, and nature is also perceived as independent, as the vague perceptions of partial events are experienced as something beyond our current perception. The body, the perceived room, the building, provide a background of events that are not the actual object of perception but persist within it and open it up to aspects that are only vaguely perceived. (Debaise, *Nature* 29)

In his later writings Whitehead went beyond the limits of his version of phenomenology to incorporate metaphysical speculations, which I discussed in Part III.

Maurice Merleau-Ponty carries this criticism of dividing nature even further than Husserl does, ending with a position comparable to the views held by the later Whitehead. In his lectures on nature, given at the Collège de France in the 1950s, for example, Merleau-Ponty treats nature as a living whole with an ingrown tendency towards change. Nature is thought as autopoietic, as self-producing and thus as capable of producing its own meaning:

> There is nature wherever there is a life that has meaning, but where, however, there is not thought; hence the kinship with

the vegetative. Nature is what has a meaning, without this meaning being posed by thought: it is the autoproduction of a meaning. Nature is thus different from a simple thing. It has an interior, is determined from within; hence the difference of 'natural' to 'accidental'. (Merleau-Ponty, *Nature* 3)

For Merleau-Ponty, nature is not only determined internally and dynamic-productive, it is also creative; it creates its own meaning, a meaning that is quite independent of human understanding and interpretation, but that can be discovered by humans. To claim that nature can *create its own meaning* can here be read as nature constituting a meaning that is not constructed by the human mind or by human consciousness, but by what there is. Nature, in creating its own meaning, structure and order, is independent of human understanding. When it comes to understanding concrete nature, all that remains for humans is to learn how to read this book of nature, while avoiding all the conceptual and intellectual distractions and preconceptions grounded in the need for precision and certainty that made such reading almost impossible for millennia.

In elaborating these thoughts, Merleau-Ponty characterises Whitehead's understanding of nature as a creative principle that brings forth recursively (in the form of self-communing), where recursion does not lead to an infinite number of unchanging repetitions, but to repetitions that differ:

> What he [Whitehead] means in speaking of the 'subject-object' is that Nature 'communes with itself', without this self-communion allowing Nature to be conceived as a creative principle. It is this outside of which is nothing, that from which is taken all spatiality and temporality. It is what always appears as already containing all that appears. In it, creature and creator are inseparable. It is with this reservation in mind that we must call Nature an 'operating presence'. (Merleau-Ponty, *Nature* 120)

However, this use of the term 'nature', as a way of understanding what there is as nature alive, remains distinguished from the traditional Newtonian, naturalistic or physicalist perspective that discloses nature as the sum and/or interactions of bits of matter occupying a specific region in infinite and homogeneous space at a (non-durational) instant. This modern, scientific understanding reduces nature to bits of matter as passive facts, which play no active role in the reality they constitute. And it seems the case that this distinction is not mediated or bridged adequately by Merleau-Ponty. The dichotomy between a materialist and a processual reading of nature thus simply reintroduces the dualism between the internal-subjective and the external-objective, and thus the initial problem reappears, albeit in a different form. This return of the objective–subjective distinction makes the adequacy of our strategy to simplify our discussion by beginning with nature at least doubtful.

The reader familiar with the Enlightenment and Romantic traditions will easily see echoes of the debates around the opposition between *natura naturata* (nature as a stable and intelligible structure) and *natura naturans* (nature as a creative process) in these descriptions. But while conceiving of nature as *natura naturata* was denounced by the Romantics as an almost inhuman attempt to erase the inherent creative value of nature in favour of an instrumental use and abuse of natural resources, process philosophers and phenomenologists tend to be less dramatic. The descriptions of nature as inert and only mechanically affected are to be avoided in our account of what there is because they are simply not adequate descriptions of the natural phenomena observed, they do not grasp what there is as it is. While there is nothing inherently wrong (or nihilistic) in considering material nature to be inert and thing-like, it is a very abstract and merely intellectual *interpretation* of what there is. Both process thinkers such as Whitehead as well as phenomenologists such as Merleau-Ponty claim that such an understanding of nature can only be reached by disregarding or abstracting from most of the experiential or phenomenological data gleaned from the actual life-world. This results in a philosophy of nature that does not merely aim to understand physical and biological nature, but also to integrate and understand history, spirit and humanity.

> But the neglect which has fallen upon the philosophy of nature embraces also a certain conception of spirit, history and man, namely, the assumption of making them appear as pure negativity. By contrast, in returning to the philosophy of nature, we only seem to be looking away from these fundamental problems; in fact, we are trying to lay the ground for a solution to them which is not immaterialist. Naturalism apart, an ontology which leaves nature in silence shuts itself in the incorporeal and for this very reason gives a fantastic image of man, spirit and history. (Merleau-Ponty, *Themes* 62)

Thus, Merleau-Ponty proposes a quite unfamiliar, but interesting understanding of nature, which is very much in line with the position defended in this book. It is an understanding that does not imply or create an opposition between subjectivity and objectivity, between experience and matter, between spirit and nature. On the contrary, it rests on the premise that only an integrated look at nature as a whole can prevent inadequate ways of understanding the role of reason, objective matter, scientific discovery or humanity. Now we have to ask ourselves, should this understanding of nature truly be upheld, is it not simply anachronistic considering the successes of modern science? And if it is the case that our experience shows us reality or nature as alive, as becoming, complex, creative and dynamic, how could the reductive Newtonian view of nature ever have established itself? And how could it be as successful as it is? As contemporary philosophers it seems inadequate simply to ignore the fact that modern science and its reductive view of nature have led to striking technological and epistemic advances. Therefore, I will return once more to an investigation of the scientific view of nature.

The old Newtonian view of nature, which still influences contemporary science education, popular physics and some strands of contemporary biology, is the result of a certain epistemic approach that interprets nature only 'by reliance on clear and distinct sensory experiences, visual, auditory and tactile' (Whitehead, *Modes* 128). However, this approach necessarily 'omits those aspects of the universe as experience, and of our modes of experiencing, which jointly lead to the more penetrating ways of understanding' (Whitehead, *Modes* 135). So, the pervasive scientific understanding of nature is, among other factors, also a result of focusing on what is given clearly and distinctly in sense perception, while ignoring further levels of more integrated phenomenological experience. Husserl provides a similar diagnosis of modern science, insofar as modern science is based on the preconceptions implied by the methods of mathematical physics that were introduced by Galileo and came to full expression in Newton. The European sciences are in crisis, Husserl claims, not because they lack conceptual unity or progress, but because lived experience and the creative input it can provide has lost its place. He points out, first, that the results of contemporary science do not reflect the world we live in, and, secondly, that all the subjective elements that are essential to actual life have been excluded a priori, and thus the sciences do not have much to contribute to any question that involves subjectivity:

> In our vital need – so we are told – this science has nothing to say to us. It excludes in principle precisely the questions which man, give over in our unhappy times to the most portentous upheavals, finds the most burning: questions of the meaning or meaninglessness of the whole of this human existence. (Husserl, *Crisis* §2)

It is precisely this striving for objectivity and clarity that has enabled many of the scientific and technological advances that make our modern lives so comfortable. But objectivity and clarity come at a price. Through the lens of a scientific approach, reality is often presented in terms of a simplicity that does not actually exist. Furthermore, as subjectivity has no active role within science, the influence of the scientific approach even on social and cultural realms has led to a society that has forgotten about the essential role of the humanities, about history, literature and art, the essential contributions of an *episteme* that explicitly reflects and investigates what it means to be a human subject in this world.

The impression that everything that there is can be disclosed in a clear and precise manner means that what cannot be disclosed in this manner remains, by the very nature of this method, in the shadows. And thus, clarity and precision bring with them the danger of overconfidence in our understanding of what there is and a loss of engagement with actual reality as it is given in experience. This sort of objectivity and clarity conceals what it does not focus on, and through focusing on specific issues that are clearly highlighted, it plunges into shadow whatever is fuzzy, unclear, relational and constantly changing. It distorts and disconnects the original interconnection of reality. Striving for even more objectivity, even more focus and even more clarity are not remedies here, since a further application of these methods leads to more distortion. Clarity or pure objectivity can never provide a full and adequate picture of what there is, because this mode of thought can only ever illuminate one piece and then the next piece, never reaching a final vista that discloses how these aspects hang together, how they relate to human life and consciousness, let alone what there is as it is in its becoming creativity.

This general difference in epistemic approaches to nature, either attempting to reach mathematically describable simplicity and thus a (restricted) explanatory clarity on the one hand, or attempting to understand and describe the complex dynamic interconnectedness of the whole on the other, might be best illuminated by a couple of anecdotes. In writing the *Principia Mathematica* Bertrand Russell and Alfred North Whitehead got to know each other quite well. At the end of this close collaboration some fundamental differences in the way they saw and approached the world were evident to both. When Russell came to Harvard in 1940 to give the William James Lectures, Whitehead introduced him by remarking that 'Bertie says that I am muddle-headed, but I say that he is simple-minded' (Hartshorne 60). Russell, on the other hand, recalled Whitehead telling him, 'You think the world is what it looks like in fine weather at noon day; I think it is what it seems like in the early morning when one first wakes from deep sleep.' Russell continues:

> I thought his remark horrid, but could not see how to prove that my bias was any better than his. At last he showed me how to apply the technique of mathematical logic to his vague and higgledy-piggledy world, and dress it up in Sunday clothes that the mathematician could view without being shocked. (Russell, *Portraits* 39–40)

While for Russell, clarity was a necessary feature of knowledge and required Whitehead to dress up his worldview in a mathematician's Sunday clothes, for Whitehead this striving after clarity for clarity's sake was a danger for philosophy. The Sunday best, the focus on a neat appearance, can ensnare thought, seducing us into believing that reality is ultimately orderly and that thought or language can express what there is perfectly or even adequately.

Looking back, an elderly Russell ultimately agreed with Whitehead:

> Although I still think that this [i.e. mathematical exactness] is scientifically the right way to deal with the world, I have come to think that the mathematical and logical wrappings in which the naked truth is dressed go to deeper layers than I had supposed, and that things which I had thought to be skin are only well-made garments. Take, for instance, numbers: when you count, you count 'things,' but 'things' have been invented by human beings for their own convenience. This is not obvious on the earth's surface because, owing to the low temperature, there is a certain degree of apparent stability. But it would be obvious if one could live on the sun where there is nothing but perpetually changing whirlwinds of gas. If you lived on the sun, you would never have formed the idea of 'things,' and you would never have thought of counting because there would be nothing to count. In such an environment, Hegel's philosophy would seem to be common sense, and what we consider common sense would appear as fantastic metaphysical speculation.

> Such reflections have led me to think of mathematical exactness as a human dream, and not as an attribute of an approximately knowable reality. (Russell, *Portraits* 40)

So how are we to understand this higgledy-piggledy world, the sort of messy, chaotic, dynamic nature that takes into account physical as well as biological aspects, while also reflecting history, humanity and life, to shed at least some light on what is chaotic, relational, confused, unclear?

The concept of *nature alive* that I presented in discussing the Greek understanding of *physis* seems to be a good candidate for this project. And since both 'nature' and 'life' have a distinct overlap when it comes to characterising what there is as concrete, dynamic and relational, we can use either concept to denote these aspects of what there is. However, nature alive has the advantage of avoiding the immediate association of nature with materialism or scientism on the one hand, as well as potentially creating a barrier to interpreting life as consciousness, subjectivity or vitalism. The concept of *nature alive* used to characterise what there is presents what there is as *unfolding (i.e. temporal)* and *relational becoming*.

Taking this idea of the fundamental becoming and relationality of life or nature seriously leads us to some quite abstract and general ontological issues, which need to be addressed in order to understand the full integration and correlation between a *dynamic or temporal* understanding of what there is and a fundamentally *relational* understanding.[17] Therefore, it is now time to move towards a more speculative and thus more metaphysical examination of these issues.

---

17. This is one of the issues that distinguishes any processual approach from power ontologies or ontologies that focus on dispositions. These approaches still presuppose some*thing* (i.e. a power or disposition or something that possesses either the power or the disposition) that is related.

12

From Phenomenology to Speculative Metaphysics

The question that seems most urgent at this point is why? Why introduce all these complexities, connections and interrelations between life and nature, internal tendencies and so on? Why even risk falling into the old traps of anthropomorphism, vitalism, panpsychism? What does all this add to traditional metaphysical approaches? Why not simply stick to essences, powers or dispositions instead? In order to come to terms with these issues two questions need to be answered. The first question is, why is the step into speculation necessary? And the second is, why the move towards metaphysics?

The step into speculation is necessary because the way *nature alive* exists as productive and creative is itself not given as a phenomenon; this description is the result of speculative generalisations. The 'how' of being that nature exhibits cannot ultimately be grasped through mere observation alone. We can only ever experience facets and aspects of this natural dynamic presence, precisely because creative and productive nature can only create and produce over time, precisely because it is alive. Nature only shows itself as being alive over time and in its relation to its environment. And while phenomenology might be able to help us come to terms with the temporal structure of nature alive, its ontological organisation is a different matter. This step again takes us somewhat outside of the phenomenological realm and pushes us towards an ontological and thus a more speculative approach.

There is a further reason for this step into speculation. The concepts of 'nature' and 'life' found and ground the possibility of understanding in the first place: it is nature alive that grounds thought, it is life that enables us to keep going and keep thinking. Nature is not merely an object for consciousness, it is the realm from which we as human subjects constantly arise, which allows for our existence, which supports and grounds every moment of our being. In this sense nature is ontologically primary and the ground for living beings, if not for all being. Nature alive is thus neither a simple phenomenon, nor a simple speculative concept; it is a necessary material condition for conscious experience to exist at all. It is a material condition that cannot be grounded in human reason or subjectivity, or reduced to it, since it is the ontological basis that gives rise to human consciousness – historically through evolution and presently by continuously regenerating an environment that is able to sustain human life.

As to the second point, the move towards metaphysics, this question is especially pressing, considering that when I use nature alive as the main way to characterise what there is, this causes some familiar ontological issues: am I not simply substituting nature alive for essences, is this move not simply a new version of the idea of the good or God as the ground of all being(s)? If this is actually the case, the present attempt is just a specific interpretation of what we mean by being, and we inherit all the problems that plagued traditional ontologies. For example, there is the problem of ontological difference – the difference between 'life' and 'living beings' or 'nature' and 'natural beings'. This ontological difference is at least analogous, if not identical, to the difference between the realm of the ontological and the realm of the ontic described by Heidegger in *Being and Time*. So, am I simply repeating the difference between *Sein* (Being) and *Seiendes* (being), just in a slightly different form?

Philosophers familiar with Heidegger's *Fundamentalontologie* will immediately see how closely the relationship between living organisms and life, between natural beings and nature mirrors the ontological difference Heidegger describes. One way to avoid the issues that result from traditional ways of understanding being (which are not limited to the ontological difference but also include, among other problems, the issues of ontotheology and the objectification of the absolute) is to consider 'life' (or 'nature') as nature alive to be somehow inherently different from other definitions of being such as mere existence, essence or matter. And there are attempts to argue precisely this. Philosophers such as Frédéric Worms in his writings on critical vitalism or Gilles Deleuze in his late work *Pure Immanence* are examples of such attempts to distinguish 'life' from traditional metaphysical approaches.

In his critical vitalism Worms does not consider life to be a unified or simple ontological principle such as 'substance' or 'idea'. For him, life always denotes something fragmented and displaced, a series of differences and relationships, a going on that can never be grasped in one simple act. This means that life is understood as 'consisting in a series of differences and oppositions, of changes and relations' (Worms 9).[1] Worms's ontology is thus characterised by a fundamental openness, including issues such as death and decay, difference and contrast, past becoming and future outcome. Any exclusions, he argues, would lead to an ideological vitalism (Worms 10). If we use Worms's understanding of life, this leads to thinking what there is as fragmented (relational) and open (temporal). This way we can avoid the traditional unifying structures of essences and ideas and thus avoid many of the problems that result from traditional ontological structures. This way of conceiving life can also, *mutatis mutandis*, be considered to apply to nature, if nature is understood as *physis* in the pre-Socratic sense.

Deleuze approaches the concept of life somewhat differently. For him, it is a fundamentally empiricist concept, which he thinks in an ontological fashion. The fundamental starting point for him is pure immanence, which is the differential plane

---

1. My translation of 'eine Reihe von Differenzen und Widerständen, von Veränderungen und Beziehungen'.

of virtuality and all becoming. This differential plane of pure becoming to him is a life. This plane is most readily conceptualised as a field of difference – think about a field of grass, about clouds in the sky or even a monochromatic wallpaper. If one stares at any of these planes long enough, patterns and figures will emerge; they can shift and transform into other patterns without any apparent conscious activity. It is important to note that these patterns are not imagined, they are present in the way the grass blades stand, in the way the fibres of the wallpaper are shaped. What there is lends itself to these appearing forms. On the other hand, these patterns are not there in an absolute sense of objective existence, they have no stable substantiality. At any moment they can transform and appear as something else – all of these patterns are, whether they appear or not, but they are virtually. While this might be a somewhat helpful analogy to understand the field of immanence and its virtual nature, it is at the same time a poor analogy as it fundamentally connects virtuality and its actualisation to an observing consciousness. The field of immanence, however, pre-exists any interpreting consciousness; it is before understanding; it is impersonal and yet singular, it is pure virtuality, it is pure sensation that can coalesce into subjects and objects, without either being or presupposing a subject or an object. So, what Deleuze calls a life, pure immanence, is a field of virtual differences of multiplicities (indicating a relational dimension) that form, dissolve and reform time and again (implying a temporal dimension).

Both of these ways of conceptualising life thus imply or suggest that what there is is *temporal* and *relational,* just as the term 'nature' understood as *physis* suggested. However, as I have stated before, nature can only show itself as creative becoming, as alive, if it is considered in its temporality, investigated and observed for a sufficient period of time. Furthermore, the hallmark properties of actually existing nature alive cannot become fully evident by simply considering how a single phenomenon appears over time; the true mode of being of life or nature (i.e. nature alive) can only come to light if it is also *considered in its interactions with and relations to its surroundings.* No aspect of nature alive exists in complete separation. The act of separating a part from a living organism (such as a cell, for example) or an aspect of nature (such as materiality) in order to study these objects in detail transforms the object of study by robbing it of the hallmark features uncovered above, namely its enduring (temporal) and relational mode of existence. Nature alive thus needs to be considered in its evolving and changing relational organisation, in order to be able to appear as such and thus to be investigated as such.

The present project now hinges on the question of whether being fundamentally dynamic and fundamentally relational suffices to distinguish life (or, *mutatis mutandis*, nature alive) sufficiently from substances or essences as to render these concepts, and the hallmark properties of what there is that they suggest, a viable path for the development of a new metaphysics that does not simply repeat the tradition and its shortcomings.

Metaphysical Consequences

So, what kind of metaphysics would result from considering relationality and dynamic temporality as the hallmark features of what there is? Since relationality and dynamic temporality depend on each other, an investigation into either is at the same time an investigation into the other. And since I emphasised the temporal approach in Part II as well as Part III, it is now time to focus on the relational aspect and demonstrate how fundamentally it is connected to the temporal aspect.

There are two issues to consider when it comes to dynamic relationality on an ontological level. The first concerns the ontological status of relations, i.e. the question as to whether relations are internal or external, whether relations are an integrative and substantial aspect of what there is, or whether they are external to the beings they relate (the relata) and thus not essential to the identity of those beings. The second issue to be addressed is the question of how we can conceive of what stands in relation to each other (i.e. the beings that are internally related).

Let me begin by discussing the first issue. In a truly dynamic reality, it is impossible to distinguish between internal and external relations, as there is no *thing* they could be (said to be) internal or external to. Thinking reality as truly dynamic or processual implies that there are no substances, that there are no things that remain self-identical through change. In a dynamic reality there are no diachronically self-identical or self-contained physical (or material) objects, so there is no thing that relations could be internal or external to. Concrete processes are open to their surroundings, that is to say, they influence and are influenced by the other processes happening in their temporal and local vicinity to such a degree that it is difficult to determine where the external influence ends and where the process itself begins and vice versa. Again, life and nature provide us with very good paradigmatic examples for this kind of ontology. It is intuitively plausible to claim that the phenomena in question are so strongly interrelated that speaking of inside and outside is just a figure of speech, the result of a chosen perspective, as Georges Canguilhem argues with regard to living beings:

> From the biological point of view, one must understand that the relationship between the organism and its environment is the same as that between the parts and the whole of an organism. The individuality of the living thing does not stop at its ectodermic borders any more than it begins at the cell [. . .] The cell is a milieu for intracellular elements; it itself lives in an interior milieu which is sometimes on the scale of the organ and sometimes of the organism, the organism itself lives in a milieu that, in a certain fashion, is to the organism what the organism is to its components. (Canguilhem 111)

Let me now move on to discuss the second, more technical issue, namely the nature of the relata, i.e. the nature of what stands in relation. This question is usually answered by introducing some type of entity that can function as the bearer of the relation; such entities tend to be essences or substances. However, in suggesting a (static) something that is the bearer of the relation as a necessary precondition for relations, the possibility of a truly dynamic understanding of reality is necessarily excluded. This presupposition of a static bearer also presupposes that these bearers are more fundamental than the relations they stand in. The idea of a bearer is thus wholly inadequate to account for relations in a dynamic reality. Again, here relations cannot have bearers, since, as I argued before, there is no *thing* to bear them.

In order to account for dynamic reality, the traditional picture of relations and the relata that bear them has to be turned on its head, so to speak. It is not a something bearing and grounding relations; on the contrary, relations ground what we perceive as things. Relations are fundamental and their relata are not substantial entities, but the results of processual intersections of various relations. So, while this position does not necessarily imply relations without relata, it does imply that the relata not be individuals. What we generally consider things can thus be thought of as nodes or intersections formed by various relations that constitute diachronically (relatively) stable points of difference. These intersections of relations have a temporal dimension. They are the result of diachronic relations between past, present and future as well as of synchronic relations between contemporaneous processes. This diachronic dimension of relationality constitutes the temporality or becoming dynamism of what there is, which I have been describing throughout this book. The synchronic intersectionality, on the other hand, I have been referring to by the term 'relational', corresponds to the structures described by ontic structural realism.

This look at the nature of relations and the processes involved in these relations shows that the distinction between dynamic temporality and relationality is not as static or absolute as I have implied so far. The temporal-dynamic dimension can be grasped as a relation, while synchronic relations too are constantly evolving through time, so one could just drop the term 'relational' or the term 'dynamic' in favour of the other term. However, to keep things understandable I will continue with the convention of using the characterisations of 'dynamic' and 'relational' in the way used throughout.

To sum up these arguments, a further hallmark feature of any dynamic reality is the fact that everything is interrelated (to varying degrees), and that what there is is a function or a result of these dynamically evolving relations. This interrelation is so fundamental that it is difficult to distinguish one process from the other, and thus it is difficult to absolutely or objectively determine what is internal and what is external to any particular process, to determine where one resulting entity ends and the other begins. This structure holds in every direction: all the way down towards the simplest entities, all the way up to the level of the universe, all the way out and all the way in. The whole of reality is integrated, but it is integrated without collapsing into a holistic block, precisely because the integration itself is 'alive' in the previously introduced sense, and thus conflicts and differences continuously re-emerge – reality is constantly evolving, changing and shifting in creative and not fully predetermined ways.

The Becoming Existence of What There Is

If this fundamental temporal interrelatedness actually pertains, then this implies that there are no ultimate distinctions to be made between living and non-living, between nature and non-nature, the use of 'life' or 'nature alive'. Thus, thinkers such as Bergson, Deleuze or Worms are operating with a concept of life that is general enough to apply not only to all living beings, not only to nature, but to all that is – be that vitality or a plane of immanence. This transforms life or nature from concepts that characterise a part of reality into a specific, not traditionally metaphysical, understanding of being – into a *concept of being*. As concepts of being, life, nature or nature alive become metaphors so general as to lose their ability to exclude anything, these concepts thus lose their ability to distinguish between living and dead, between nature alive and inert nature. If we used life or nature as concepts of being, we would render any conceptual engagement with death or inert nature as difficult as the concepts of 'nothing' or 'not-being'. While such a strategy might suit our modern preference for avoiding death, this does not seem a price worth paying. Thus, while the terms 'life' or 'nature' are themselves problematic if used in an overly general ontological sense, they can provide us with a set of characteristics that shape or define all of being, the hallmarks of the real. Therefore, I will develop a general and abstract concept of being, based on the discoveries so far – a concept of being that is rooted in direct engagement and experience of what there is, namely the concept of becoming existence.

In the following paragraphs, I will introduce an understanding of being as becoming existence that takes all of these hallmark features into account, while leaving the well-used and reused and thus maybe distracting terminology of 'life' and 'nature', of 'immanence' and 'transcendence', of 'subject' and 'object' as well as the 'virtual' and the 'actual', behind. This means that I now move on to the level of ontology proper. In doing so I use the expression 'becoming existence' to express the hallmark features discovered in the investigation of life/ nature as a concept of being. What there is is then characterised by a generative relational growth – in all directions – that is co-guided by internal aims or an internal perspective, that is a result of all the relations and influences constituting the dynamic processes. Since this being is fundamentally relational, it can only be conceived as radically immanent; only non-being can be transcendent. The resulting characteristics are thus immanence, dynamicity and relationality, which create continuity and relative stability, i.e. becoming existence as a concept of being.

If becoming existence is to be considered a concept of being, then living organisms *and* reality as such are to be characterised by the same traits. In that case, it turns out that human beings are no exception to the natural order, but merely an example – maybe an outstanding one – of what there is. At first it seems rather far-fetched to characterise stones, human beings, cars and drops of water as dynamic and fundamentally interrelated. And of course, the way humans express becoming existence (their how of becoming existence) is about as removed from how stones embody becoming existence as white is removed from black on the colour spectrum. But still, the fact remains that black and white, as far apart as they are, still share their form of existence (as colours) just as rocks and humans share their form of becoming existence – as *becoming existents*. This 'sameness' of existence as becoming existents is presupposed in dynamic ontology, but this does not imply a qualitative sameness in all there is; in other words, it does not imply sameness in the concrete qualities that beings embody. Sameness of being does not imply qualitative sameness in the way this being is concretised, expressed or dynamically actualised, i.e. the way this is being 'lived'. There is a huge array of qualitative differences possible in becoming existence as a concept of being. Stones or planets, for example, go through this process at a much slower pace and with a lot less freedom or creativity than animals or human beings do. If we emphasise that becoming existence allows for almost infinite degrees in the quality of actualisation, it is not difficult to argue that stones go through the process of becoming, being and perishing just as human beings do. And this is the reason why dynamic ontology as an ontology of immanence can presuppose that all of concrete reality has the same form of being, namely becoming existence.

As I have implied before, in all of our experience of physical reality there is not one being, entity or thing that has stood the test of time without changing, without becoming, changing and perishing. While it is true that we also experience continuity and stability, much of modern science seems to indicate that this experience of stability is the result of changes that are too minute, too slow or too fast to be perceived. From quantum physics to astrophysics, not to mention other even more dynamic sciences such as biology, scientific results seem to confirm that change and movement are more fundamental than stability; they seem to ground the apparent stability that we are able to experience if we do not look too closely. So, if we take actual experience as well as the results of contemporary science seriously, we seem to possess a good basis for the claim that nothing in our physical universe is unchanging, that nothing that is part of this physical reality is eternal or timeless. Everything has become at one point, is undergoing changes now – these changes can either be so fast as to be almost instantaneous or almost imperceptibly slow – and will perish some time in the future. The same transient nature that shapes what there is becomes evident if we look closely at our own lives, if we seriously consider our bodily being. We exist as temporal beings, we are changing, evolving and unfolding in time. Our bodies have a duration, a concrete temporality just like any other being in the world. We have become, just like all beings, we are living and existing now, and we will share the fate of the world and perish one day. Even if we cannot remember our coming into being and are not usually very good at accepting our likely demise in the future, we constantly embody and enact bodily processes and changes. These physical or biological processes are going on while we experience changes in our stream of consciousness and in the world around us. We are inundated by change, from within and without. While it would be impossible to truly argue for a dynamic and relational understanding of physical reality in this book,[2] as it would challenge some of our most dearly held beliefs and necessitate some lengthy discussions which would have led us too far off topic, I hope that I have been able to show that it is at least somewhat intuitive to consider physical reality to be immanent, dynamic and relational – if we take our experiences seriously and investigate them closely enough and for a sufficient amount of time.

Therefore, modern science as well as our own conscious experience (of our minds and of the world) as well as our physical and biological existence all provide a similar picture: the entirety

---

2. These arguments are made by Alfred North Whitehead, Henri Bergson and Gilles Deleuze in various books. I have tried to give an account of this nature in Röck, *Physis*.

of concrete reality is continuously changing, continuously going through the processes of becoming, being and perishing – however minute or slow these changes might be. I hold this to be the most adequate description of what there is. This assessment suggests that in order to get a handle on such a world we should at least attempt to develop a metaphysics that can actively engage and account for the dynamic and relational character of the world, in order to 'enable us to conceive of nature more concretely, without abstraction' (Whitehead, *Modes* 147). If there is any use to the concept of becoming existence, then it is this. And even if the reader is not convinced that dynamic realism and becoming existence are adequate ways of capturing what there is, she might agree that the emerging world of technology is a world full of change, and we need to develop a conceptual scheme that can do justice to the complex, fast, dynamic and networked hybrid reality that we are living in today.

Any ontology or metaphysics is an attempt to describe what there is. The tool that we use to spell out and communicate such a description is the conceptual scheme,[3] developed with or as ontology, that we use to order what there is into understandable categories. The characterisation of what there is as fundamentally relational, dynamic and immanent implies the rejection of the idea that there is an ultimate conceptual scheme adequate for capturing concrete reality. It is thus the rejection of the claim that all people of all cultures and all times would fundamentally agree to the main differentiations implied by any scheme. Why? Even

---

3. The term 'conceptual scheme' is not used here in the sense that in knowledge or experience there are two aspects that can be distinguished, namely the 'conceptual scheme' and the 'empirical content'; this would imply the possibility of a clean distinction of the ontological from the epistemological. Since we have shown that such a distinction is impossible, conceptual scheme is used to mean an account of what is given that is explicitly based on a perspective, on certain preconceptions and a certain selectivity around what empirical data or what aims are most relevant. A conceptual scheme as it is understood here is thus never neutral, nor is it unaffected by the given, experienced empirical.

if all people of all cultures were to agree to the processual nature of reality, this cannot be translated into one ultimate conceptual scheme, due to the internal dynamic openness of processes. There would be schemes more or less adequate to grasp concrete reality and this adequacy would again be determined by the perspective and the aim of the investigation. This means that 'we are at liberty to substitute' one conceptual scheme for 'another more adequate for the purpose' (McHenry, *Event* 24) in question. This ability to substitute conceptual schemes does not, however, imply that we can do so at will, i.e. without being pushed by the phenomena; nor does it imply relativism, since it is not the case that any conceptual scheme can be substituted for any other conceptual scheme. The conceptual scheme substituted has to be more adequate for the purpose or investigation. The various degrees of adequacy are of course debatable, but they do provide an at least potentially determinable standard that is not relativistic.

Each conceptual scheme, each perspective and each translation has strengths and weaknesses. These strengths and weaknesses have many contributing factors: the structures and presuppositions employed, the aims, the phenomena investigated and so on. However, in the case of concrete dynamic reality, there is no 'original', no unchanging basis to which conceptual schemes, perspectives or translations can be compared. Thus, for our conceptual schemes, we have to give up the 'dependence on the *concept* [my emphasis] of an uninterpreted [objective and ultimate] reality, something outside all schemes and science' (Davidson 20). We have to give up on the idea of an absolute, objective reality against which we can measure our interpretations, but in doing so 'we do not relinquish the notion of objective truth - quite the contrary' (Davidson 20). I would argue that there remains the realm of experience which can – and here I am misusing Davidson's words - 'reestablish unmediated touch with the familiar objects whose antics make our sentences and opinions' (Davidson 20) about these objects adequate or inadequate.

So, while there is no ultimate original, no static, final or ultimate stable reality, the fact remains that every translation, every language, every conceptual scheme has conceptual, explanatory or descriptive strengths and weaknesses, phenomena or aspects it grasps well and phenomena or aspects that are very difficult to situate within the given scheme. Many traditional conceptual schemes excluded temporality, change or creativity, or considered these aspects ephemeral, mere appearance. With this in mind, it is not the aim of this book to revise or replace all forms of metaphysics, or to propose one specific conceptual scheme to eradicate all others, since no conceptual scheme is able to capture the full temporal complexity of what there is. The aim can only be to propose an additional conceptual scheme more adequate to come to terms with concrete reality as it is experienced.

I would like to end with the words of George Santayana:

> Here is one more system of philosophy. If the reader is tempted to smile, I can assure him that I smile with him [. . .] In the first place, my system is not mine, nor new. I am merely attempting to express for the reader the principles to which he appeals when he smiles. There are convictions in the depth of his soul, beneath all his overt parrot beliefs, on which I would build our friendship. (Santayana v)

Bibliography

Aeschylus. *Prometheus in Fesseln: Bilingual Edition*. Ed. D. Bremer. Frankfurt: Insel Verlag, 1988.
Aristotle. *The Complete Works of Aristotle*. Ed. J. Barnes. 2 vols. Princeton: Princeton University Press, 1984.
Augustine. *Confessions*. Ed. J. Henderson. Cambridge, MA: Harvard University Press, 2016.
Berghofer, Philipp. 'Why Husserl is a Moderate Foundationalist'. *Husserl Studies* 34.1 (2018): 1–23.
Bergson, Henri. *Creative Evolution: An Alternate Explanation for Darwin's Mechanism of Evolution*. Trans. A. Mitchel. New York: The Modern Library, Random House, 1944.
—. *The Creative Mind: An Introduction to Metaphysics*. New York: Kensington Books, 2002.
—. *Matter and Memory*. Trans. W. S. Palmer and N. M. Paul. New York: Zone Books, 1991.
—. *Time and Free Will: An Essay on the Immediate Data of Consciousness*. Trans. F. L. Pogson. London: George Allen and Unwin, 1910.
Bernet, Rudolf. 'Husserls Begriff des Noema'. In S. Ijsseling, ed., *Husserl-Ausgabe und Husserl-Forschung*. Dordrecht: Kluwer, 1990. 61–80.
Bernet, Rudolf, Iso Kern and Marbach Eduard. *An Introduction to Husserlian Phenomenology*. Evanston, IL: Northwestern University Press, 1993.
Berto, Francesco, and Matteo Plebani. *Ontology and Metaontology*. London: Bloomsbury, 2015.
Blanshard, Brand. *The Nature of Thought, Vol. 2*. New York: Humanities Press, 1969.
Boethius, A. M. S. *Aristoteles Latinus, Categoriae vel praedicamenta*. Ed. L. Minio-Paluello. Bruges: Desclée de Brouwer, 1961.
Bradley, F. H. *Appearance and Reality: A Metaphysical Essay*. Oxford: Clarendon Press, 1897.
—. 'Relations'. In *Collected Essays, Vol. II*. Oxford: Clarendon Press, 1935. 642–3.
Bremer, Dieter. 'Von der Physis zur Natur. Eine griechische Konzeption und ihr Schicksal'. *Zeitschrift für philosophische Forschung* 43 (1989): 241–64.

BIBLIOGRAPHY

Brentano, Franz. *Descriptive Psychology*. Trans. B. Müller. London: Routledge, 1995.
—. *Psychology from an Empirical Standpoint*. London: Routledge, 1973.
Broad, D. C. *Scientific Thought*. London: Routledge and Kegan Paul, 1923.
Brower, Jeffrey E. 'Aristotelian vs. Contemporary Perspectives on Relations'. In Anna Marmodoro and David Yates, eds, *The Metaphysics of Relations*. Oxford: Oxford University Press, 2016. 36–54.
Cairns, Huntington. 'Introduction'. In *The Collected Dialogues of Plato*. Ed. Edith Hamilton and Huntington Cairns. Trans. Lane Cooper. Princeton: Princeton University Press, 1961. xiii–xxv.
Canguilhem, Georges. *Knowledge of Life*. Ed. P. Marrati and T. Meyers. Trans. S. Geroulanos and D. Ginsburg. New York: Fordham University Press, 2008.
Chapman, H. M. 'Realism and Phenomenology'. In M. Natanson, ed., *Essays in Phenomenology*. Dordrecht: Springer, 1966. 79–115.
Chernyakov, A. *The Ontology of Time: Being and Time in the Philosophies of Aristotle, Husserl and Heidegger*. Dordrecht: Springer, 2002.
Cooper, Ron L. *Heidegger and Whitehead: A Phenomenological Examination into the Intelligibility of Experience*. Athens, OH: Ohio University Press, 1993.
Cresswell, M. J. 'Why Objects Exist but Events Occur'. *Studia Logica* 45.4 (1986): 371–5.
Davidson, Donald. 'The Very Idea of a Conceptual Scheme'. *The American Philosophical Association* 47 (1974): 5–20.
De Palma, Vittorio. 'Eine peinliche Verwechslung. Zu Husserls Transzendentalismus'. *Metodo. International Studies in Phenomenology and Philosophy* 1.1 (2015): 14–45.
de Vries, Willem A. *Wilfrid Sellars*. Chesham: Acumen, 2005.
Debaise, Didier. *Nature as Event: The Lure of the Possible*. Trans. Michael Halewood. Durham, NC: Duke University Press, 2017.
—. *Speculative Empiricism: Revisiting Whitehead*. Trans. Thomas Weber. Edinburgh: Edinburgh University Press, 2017.
Deleuze, Gilles. *Dialogues, Gilles Deleuze and Claire Parnet*. Trans. H. Tomlinson and B. Habberjam. London: Athlone Press, 1987.
—. *Difference and Repetition*. New York: Columbia University Press, 1994.
—. *Pure Immanence: Essays on a Life*. Trans. Anne Boyman. New York: Zone Books, 2001.
Derrida, Jacques. *The Problem of Genesis in Husserl's Philosophy*. Trans. Marian Hobson. Chicago: University of Chicago Press, 2003.
Descartes, René. *The Philosophical Writings of Descartes*. Trans. Robert Stoothoff, Dugald Murdoch, Anthony Kenny and John Cottingham. 3 vols. Cambridge: Cambridge University Press, 2005.
Dewey, John. *Experience and Nature*. La Salle, IL: Open Court, 1986.
Dod, Bernhard G. 'Aristoteles latinus'. In A. Kenny, J. Pinborg, N. Kretzmann and E. Stump, eds, *The Cambridge History of Later Medieval Philosophy: From the Rediscovery of Aristotle to the Disintegration of Scholasticism, 1100–1600*. Cambridge: Cambridge University Press, 1982. 45–80.

Dolbeault, Joel. 'From Mind to Matter: How Bergson Anticipated Quantum Ideas'. *Mind & Matter* 10.1 (2012): 25–45.
Dolev, Yuval. 'Motion and Passage: The Old B-Theory and Phenomenology'. In L. N. Oaklander, ed., *Debates in the Metaphysics of Time*. New York: Bloomsbury, 2014. 31–50.
Drost, Mark P. 'The Primacy of Perception in Husserl's Theory of Imagining'. *Philosophy and Phenomenological Research* 50.3 (1990): 569–82.
Drummond, John J. *Husserlian Intentionality and Non-Foundational Realism: Noema and Object*. Dordrecht: Kluwer, 1990.
Dukic, Vladimir, and Marie-Eve Morin. 'Introduction'. In Marie-Eve Morin, *Continental Realism and its Discontents*. Edinburgh: Edinburgh University Press, 2017. 1–20.
Duncombe, Matthew. *Aristotle on the Distinction between Substances and Relatives*. Oxford: Oxford University Press, 2020.
Eisler, Rudolf. 'Stichwort: Anschauung, intellektuale'. In R. Eisler, *Wörterbuch der philosophischen Begriffe in 2 Bänden*. Berlin: Verlag Ernst Siegfried Mittler und Sohn, 1904.
Føllesdal, Dagfinn. 'Husserl on Evidence and Justification'. In Robert Sokolowski, ed., *Edmund Husserl and the Phenomenological Tradition*. Washington, DC: Catholic University of America Press, 1988. 107–30.
———. 'Husserl's Notion of Noema'. *Journal of Philosophy* 66.20 (1969): 680–7.
Ferraris, Maurizio. *Manifesto del nuovo realismo*. Rome: Laterza, 2012.
———. *Positive Realism*. Winchester: Zero Books, 2015.
Gabriel, Markus. *Fields of Sense: A New Realist Ontology*. Edinburgh: Edinburgh University Press, 2015.
Gloy, Karen. *Komplexität. Ein Schlüsselbegriff der Moderne*. Paderborn: Wilhelm Fink, 2014.
Godfrey-Smith, Peter. *Philosophy of Biology*. Princeton, NJ: Princeton University Press, 2016.
Grant, Iain Hamilton. *Philosophies of Nature After Schelling*. London: Continuum, 2006.
Gratton, Peter. *Speculative Realism*. London: Bloomsbury, 2014.
Greenough, Patrick, and Michael P. Lynch. *Truth and Realism*. Oxford: Clarendon Press, 2006.
Gurwitsch, Aron. *The Structure of the Perceptual Noema*. In *The Collected Works of Aron Gurwitsch (1901–1973)*. Ed. J. García-Gómez. Phaenomenologica (Published under the Auspices of the Husserl-Archives), vol. 192. Springer, Dordrecht, 2010.
Haag, J. 'A Kantian Critique of Sellars' Transcendental Realism'. In P. J. Reider, ed., *Wilfrid Sellars, Idealism, and Realism: Understanding Psychological Nominalism*. London: Bloomsbury, 2017. 149–72.
Hacker, P. M. S. 'Events, Ontology and Grammar'. *Philosophy* 57.222 (1982): 477–86.
Hägglund, Martin. 'Radical Atheist Materialism: A Critique of Meillassoux'. In Levi Bryant, Nick Srnicek and Graham Harman, eds, *The Speculative Turn: Continental Materialism and Realism*. Melbourne: re.press, 2011. 114–29.

Hartshorne, Charles. 'Whitehead's Philosophy of Reality as Socially Structured Process'. *Chicago Review* 8.2 (1954): 60–77.
Heffernan, George. 'A Tale of Two Schisms: Heidegger's Critique of Husserl's Move into Transcendental Idealism'. *The European Legacy* 21 (2016): 556–75.
Heidegger, Martin. *Being and Time*. Trans. Joan Stambaugh. Albany: State University of New York Press, 2010.
——. *Die Grundprobleme der Phänomenologie (1919/1920)*. Ed. H.-H. Gander. Vol. GA 58. Frankfurt: Klostermann, 1992.
——. *History of the Concept of Time: Prolegomena*. Trans. Theodore Kisiel. Bloomington: Indiana University Press, 1985.
——. *Introduction to Metaphysics*. Trans. Gregory Fried and Richard Polt. New Haven, CT: Yale University Press, 2000.
——. 'On the Question of Being'. In Martin Heidegger, *Pathmarks*. Ed. W. McNeill. Cambridge: Cambridge University Press, 1998. 291–323.
Heidel, William A. 'Peri Physeos. A Study of the Conception of Nature among the Pre-Socratics'. *Proceedings of the American Academy of Arts and Sciences* 45 (1910): 79–133.
Heinemann, Gottfried. *Studien zum griechischen Naturbegriff I. Philosophische Grundlegung: der Naturbegriff und die 'Natur'*. Trier: Wissenschaftlicher Verlag Trier, 2001.
Hume, David. *A Treatise of Human Nature*. Ed. P. H. Nidditch and L. A. Selby-Bigge. 2nd edn. Oxford: Clarendon Press, 1978.
Husserl, Edmund. *Analyses Concerning Passive and Active Synthesis: Lectures on Transcendental Logic*. Trans. A. J. Steinbock. Dordrecht: Kluwer, 2001.
——. *Briefwechsel – Wissenschaftlerkorrespondenz*. Ed. K. Schuhmann. Vol. Husserliana Dokumente III/7. Dordrecht: Kluwer, 1994.
——. *Cartesian Meditations: An Introduction to Phenomenology*. Trans. Dorion Cairns. The Hague: Martinus Nijhoff, 1960.
——. *The Crisis of European Sciences and Transcendental Phenomenology*. Trans. David Carr. Evanston, IL: Northwestern University Press, 1970.
——. *Einleitung in die Logik und Erkenntnistheorie, Vorlesung 1906/7*. Ed. Ulrich Melle. Vol. HUA 24. Dordrecht: Martinus Nijhoff, 1984.
——. *Formal and Transcendental Logic*. Trans. D. Cairns. Vol. HUA 17. The Hague: Martinus Nijhoff, 1969.
——. *The Idea of Phenomenology*. Trans. Lee Hardy. Vol. HUA 2. Dordrecht: Kluwer, 1999.
——. *Ideas: General Introduction to Pure Phenomenology*. Ed. Dermot Moran. Trans. W. R. Boyce Gibson. London: Routledge, 2012.
——. *Ideas Pertaining to a Pure Phenomenology and to a Phenomenological Philosophy, Book I*. Trans. F. Kersten. Vols. HUA 3/I, 3/II. Dordrecht: Kluwer, 1983.
——. *Ideas Pertaining to a Pure Phenomenology and to a Phenomenological Philosophy, Book II*. Trans. A. Schuwer and R. Rojcewicz. Dordrecht: Kluwer, 1989.
——. *Introduction to Logic and the Theory of Knowledge. Lectures 1906/07*. Trans. Claire Ortiz Hill. Dordrecht: Springer, 2008.

—. *Logical Investigations*, Vol. *I*. Ed. Dermot Moran. Trans. J. N. Findlay. Vol. HUA 18. London: Routledge, 2001.

—. *Logical Investigations*, Vol. *II*. Ed. Dermot Moran. Trans. J. N. Findlay. Vols. HUA 19/1, 19/2. London: Routledge, 2001.

—. *On the Phenomenology of the Consciousness of Internal Time (1893–1917)*. Ed. J. B. Brough. Vol. HUA 10. Dordrecht: Kluwer, 1991.

—. *Thing and Space: Lectures of 1907*. Dordrecht: Kluwer, 1997.

—. *Vorlesungen über Bedeutungslehre: Sommersemester 1908*. Ed. Ursula Panzer. Vol. HUA 26. Dordrecht: Kluwer, 1986.

—. *Zur Phänomenologie der Intersubjektivität. Erster Teil 1905–1920*. Ed. Iso Kern. Vol. HUA 13. The Hague: Martinus Nijhoff, 1973.

Jansen, Julia. 'On Transcendental and Non-Transcendental Idealism in Husserl: A Response to De Palma and Loidolt'. *Metodo. International Studies in Phenomenology and Philosophy*, special issue, 1.2 (2017): 27–39.

Kahn, C. *Anaximander and the Origins of Greek Cosmology*. New York: Columbia University Press, 1960.

Kant, Immanuel. *Critique of Pure Reason*. Ed. and trans. Allen W. Wood and Paul Guyer. Cambridge: Cambridge University Press, 1998.

Kirk, G. S. *Heraclitus. The Cosmic Fragments*. Cambridge: Cambridge University Press, 1962.

Kortooms, Toine. *Phenomenology of Time*. Dordrecht: Kluwer, 2002.

Ladyman, James, and Don Ross. *Every Thing Must Go: Metaphysics Naturalised*. Oxford: Oxford University Press, 2010.

Leibniz, G. F. *New Essays*. Trans. P. Remnant and J. Bennett. Cambridge: Cambridge University Press, 1985.

Levine, Steven. *Pragmatism, Objectivity and Experience*. Cambridge: Cambridge University Press, 2019.

Levins, Richard. 'The Strategy of Model Building in Population Biology'. *American Scientist* 54.4 (1966): 421–31.

Lohmar, Dieter. 'Husserl's Concept of Categorial Intuition'. In D. Zahavi and F. Stjernfelt, eds, *One Hundred Years of Phenomenology: Phaenomenologica*. Dordrecht: Springer, 2002. 125–45.

Loidolt, Sophie. 'Transzendentalphilosophie und Idealismus in der Phänomenologie. Überlegungen zur phänomenologischen "Gretchenfrage"'. *Metodo. International Studies in Phenomenology and Philosophy*, special issue, 1.1 (2015): 103–35.

Markosian, Ned. 'Against Ontological Fundamentalism'. *Facta Philosophica* 7 (2005): 69–84.

Marmodoro, Anna, and David Yates. 'Introduction'. In Anna Marmodoro and David Yates, eds, *The Metaphysics of Relations*. Oxford: Oxford University Press, 2016. 1–19.

Maudlin, Tim. *Philosophy of Physics*. Princeton, NJ: Princeton University Press, 2012.

McDowell, John. *Mind and World*. Cambridge, MA: Harvard University Press, 1996.

McHenry, Leemon B. *The Event Universe: The Revisionary Metaphysics of Alfred North Whitehead*. Edinburgh: Edinburgh University Press, 2020.
—. 'Quine and Whitehead: Ontology and Methodology'. *Process Studies* 26.1/2 (1997): 2–12.
McTaggart, John. 'The Unreality of Time'. *Mind. A Quarterly Review of Psychology and Philosophy*, NS, 17.68 (1908): 457–74.
Meillassoux, Quentin. *After Finitude: An Essay on the Necessity of Contingency*. Trans. Ray Brassier. London: Continuum, 2011.
—. 'The Contingency of the Laws of Nature'. *Environment and Planning D: Society and Space* 30 (2012): 322–34.
Merleau-Ponty, Maurice. *Nature: Course Notes from the Collège de France*. Ed. Dominique Séglard. Trans. Robert Vallier. Evanston, IL: Northwestern University Press, 2003.
—. *Themes from the Lectures at the College de France 1952–1960*. Trans. John O'Neill. Evanston, IL: Northwestern University Press, 1970.
Mignucci, Mario. 'Aristotle's Definitions of Relatives in "Cat." 7'. *Phronesis* 31.2 (1986): 101–27.
Moran, Dermot. *Edmund Husserl, Founder of Phenomenology*. Cambridge: Polity Press, 2005.
Moran, Dermot, and Joseph Cohen. *The Husserl Dictionary*. London: Continuum, 2012.
Morin, Marie-Eve. 'Merleau-Ponty and the Challenge of Realism'. In Marie-Eve Morin, *Continental Realism and its Discontents*. Edinburgh: Edinburgh University Press, 2017. 137–54.
Nietzsche, Friedrich. 'On Truth and Lie in a Nonmoral Sense'. In *On Truth and Untruth: Selected Writings*. Ed. and trans. Taylor Carman. New York: HarperCollins, 2010. 15–50.
Peirce, Charles Sanders. *Chance, Love and Logic: Philosophical Essays*. London: Kegan Paul, Trench, Trubner, 1923.
—. *Collected Papers of Charles Sanders Peirce: Science and Philosophy, and Reviews, Correspondence and Bibliography*, Vol. 7. Ed. Arthur W. Burks. Cambridge, MA: Harvard University Press, 1966.
Pihlström, Sami. 'Metaphysics'. In Sami Pihlström, ed., *The Continuum Companion to Pragmatism*. London: Continuum, 2011. 92–101.
—. 'New Directions'. In Sami Pihlström, ed., *The Continuum Companion to Pragmatism*. London: Continuum, 2011. 201–16.
Ramey, Joshua. 'Contingency Without Unreason'. *Angelaki* 19.1 (2014): 31–46.
Ricœur, Paul. *A Key to Husserl's Ideas I*. Marquette, WI: Marquette University Press, 1996.
—. *Temps et récit, 1: l'intrigue et le récit historique*. Paris: Éditions du Seuil, 1991.
Röck, Tina. 'The Concept of Nature: From Presocratic Physis to the Natural Kosmos of the Timaeus'. *Philosophica* 47 (2016): 9–27.
—. 'Experiencing Reality Alive: Bergson and Whitehead on Engaged Experience'. In D. Kreps, ed., *Understanding Digital Events: Bergson, Whitehead, and the Experience of the Digital*. Oxford: Routledge, 2019. 97–113.

—. *Physis als bewegte Existenz. Eine Ontologie des Konkreten*. Berlin: Duncker & Humboldt, 2016.
—. 'Time for Ontology? The Role of Ontological Time in Anticipation'. *Axiomathes* 29 (2017): 33–47.
Russell, Bertrand. *A History of Western Philosophy*. New York: Simon and Schuster, 1945.
—. *Portraits from Memory and Other Essays*. New York: Simon and Schuster, 1956.
—. *Principles of Mathematics*. 2nd edn. London: George Allen and Unwin, 1937.
—. *The Problems of Philosophy*. Oxford: Oxford University Press, 1980.
Sachs, Carl B. *Intentionality and the Myths of the Given: Between Pragmatism and Phenomenology*. New York: Routledge, 2016.
Santayana, George. *Scepticism and Animal Faith*. New York: Scribner's, 1923.
Seibt, Johanna. 'How to Naturalise Sensory Consciousness and Intentionality within a Process Monism with Normativity Gradient. A Reading of Sellars'. In James R. O'Shea, ed., *Sellars and his Legacy*. Oxford: Oxford University Press, 2016. 186–222.
Sellars, Wilfrid. 'The Lever of Archimedes'. *The Monist* 64.1 (1981): 3–37.
—. *Science, Perception and Reality*. Atascadero, CA: Ridgeview, 1991.
—. 'The Structure of Knowledge'. In Hector-Neri Castañeda, ed., *Action, Knowledge and Reality: Studies in Honor of Wilfrid Sellars*. Indianapolis, IN: Bobbs-Merrill, 1975. 295–347.
—. 'Truth and "Correspondence"'. *The Journal of Philosophy* 59.2 (1962): 29–56.
Shaviro, Stephen. *The Universe of Things: On Speculative Realism*. Minneapolis: University of Minnesota Press, 2014.
Simons, Peter. 'Events'. In M. J. Loux and D. W. Zimmerman, eds, *The Oxford Handbook of Metaphysics*. Oxford: Oxford University Press, 2003. 358–85.
—. 'Metaphysics in Analytic Philosophy'. In Michael Beaney, ed., *The Oxford Handbook of the History of Analytic Philosophy*. Oxford: Oxford University Press, 2013. 709–29.
Smith, David Woodruff. *Husserl*. New York: Routledge, 2007.
Soffer, Gail. 'Revisiting the Myth: Husserl and Sellars on the Given'. *The Review of Metaphysics* 57.2 (2003): 301–37.
Sokolowski, Robert. 'Intentional Analysis and the Noema'. *Diacritica* 38.2–3 (1984): 113–29.
—. *Introduction to Phenomenology*. Cambridge: Cambridge University Press, 2000.
Sparrow, Tom. *The End of Phenomenology. Metaphysics and the New Realism*. Edinburgh: Edinburgh University Press, 2014.
Staiti, Andrea. 'Pre-Predicative Experience and Life-World: Two Distinct Projects in Husserl's Late Phenomenology'. In Dan Zahavi, ed., *The Oxford Handbook of the History of Phenomenology*. Oxford: Oxford University Press, 2018. 155–73.
Strawson, Peter. *Individuals: An Essay in Descriptive Metaphysics*. London: Methuen, 1959.

Tegtmeier, Erwin. 'Temporal Succession and Tense'. In L. N. Oaklander, ed., *Debates in the Metaphysics of Time*. New York: Bloomsbury, 2014. 73–86.

Thacker, Eugene. *After Life*. Chicago: University of Chicago Press, 2010.

Unger, Roberto, and Lee Smolin. *The Singular Universe and the Reality of Time: A Proposal in Natural Philosohpy*. Cambridge: Cambridge University Press, 2015.

van Fraassen, Bas. *Scientific Representation: Paradoxes of Perspective*. Oxford: Oxford University Press, 2008.

van Inwagen, Peter. 'Meta-ontology'. *Erkenntnis* 48 (1998): 33–250.

Vanzago, Luca. *L'Evento del Tempo*. Milan: Mimesis, 2005.

—. 'Introduzione'. In Alfred North Whitehead, *Processo e realtà*. Florence: Bompiani, 2019. 7–63.

—. *Modi del Tempo. Simultaneità, processualità e relatzionalità tra Whitehead e Merleau-Ponty*. Milan: Mimesis, 2001.

Westerlund, Frederik. 'Phenomenology as Understanding of Origin. Remarks on Heidegger's First Critique of Husserl'. In Frederike Rese, ed., *Heidegger und Husserl im Vergleich*. Frankfurt: Klostermann, 2010. 34–56.

Whitehead, Alfred North. *Adventures of Ideas*. Cambridge: Cambridge University Press, 1933.

—. *The Aims of Education and Other Essays*. London: Williams and Norgate, 1929.

—. *The Concept of Nature*. Cambridge: Cambridge University Press, 1920.

—. *Modes of Thought*. New York: The Free Press, 1966.

—. *Process and Reality*. Corrected edition. New York: Macmillan, 1978.

—. *Science and the Modern World*. New York: Macmillan, 1948.

Wiesing, Lambert. *The Philosophy of Perception*. Trans. Nancy Ann Roth. London: Bloomsbury, 2014.

Williams, D. C. 'The Myth of Passage'. *Journal of Philosophy* 48.15 (1951): 457–72.

Williams, James. *Gilles Deleuze's Philosophy of Time: A Critical Introduction and Guide*. Edinburgh: Edinburgh University Press, 2011.

Worms, Frédéric. *Über Leben*. Berlin: Merve, 2013.

Zahavi, Dan. 'The End of What? Phenomenology vs. Speculative Realism'. *International Journal of Philosophical Studies* 24.3 (2016): 289–309.

Index

Note: page numbers followed by 'n' indicate footnotes.

4D theorists, 147

a priori correlations, 52–3, 98–100, 102–3, 118
Abschattungen (adumbrations), 225
absolute idealists, 94
absolute knowledge, 179, 182
absolute understanding, 63–4
abstractions, 33, 220, 251
actual occasions/actual entities, 186–7
ad-aequatio, 36
adequacy, 34–7
adumbrations, 225
aeroplane, flight of, 43–4
After Finitude (Meillassoux), 53–4, 114, 115–16, 117
Aims of Education (Whitehead), 25
aletheia, 35
Analyses Concerning Passive and Active Synthesis (Husserl), 102
analysis, 179–82
analytic metaphysics, 50–1
analytic philosophy, 2, 21–3, 50, 177, 205–6, 207, 237
ancestrality, 115–17
appearance, 78–9
Appearance and Reality (Bradley), 57
arche-fossils, 115–16
Aristotle
   asyntheta, 35, 106–7n
   change, 125, 144, 148
   life, 261–6, 268
   master-slave relation, 56, 58
   nature, 144, 197, 270–3
   prote philosophia, 201
   relations, 54–5

   substances, 55, 204–5
   time, 125, 148
asyntheta, 35, 106–7n
attitudes, 81–4
Augustine, 151, 157

Basic Problems of Phenomenology (Husserl), 104
becoming
   dynamic event ontologies, 162
   growth and becoming metaphor, 153–8
   and prehension, 185–7
   Whitehead, 158–61
becoming existence, 203–8, 289–95
beginnings, 40
being, 23, 27–9, 200–3
   as becoming existence, 289–95
   and experience, 17, 184
   as process, 59
   temporal, 203–8
   and temporality/time, 34, 138, 141–5, 153–4
   and thinking, 4, 6, 60–5
   see also existence; *nature alive*
Being and Time (Heidegger), 7, 69, 78, 142, 283
Bergson, Henri, 8, 9, 137
   duration, 30, 143, 172
   experience, 171–2: engaged, 228
   intuition, 172–9: and knowledge, 179–84
   life, 265–6
   matter, 239–41
   motion, 152
   perception, 16, 173
   reality, 245
   science, 219, 220
Berkeley, George, 240, 261

Berto, Francesco, 19
biochemistry, 22
biology, 205
Blanshard, Brand, 57
bodily awareness, 193
bodily feeling, experience as, 184–9
  causal efficacy and presentational immediacy, 191–5
  epistemology v. ontology, 189–91
Bradley, Francis Herbert, 57–8
Brentano, Franz, 8, 119
Briefwechsel (Husserl), 67, 85
Broad, D. C., 43, 161
broken straw illusions, 75–6
building-block ontologies, 162–3

Cairns, Huntington, 269
Cambridge change, 24–5
Canguilhem, Georges, 287
Cartesian Meditations (Husserl), 77, 80, 94–5, 103, 109–10, 117, 123
Categories (Aristotle), 54, 55, 270–1
causal efficacy, 190, 191–5, 228
causality, 190, 193, 194
Chance, Love and Logic (Peirce), 39
change, 23–7, 270–2
  dynamic event ontologies, 162
  scientific view of, 291–3
  and stability, 199–200
  and temporality/time, 120–1, 124: Aristotle, 125, 144, 148; Husserl, 119, 126, 127–33; McTaggart, 146, 149–50; Parmenides, 143; Plato, 143–4; Shoemaker, 31–3, 42–3
  see also becoming
chaos, 26, 99–100
Chapman, H. M., 226
Chernyakov, A., 142
clarity, 278, 279
clock time, 30, 125, 147, 155; *see also* objective time
Collected Papers (Peirce), 219n
composite parts, 181
'Concept of Nature' (Röck), 271
Concept of Nature (Whitehead), 188–9, 215, 274
concepts, 215, 216, 218
conceptual prehensions, 184n
conceptual schemes, 293–5
concrescence, 186
concrete reality, 215
conditio humana, 2

Confessions (Augustine), 157
conscious temporality, 122
consciousness, 17, 18, 226
  foundationalism, 112
  intentional object of, 109–10
  pure, 97, 98–101
  and temporality/time, 120, 126, 146
  time-consciousness, 152
  and world, 95–6
constitution, 102
constructivism, 62
continental philosophy, 2–3
'Contingency of the Laws of Nature' (Meillassoux), 167
continuity, 40
Cooper, Ron L., 139, 142–3, 154, 189, 192
Copenhagen interpretation, 241–2
copula, 5
correlated transcendental realism, 92, 101–3
  critical perspectives, 103–13
correlationism, 113–18
correlations, 52–4, 60; *see also* a priori correlations; relations
cosmology, 235
Cratylus (Plato), 23–4
Creative Evolution (Bergson), 241, 265–6
Creative Mind (Bergson), 16, 152, 172, 173, 174–5, 177, 180, 183, 220, 226n
creativity, 3–4
Crisis of European Sciences (Husserl), 47, 52, 82, 84, 90, 256–7, 273, 278

Davidson, Donald, 163, 294
De anima (Aristotle), 262, 263, 264, 266, 271
de Vries, Willem A., 250
Debaise, Didier, 35, 45, 134, 185, 187, 253, 274
Deleuze, Gilles, 137–8, 157, 169, 171–2, 202, 284–5
Denkmöglichkeiten (possibilities of thought), 42–3
Derrida, Jacques, 91, 141
Descartes, René, 184–5
descriptions, 217–18
descriptive metaphysics, 20
dianoia, 34
Dick, Philip K., 210
Difference and Repetition (Deleuze), 157, 202

INDEX

direct experience, 4; *see also* engaged experience
Dolev, Yuval, 151–2
Drummond, John J., 87
Dukic, Vladimir, 114
Duns Scotus, John, 202
duration (*durée*), 120, 137, 143, 148n, 172, 177
dynamic ontologies, 161–8, 200, 205, 291
dynamic realism, 6–8, 18, 41, 86, 244, 246
dynamic reality, 21, 29, 59, 247–52
dynamic relationality, 286–9
dynamic temporality, 288–9

effective differences, 3
efficacy, 232
  causal, 190, 191–5, 228
Einleitung in die Logik (Husserl), 71, 102
ekstatic temporality, 143
empiricism, 62, 169, 171, 214
  minimal, 211
'Empiricism and the Philosophy of Mind' (Sellars), 105
End of Phenomenology (Sparrow), 113
engaged experience, 4, 214, 218–29
  moving towards, 221–6
  what it is not, 219–21
epistemic realism, 4–6
epistemology, 4, 6, 60–5, 189–91
epoch, 160
epochal time, 143, 158–61
epochē, 83, 84, 85, 93
Erfahrung, 15–16, 70
Erlebnis (lived experience), 15, 16, 45, 134, 217
eternal entities, 29–30
event ontologies, 161–8
Event Universe (McHenry), 159, 160, 164, 186, 215, 220, 294
events, 181, 202, 273–4
'Events' (Simons), 166
everyday world, 38, 61–2, 64, 209, 213, 253, 255
  and science, 251
existence, 23, 27, 28–9
  becoming existence, 203–8, 289–95
  mere existence, 29, 202, 206–7
  see also being
experience, 7, 14–19, 214–18, 294
  and ancestrality, 116–17
  and being, 17, 184

as bodily feeling, 184–9: causal efficacy and presentational immediacy, 191–5; epistemology v. ontology, 189–91
and consciousness, 97
and immanent transcendence, 46
as intuition, 172–9: and knowledge, 179–84
and knowledge, 106
of matter, 239–40
phenomenological tradition, 70, 71–6: object of experience, 76–9
pre-predicative, 107–8
and scientific method, 252
and speculation, 44–5
and temporality, 120, 138–9, 169–72
and the world, 258
see also engaged experience; *Erlebnis* (lived experience)
Experience and Judgement (Husserl), 107–8
external relations, 57–8, 287

fallacy of misplaced concreteness, 32–3, 220, 238
fallacy of simple location, 238
feeling, 138, 171, 220
  experience as, 184–9: causal efficacy and presentational immediacy, 191–5; epistemology v. ontology, 189–91
Ferraris, Maurizio, 41, 51, 210–11, 216
Fields of Sense (Gabriel), 38
flight of an aeroplane, 43–4
flow, 148, 149, 151–3
  of consciousness, 146
  of nows, 122, 123, 124, 132, 150
  see also change; temporality/time
Formal and Transcendental Logic (Husserl), 71, 88
foundationalism, 103, 112
Frege, Gottlob, 8, 87
fundamental physics, 245–6

Gabriel, Markus, 38, 39
Gegenstandssinn (object meaning), 102
general positioning, 82
Generalthesis, 82, 83
genesis, 90–1, 134
genetic phenomenology, 90, 115, 134–5
German Idealism, 232
given, myth of the, 103, 105–13
givenness, 46, 52, 70, 77, 79, 98–9, 179
  in the everyday world, 255

INDEX

physical, 192
pre-intentional, 260n
temporal, 122
Gloy, Karen, 100
Godfrey-Smith, Peter, 33
Gratton, Peter, 213
Greenough, Patrick, 231
growth and becoming metaphor, 153–8
Gurwitsch, Aron, 87

Haag, J., 244
Hartmann, Nicolai, 42
Hegel, G.W.F., 40–1
Heidegger, Martin
　being, 203, 283: and time, 142–3, 153–4, 155
　constitution, 102
　events, 202
　experience, 46
　hermeneutics, 134
　object of experience, 78
　ontology and phenomenology, 7
　perception, 73, 75
　phenomenology, 69
　philosophy, 183–4
　pure consciousness, 101
　truth, 35
Heidegger and Whitehead (Cooper), 189
Heidel, William A., 270
Henry, Michel, 260–1n
Heraclitus, 58
History of the Concept of Time (Heidegger), 73, 75, 101, 102
History of Western Philosophy (Russell), 162
horizons, 253–4
human body, 17, 292; *see also* bodily awareness; bodily feeling
humanity-in-the-world, 248–50
Hume, David, 193, 194
Husserl, Edmund, 7, 8
　absolute understanding, 63–4
　consciousness, 116, 117
　correlated transcendental realism, 92, 101–3: critique, 103–13
　correlations, 52–3
　experience, 118
　givenness, 179
　immanent transcendence, 46
　intentionality, 47
　intuition, 70
　nature, 273
　phenomenalism, 103–5

phenomenological experience, 71–3, 74: 'object as intended', 76–9
phenomenological idealism, 67
positing sentences, 35
science, 251, 278
sense experience, 223–6
sense perception, 71, 74
temporality, 119–35: and genetic phenomenology, 134–5; objective time and time-consciousness, 152–3; in phenomenology, 121–7; *Thing and Space* lectures, 127–33
transcendental idealism, 80–1, 92: from natural to phenomenological attitude, 81–6; *noema*, 86–91
transcendental idealism and the a priori correlation, 93–6 (correlated transcendental realism, 101–3; pure consciousness, 97–101)
world, 118: as horizon of all horizons, 253–9, 265–6
world-in-itself, 97–101
hypokeimenon, 204

Idea of Phenomenology (Husserl), 83, 85
ideal entities, 29–30
ideal objects, 33–4, 212–13
idealised reality, 215
idealism, 93, 94
　phenomenology as, 80–1: from natural to phenomenological attitude, 81–6; *noema*, 86–91
Ideas I (Husserl)
　consciousness, 95–6, 116: pure, 97–9
　Generalthesis, 82
　intentionality, 47
　intuition, 70
　natural attitude, 83
　noema, 80–1, 86, 87–8
　world as horizon of all horizons, 253, 254
Ideas II (Husserl), 128, 129, 132, 251, 256, 273
identity, 59, 133, 267–8
images, 224n, 239, 240
imaginative generalisation, 43–4
immanence, 94, 285
immanent objects, 76
immanent transcendence, 46, 74
immediacy, 105, 107
　presentational, 191–5
immediate experience, 170
individuality, 59

INDEX

Individuals (Strawson), 163–4
information/information technology, 1
inner episodes, 105–6, 110
inner temporality, 124–7
intellect, 102, 178
intentional acts, 79, 87, 90
intentional matter, 79
intentional object, 86–91
intentionality, 47–8, 49, 53, 92, 95
internal relations, 55–9, 287; *see also* correlations
internal time, 121
internality, 266, 267
Introduction to Metaphysics (Heidegger), 153–4, 183–4
Introduction to Phenomenology (Sokolowski), 87
intuition, 172–9
  and knowledge, 179–84

James, William, 219n
judgement, 107–8

Kant, Immanuel, 4, 77, 93, 176
Kinaesthesen, 224
knowledge, 2, 63
  as adequate, 35, 36
  correlationist approach to, 114
  and experience, 106–7
  and inner episodes, 110
  and intellect, 178
  and intuition, 176, 179–84
  in Western philosophy, 62
Kortooms, Toine, 130
Kripke, Saul, 50, 51

Lacan, Jacques, 38
Ladyman, James, 231–2, 237–8, 245, 246
language, 2, 36–7, 216, 217
laws, 33–4
Leibniz, G. F., 56
Levins, Richard, 22–3
Lewis, David, 50–1
life
  Aristotelian understanding of, 261–6, 268
  as concept of being, 289–90
  in Deleuze, 284–5
  phenomenological issues, 259–61
  in process thought, 266–9
  in Worms, 284
  see also nature; *nature alive*

life-world, 256–9
  and Aristotelian understanding of life, 265–6
  historical roots, 258n
lived experience (*Erlebnis*), 15, 16, 45, 134, 217
living beings, 287
logic, 2, 36–7
Logical Investigations (Husserl), 8, 74, 79, 88, 89–90, 118
Lynch, Michael P., 231

McDowell, John, 17–18, 108, 111, 211
Mach, Ernst, 104
McHenry, Leemon B., 159, 160, 164, 186, 215, 220, 294
McTaggart, John, 146, 149–50
Manifesto (Ferraris), 51
Marmodoro, Anna, 58
master-slave relation, 56, 58–9
materialism *see* naturalism; physicalism
mathematics, 2, 32–3, 212, 242–3
matter, 222n, 237–43
Matter and Memory (Bergson), 173, 224n, 240
Maudlin, Tim, 30–1
meaning, 102, 108
measurability, 232
measurable time, 147–51; *see also* clock time; objective time
measurements, 31
measuring tools, 30–1
mediated appearance, 78
Meditation (Descartes), 184–5
Meillassoux, Quentin, 53–4, 114, 115–17, 167, 212
mentality, 267
mere appearance, 78
mere existence, 29, 202, 206–7
Merleau-Ponty, Maurice, 274–7
meta-ontology, 20–3
'Meta-ontology' (Inwagen), 28
metaphysics, 4, 174, 283
  analytic, 50–1
  descriptive, 20
  versus ontology, 19–20
Metaphysics (Aristotle), 35, 107n, 201, 270–1
'Metaphysics in Analytic Philosophy' (Simons), 50, 51
methodology, 39–49
  beginning, 40–3

INDEX

phenomenology, 45–9
speculation, 43–5
Mignucci, Mario, 55
mind, 92, 241
Mind and World (McDowell), 211
minimal empiricism, 211
misplaced concreteness, fallacy of, 32–3, 220, 238
modal realism, 51
Modes of Thought (Whitehead), 170, 220, 238, 267, 277, 278, 293
Moran, Dermot, 72, 74, 80, 82, 83, 84, 94
Morin, Marie-Eve, 46, 114
motion/movement, 152, 262–4, 270–1
scientific view of, 291–2
myth of the given, 103, 105–13
'Myth of Passage' (Williams), 147

Nagarjuna, 4, 58
naïve realism, 75
Naming and Necessity (Kripke), 50
natural attitude, 82, 83, 84
natural beings (*physei onta*), 262–3, 270, 271–2
naturalism, 230, 248; *see also* physicalism
nature, 220
Aristotle, 144, 197, 270–3
bifurcation of, 214–15, 222, 249
as concept of being, 289–90
Husserl, 273
Merleaux-Ponty, 274–7
Newtonion view of, 275–6, 277–9
as process, 41
scientific materialism, 236–7
and 'what there is', 269–81
Whitehead, 188–9, 248, 273–4, 275
see also life
Nature (Merleau-Ponty), 274–5
nature alive, 273, 275–6, 281, 282–4, 285–6
Nature as Event (Debaise), 185, 187, 253, 274
'New Directions' (Pihlström), 249
Newtonian paradigm, 235
Newtonian view of nature, 275–6, 277–8
Nietzsche, Friedrich, 216
nihilism, 3
noema, 80–1, 86–91, 108
noesis, 34, 80–1
nows, flow of, 122, 123, 124, 132, 150

'object as intended', 76–9

object meaning (*Gegenstandssinn*), 102
objective temporality, 122
objective time, 120, 122–3, 124, 125–6, 152, 153, 154–5, 157; *see also* clock time; measurable time
objectivity, 278, 279
On the Phenomenology of the Consciousness of Internal Time (Husserl), 120, 121, 123, 129, 130
On the Plurality of Worlds (Lewis), 51
ontic structural realism, 243–4, 245–7
ontological change, 25
ontological commitment, 50
ontological growth, 146
ontological realism, 4–6
ontological temporality/time, 138, 143, 153–8
Whitehead's understanding of, 158–61
ontology, 203–5, 250
dynamic, 200, 205, 291
and epistemology, 4, 6, 60–5, 189–91
versus metaphysics, 19–20
and time, 141–5
open creativity, 3–4
order, negation of, 99–100
ousia, 204

Parmenides, 143, 206
particle physics, 240–1
particle-wave dualism, 159–60
part/whole distinction, 245
Peirce, Charles Sanders, 39, 219n
perception, 16, 70–1, 71–6, 80, 173, 184–5, 191, 192
personal time, 123
phenomenalism, 103–5
phenomenological attitude, 82–3, 84
phenomenological contradiction, 98
phenomenological descriptions, 217–18
phenomenological experience, 70, 71–6
object of, 76–9
phenomenology, 41–2, 45–9, 69–70, 93, 102–3, 219n
as correlationism, 113–18
and dynamic realism, 6–8
genetic, 90, 115, 134–5
as idealism, 80–1: from natural to phenomenological attitude, 81–6; noema, 86–91
as *sui generis* position, 92
temporality/time, 121–7, 142, 151–3
v. process thought, 189–91
philosophical attitude, 83

INDEX

Philosophie der Arithmetik (Husserl), 8
philosophy, 43, 183–4
  analytic, 2, 21–3, 50, 177, 205–6, 207, 237
  continental, 2–3
  reductive, 21–3, 248
physei onta, 262–3, 270, 271–2
physical prehensions, 184n
physical time, 125; *see also* clock time; objective time
physicalism, 236–43; *see also* naturalism
physicist, 231–2
physics, 30–1, 141, 158–60, 245
  fundamental, 245–6
Physics (Aristotle), 125, 144, 148, 197, 262–3, 270, 271–2
physis (nature), 270–3, 284
picturing, 35
Pihlström, Sami, 249
Plato, 4, 23–4, 143–4, 176, 232
Plebani, Matteo, 19
Portraits from Memory (Russell), 280–1
positing sentences, 35
Positive Realism (Ferraris), 41, 211, 216
possibilities of thought, 42–3
possibility, 94–5
postmodernism, 51
pragmatism, 62, 142, 219n
prehension, 138, 184–8
pre-phenomenological temporality, 122, 123
pre-predicative experience, 107–8
presentational immediacy, 191–5
primary properties, 222–3
primary substances, 204–5
Principles of Mathematics (Russell), 24
Problem of Genesis in Husserl's Philosophy (Derrida), 91
process, 59
Process and Reality (Whitehead), 7, 11
  actual entities, 185, 186–7
  becoming, 159, 161
  being and temporality, 142–3
  causal efficacy, 192, 193, 194–5
  causation, 190–1
  experience, 45, 170, 171
  intellect, 178
  language, 217
  philosophical process, 43
  speculation, 44
process ontology, 14, 247; *see also* dynamic ontologies
process thinkers, 247–8

process thought, 8, 40–1
  experience, 169, 170–1
  life, 266–9
  nature, 276
  reality, 266
  time, 142
  v. phenomenology, 189–91
processes, 40, 167, 186–7, 287
process-objects, 186
process-subjects, 186
proprioception, 193
pros ti, 54
prote philosophia, 201
protention, 224
psychē, 263–5, 265–6, 268, 270
pure consciousness, 97, 98–101
pure difference, 3

quantity terms *see* measurements
quantum physics, 42, 159–60, 241–2
quantum theory, 162
questions, 209
Quine, Willard Van Orman, 8, 9n, 50, 161

Ramey, Joshua, 59
rational intuition, 176
rationality, 249
real, 38, 230, 231–4
real possibilities, 42–3
realism, 50–1, 118, 198, 213
  correlated transcendental, 92, 101–3: critical perspectives, 103–13
  dynamic, 6–8, 18, 41, 86, 244, 246
  epistemic v. ontological, 4–6
  modal, 51
  naïve, 75
  ontic structural, 232–4, 245–7
  transcendental scientific, 244, 247–50
realist phenomenology, 114
reality, 58, 61, 63, 198, 210–14
  building-block ontologies, 162
  concrete v. idealised, 215
  as dynamic, 21, 29, 59, 247–52
  German Idealism, 232
  immanent nature of, 169
  as internally related, 245–7
  perception v. science, 220, 251
  as process, 13–14, 266 (*see also* process thought)
  as world-in-itself, 97–8
  see also 'what there is'
Realmöglichkeiten (real possibilities), 42–3

310

INDEX

reason, 1, 2, 4, 20, 178, 249
reductions, 80, 83, 84–6
reductive philosophy, 21–3, 248
reification, 32–3
relatedness, 48–9n
relations, 54–60, 286–8; *see also* correlations
'Relations' (Bradley), 57
relativism, 294
relativity, 162
religious attitude, 81
retention, 224
revolution, 40
Röck, T., 271
Ross, Don, 231–2, 237–8, 245, 246
Russell, Bertrand, 24, 161, 162, 225n, 279–81

Sachs, Carl B., 111
Santayana, George, 13, 24, 26, 36–7, 295
scale, 164
scepticism, 214–15
science, 2
 ancestrality, 115–16
 change, 291–3
 description of reality, 250
 life-world, 258–9, 265
 primary and secondary qualities, 223
 understanding of nature, 214–15, 243, 248–9, 276, 278–9
 v. perception, 220, 251
Science, Perception and Reality (Sellars), 105, 106, 108–9, 248
Science and the Modern World (Whitehead), 238
scientific attitude, 81
scientific materialism, 236–43
scientific method, 219–21, 230, 231, 250–2
scientific realism, 230–1, 230–5
 ontic structural realism, 243–4, 245–7
 transcendental scientific realism, 247–50
scientific theories, 243–4
secondary properties, 222–3
Seibt, Johanna, 247–8n, 250
self-causation, 268
Sellars, Wilfrid, 35, 104–5
 myth of the given, 103, 105–13
 transcendental scientific realism, 244, 247–50

sensations, 109, 120
sense (*Sinn*), 86, 87
sense data, 104, 106, 223
sense experience, 225
sense-datum theorists, 106–7
sensibility, 102
sensual intuition, 177
Shoemaker, Sidney, 31–2, 42–3
Simons, Peter, 50, 51, 166
simple location, fallacy of, 238
simplicity, 86
Sinn (sense), 86, 87
slaves *see* master-slave relation
Smith, David Woodruff, 71, 77, 97, 261
Smolin, Lee, 33, 144, 234, 235, 242–3
Socrates, 23–4
Soffer, Gail, 104, 105, 118
Sokolowski, Robert, 87
Sophist (Plato), 232
space-time, 147–8, 155
Sparrow, Tom, 113, 118
spatiotemporal location, 56
spatiotemporal objects, 120–1, 123, 127, 129–31, 132
speculation, 43–5, 282–3
Speculative Empiricism (Debaise), 35, 45
Speculative Realism (Gratton), 213
speculative realists, 53
Spinoza, Baruch, 176
stability, 199–200, 205, 271, 291
static event ontologies, 161–8
Strawson, Peter, 50, 163–4
strong correlationism, 117
structural realism, 243–4; *see also* ontic structural realism
'Structure of Knowledge' (Sellars), 250
subjective idealist, 94
subjective objectivity, 103
subjective time, 157
subjective time experience, 123, 124, 125
subjectivity, 220, 242, 278
 transcendental, 95
substances, 55, 204–5
symbolisation, systems of, 36–7
sympathy, 228
synholon, 204

technē onta, 262–3, 270
Tegtmeier, Erwin, 29, 151, 206
temporal being, 203–8
temporal objects, 120–1, 129–30, 131

INDEX

temporality/time, 7, 27, 29–34, 119–35
  and being, 34, 138, 141–5, 153–4
  building-block ontologies, 162–3
  and change, 120–1, 124: Aristotle, 125, 144, 148; Husserl, 119, 126, 127–33; McTaggart, 146, 149–50; Parmenides, 143; Plato, 143.144; Shoemaker, Sidney, 31–3, 42–3
  conscious, 122
  dynamic, 288–9
  and genetic phenomenology, 134–5
  inner, 124–7
  intuitions and metaphors about, 145–7: flow metaphor, 151–3; growth and becoming metaphor, 153–8; timeline metaphor, 147–51
  in phenomenology, 121–7, 151–3
  Thing and Space lectures, 127–33
  Whitehead's understanding of, 158–61
terminology, 199
Thacker, Eugene, 262
Themes from the Lectures at the College de France (Merleau-Ponty), 277
Theory of Meaning (Husserl), 80n
Thing and Space (Husserl), 80, 118, 121, 122–3, 126, 127–33
thinking, 4, 6, 60–5
though experiments, 31–2, 42–3
Timaios (Plato), 143–4
time *see* temporality/time
time-consciousness, 119n, 124n, 152
timeline metaphor, 146, 147–51
tode ti, 204–5
transcendence, 94
  immanent, 46, 74
transcendent objects, 76
transcendental attitude, 83
transcendental idealism, 80–1, 92
  from natural to phenomenological attitude, 81–6
  noema, 86–91
  and the a priori correlation, 93–6: correlated transcendental realism, 101–3; pure consciousness, 97–101
transcendental phenomenology, 114
transcendental realism *see* correlated transcendental realism
transcendental scientific realism, 244, 247–50
transcendental subjectivity, 95

truth, 1, 2, 35–7, 86
'Truth' (Sellars), 35

Unger, Roberto, 33, 144, 234, 235, 242–3
universal thesis, 82

van Fraassen, Bas, 31
van Inwagen, Peter, 28–9
visceral feelings, 192
vision, 191

Wahrnehmung, 70; *see also* perception
weak correlationism, 117
'what there is', 37–8, 269–81
Whitehead, Alfred North, 7, 8–9, 11
  and Bertrand Russell, 279–81
  causal efficacy, 228
  change, 25
  experience, 45, 170, 171–2: as bodily feeling, 184–9 (causal efficacy and presentational immediacy, 191–5; epistemology v. ontology, 189–91)
  fallacy of misplaced concreteness, 32
  intellect, 178
  language, 217
  life, 267
  matter, 238
  naturalism, 248
  nature, 188–9, 248, 273–4, 275
  philosophical process, 43
  Process and Reality, 274
  process thought, 137, 138, 202
  science, 215, 219, 220
  speculation, 44
  temporality, 158–61
  temporality and being, 142–3, 154
Wiesing, Lambert, 16
Williams, D. C., 147
world, 38–9, 94–6, 213–14, 220
  as horizon of all horizons, 253–9
  and Aristotelian understanding of life, 265–6
  see also everyday world; nature; reality
world-in-itself, 97–101
Worms, Frédéric, 284

Yates, David, 58

Zahavi, Dan, 89

EU representative:
Easy Access System Europe
Mustamäe tee 50, 10621 Tallinn, Estonia
Gpsr.requests@easproject.com

www.ingramcontent.com/pod-product-compliance
Lightning Source LLC
Chambersburg PA
CBHW050203240426
43671CB00013B/2228